For Gillian -
after fifty years -
pure gold.

Books by the same author:

Introduction to General Practice with Michael Drury 1979
Infective Disease, 1987
Teamwork in Palliative Care with Vicki Sargent & Mary Ellis, 1989
Pocketbook of Palliative Care, 1994.
Just a GP. Biography of Professor Sir Michael Drury PRCGP. 1994
A Schoolboys War Published by GPWA. 1994
Scottish Birds; Culture & Tradition: 2001
Ravens over the Hill: The History of Dun Coillich. 2004
The Healing Island. A Novel. 2004
Silver Sea, Sequel to The Healing Island, 2007
Scottish Mammals 2007

Many chapters in multi-authored medical books

About 1000 articles, papers, reviews, broadcast & television
scripts and crosswords in journals worldwide.

Foreword: Medical Chequers

David Haslam

Part of the joy of being a family doctor comes from the unpredictability and the surprise. You think you really know someone, and then discover you hardly know them at all. I will never ever forget a patient of mine whom I must have seen fifty times over many years, and whom I had simply filed mentally away in an exceedingly patronising way as "just an average middle aged woman". And then one day I visited her home when her husband was ill, and as I left the house I noticed an extraordinarily large greenhouse in her entirely average garden. I made a comment, was offered the chance to have a look, and discovered that my patient was one of the UK's foremost experts on the rarest of carnivorous plants. In a moment, my picture of a woman that I thought I knew was changed forever.

I thought I knew Robin Hull well. Our paths have kept crossing for well over 30 years, and I have long enjoyed his wit and wisdom, his generosity and his friendship. And then I read this beautifully written book and realised that - as with my remarkable patient - I was really only glimpsing the surface. Robin has led a truly remarkable life. The overwhelming picture one is left with is that of one of life's enthusiasts, with more than his fair share of fascinating enthusiasms.

It is traditional when looking back on a remarkable life to say "and we shall not see his like again" and I've never believed it. Every generation produces remarkable men and women. If it did not, humanity would stagnate. And stagnation is the one thing Robin would be incapable of.

Those of us who have known him can now fully appreciate what a remarkable friend and colleague we have had. Medical Chequers is a great title for someone who has played a great game. And there is little doubt that it was a game that he won.

*****

Professor David Haslam, CBE
President, Royal College of General Practitioners

Apologia–The man on the sitooterie

His age is suggested by his white hair and beard as he dozes in a comfortable deck chair. The sitooterie is a mass of colour from plants from the many countries of this much travelled gardener. Climbing plants from both Americas, abutilons from Morocco, scaveola or fan flower from Australia and pelargonium species from South Africa flower amidst embothrium from Chile, rhododendrons from Asia, Japanese maples and phormium from New Zealand.

Beside him, on the garden table, his binoculars are ever ready to focus on the creatures that share the garden. The sitooterie is surrounded by drystane dykes, home to hundreds of wood mice. These attractive creatures lure stoats and weasels to the garden, occasionally pine martens visit and 100 yards away the biggest river of Scotland provides a playground for otters. Other creatures inhabit the garden, roe deer eat the roses and rabbits everything else, which makes the stoats doubly welcome. There are soprano and bandit pipistrelles in the roof and occasional Daubenton's bats fly so close to the river that they are indistinguishable from their own reflections. Everyone's favourites are the red squirrels who believe they own the garden. Sometimes when the old man sits quite still, dram in hand, the squirrels pause in their passage across the sitooterie and, sitting by his feet, seem to contemplate the old fellow, perhaps hoping for a handout of the nuts he likes with his whisky. In winter when it is too cold for him to use the patio, the squirrels steal nuts from the bird feeder. Then, as he watches from a warm conservatory full of plants, they hang, upside down beside great spotted woodpeckers, each oblivious of the other as they feed.

This garden is alive with birds throughout the seasons; mostly tits and siskins in winter, then chaffinches singing on April boughs, before the warblers arrive from Africa to fill the birches with song all summer. Overhead buzzards mew as they circle on the thermals, sometimes ospreys fly along the river where dippers display and kingfishers flash electric blue as they arrow upstream.

The sitooterie is a good place for watching wildlife; a good place to sip a malt, to remember and doze in the sunshine. Dreams can be prophetic. Was it not it the chemist Kekule who, puzzled by the chemical problem of balancing the hydrogen and carbon atoms of benzene, dreamt of a serpent that crawled to his feet and then seized its tail in its mouth? The scientist woke abruptly realising the imbalance of atoms was caused by them forming a ring.

Pondering this, the old man saw his life as a ring, just like the atomic structure of an organic hydrocarbon. Kekule's dream solution applied equally well to his life, for it too was annular in time and space.

He had always been a naturalist since childhood, fascinated by the world he lived in. This dominated his life leading him to natural sciences, especially biology. This, in turn was the route to medicine, to the study of the natural history of his own species. Then he wished to impart what he had learned to others as a teacher and writer before coming full circle to watch and wonder at the wild creatures of Scotland, gradually focussing on the garden he had created and on the creatures who shared it with him.

When it was suggested he write his autobiography, he shuddered at the egocentricity of such an action–anyway whoever would read that? He pondered on autobiographical memoirs he had read of people who had either been great or, more commonly, thought they had been. So often these made interesting reading until the subject of the tale became 'successful' (whatever that meant) and thereafter became a dull catalogue of riches, power, honours and self satisfaction. The old man stirred uneasily. Perhaps he was too unsuccessful; certainly he was not rich, nor powerful, had had no honours thrust upon him and such self satisfaction as he felt came chiefly when a trout took a fly he had tied himself or when an unusual plant burst into bloom.

He looked round him at the sitooterie: these flowers, birds and mammals had become the subject of his writing; perhaps the idea of the chequer board of life really was worth recording; if only as the recurrence of a Kekulean dream.

So, for what it's worth, here it is.

Preface

John Alfred Ryle, (1889-1950). was a physician at Guy's Hospital from 1924 till 1930. In 1935 he was appointed to the chair of physic in Cambridge, but returned to work in London during the war until made professor at Oxford in 1943 when he became a pioneer of social and preventive medicine. In April 1931, some six months before I was born, he gave a seminal address to Cambridge University Medical Society entitled *The Physician as Naturalist*.

I did not become aware of Ryle's famous lecture until I was well advanced in my own medical career. Despite that he could have drawn the blueprint of my life in medicine: I came to medicine because of a love of natural history; medicine taught me more about that love, enabled me to travel the world seeking greater insight into and understanding of man and other creatures of the earth and which ultimately led me to a fulfilled retirement in one of the wildest, most beautiful countries on earth.

In these days of deficient ozone, desertification, pollution of river and ocean and the omnipresent threat of global warming it is fashionable to be Green. It is essential to those whose daily task is to teach improvement in the health of populations. Such medical greenness is nothing new. The founder of medicine, Hippocrates, was as green as they come, as revealed in his *Airs, Waters and Places*.

Since then medical history has resounded with names of people who have followed in spreading the message from Cos: Harvey, Boerhaave, Pasteur, Osler and, among my own teachers, George Pickering and Alexander Fleming. I especially cherish Ryle's writings for he pointed out that Britain has been particularly rich in naturalists and that medicine and the observation of natural phenomena have always gone hand in hand. He cites the patronage of organisations such as geographical foundations, botanical clubs, gardening associations or natural history societies where you will find many doctors. This interest is not simply confined to leisure for the whole of medicine turns on the relationship between man and a hostile environment filled with toxins and organisms threatening his existence. Nature strikes back here and there exploiting a niche that man has created to turn it into a threat against him. The cause of Legionnaire's disease in our cooling systems, multiply-resistant staphylococci in our hospitals and the adaptation of retroviruses to increased means of transfusion of lymphocytes between individual humans leading to AIDS provide examples of ecology striking back.

Examples from the heroic figures of natural philosophy include Darwin, Huxley and Gilbert White of Selbourne. Of Darwin, Ryle noted that "his boyhood education was altogether a failure; he hated being taught and could not learn in the traditional way. Experience was his sole school. He observed, he collected, he recorded, and he deduced. His knowledge extended over fields immeasurably wide and applied itself to details infinitely small. Had medicine not been distasteful to him he might have become the greatest physician that ever lived, for he would have left no stone unturned in his will to discover everything knowable about man in health and disease, about man in relation to his environment, his ancestry, and to his natural enemies in the shape of sickness and injury."

Huxley was another giant but of a different kind. "He too had an amazing intellectual grasp and clarity of vision, and added to these a fine combativeness. We know him for zoologist, physiologist, and palaeontologist, very much a naturalist and in no sense specialized. A great opponent of dogma and tradition in education, a staunch advocate for giving the natural sciences an ever more prominent place in our educational system, and possessed of a literary ability rare in scientists, he will remain for all time one of the great and progressive influences in naturalistic thought. What a fine Professor of Medicine he would have made!"

Gilbert White of Selbourne, "that peaceful, parochial sage, watching his birds and his seasons, his flowers and his weather-signals; noting all down in his diaries with minute care as to time and dates; observing behaviour in wild things; experimenting with echo and dewponds; tilting at superstitions; and handing down to a grateful posterity his homely and truthful records. He would, in medicine, have supported all that is finest in the history of general practice."

Ryle spent care on selecting entrants to medicine, choosing men and women who from childhood had been so interested in birds and beasts, or fossils or flowers that they filled notebooks with observations or made careful collections of specimens; and so were thoughtfully and widely informed in natural lore. Such youngsters he loved to teach, advising them to think of the physician's life as their destiny.

Though I did not discover Ryle till my forties it seemed as though he had written his message just for me... and that is why I have chosen to write this Physician's Natural History.

'Tis all a chequer-board of nights and days
Where destiny with men for pieces plays
Here moves and mates and slays
Then, one by one, back in the closet lays

Rubáiyát of Omar Khayyám

Fortune favours the mind prepared

Louis Pasteur

I have left Robin to the end–some might say best place to leave him–he has been support in times of trouble, an inspiration when in doubt, bawdy and irreverent when we needed someone sober and discreet... At any rate he has been a constant source of laughter with us and at us–and that has been especially good.

Sir Michael Drury, retirement speech, July 1991

Introduction

Old Khayyam was right; life is indeed a chequer-board and serendipity seems to have played an enormous part in mine. Chance took me to a fine school which I nearly wasted but nothing short of monumental luck saved my bacon. I got to medical school on the chance recommendation of my school doctor. Joining the Royal Navy turned on a fortunate meeting with a namesake and if I hadn't got very drunk on leaving my ship I would not have met the best companion in life that I could have wished for. Arrival in Warwickshire was pure happenstance as were the events which altered the course of my life in North Carolina. Then a throw of dice started me at Birmingham and as for Holland that would be unbelievable in a novel. I was lucky to emerge from the academic disaster of my Dutch flirtation when the Goddess of fortune smiled upon me bringing me back to 'Brum'. After that one thing led to another retuning to where I started as a little boy who loved fishing and nature.

Part I A childhood of natural history

Chapter I Beginnings

On a May evening in Forfar in 1728 three gentlemen were walking home together after drinking in the town. Two of them were arguing; the argument grew into a quarrel and swords were drawn. The third man, upset to see his friends quarrelling, stood between them and was fatally stabbed.

The dead man was Charles, 5th Earl of Strathmore and husband of Lady Susanna Cochrane, granddaughter of Lord Charles Murray, second son of the First Marquis of Atholl. The distraught widowed Lady Susanna waited a decent time before remarrying. On 2nd July 1745 she must have scandalised the aristocracy of what was to become Tayside by marrying her factor and coachman, plain George Forbes.

What, you may ask has this to do with this history? Plain George Forbes was my great-great-great-great-grandfather and with the help of Lady Susanna he passed on to me a drop or two of the bluest blood in Scotland. Perhaps these few Scottish corpuscles

Mother at 80

have had more influence on the course of my life than anyone could have imagined.

On 6th June 1892 a daughter was born to daguerreotypist Stephen Chalmers of Dunoon. She was his ninth and last child and she was the great-great-great-granddaughter of George Forbes, second husband of Lady Susanna Cochrane, who was rarely referred to in the family and then only as 'the Coachman'. The baby girl was christened Charlotte but was always called Lottie. She had an idyllic childhood on the Clyde spoiled by older siblings, however, when she displeased them, she was reminded that she had better mind her 'ps and qs' for she was only 'The Coachman's brat'!

My family is complicated by my mother having married twice, each time tumultuously. Charlotte Maxwell Chalmers was a typical Scot, round, dumpy and very fond of sweeties. She was born in Dunoon, Argyllshire where her father, a photographer from Glasgow, produced daguerreotypes. Though reasonably comfortably off his liking for whisky may have diminished funds available for the family. He died at the age of 52. Mother always hinted that alcohol was his undoing, but her accounts of the cause of death of many of her family are doubtful (as indeed were many certified causes in those days). Looking back years later in a tape-recorded discussion with her eldest son she thought her father may have had throat cancer perhaps brought on by the chemicals he used in photography.

By all accounts, her upbringing was religious, Victorian and strict but, as the last child of a large family of older brothers and sisters, was fun. Mother often quoted a notice one of her brothers had made for the single lavatory of their overcrowded home:-

> Hasten! Hasten! For in a moment more
> The next will thunder at the door!

Lottie lived a stone's throw from the shore of the Firth of Clyde with a view of the distant Arran hills; she seldom wore shoes in summer for she was more in the sea than out of it. The family had a boat called *The Howling Hottentot** in which she must

---

*This bizzare name was used for a boat in *The Healing Island*

have spent many summer hours for, even as an old woman, she would occasionally row for pleasure. Her upbringing was as rigid as Scottish Victorianism demanded. Her father, a devotee of Shakespeare, seems to have imbued his youngest child with a love of poetry; she could recite Robbie Burns interminably and almost unintelligibly. Though of fairly simple education, she was nobody's fool and fierce in the defence of her children.

In 1912, she was introduced to a student on Dunoon esplanade by a clerical acquaintance. The student, Charles Quin was visiting Argyllshire to attend a course on Greek at a college in Kirn. They married in September 1912 when Lottie was twenty. Charles Quin moved on to Nottingham College from where he was ordained as a deacon on 4th October 1914*. His ordination as a priest was at St Mary's Cathedral, Chelmsford the following May. Shortly after their marriage, Lottie and Charles crossed the border to Carlisle, and she was never to live in Scotland again. There, her first child, Sidney, was born in 1913. Charles, her second son, followed in 1915 when her husband was working in the East End of London. She loved the cockneys though life in Plaistow cannot have been easy. Certainly it was verminous and the visiting priest sometimes brought livestock back home from his parishioners. The War took Mr Quin away as an army padre. For a long time, as I grew up, I would come across cherished military vestments in which my unknown stepfather ministered to the troops. He was a mason who, my mother told me, became a Provincial Grand Chaplain.

War has its contraceptive qualities and the vicar's absence left a gap in the family soon to be filled by Eric in 1922 and Pat in 1924. At some time, Stephen put in a brief appearance. Sidney remembers seeing him with pennies on his eyes, dead at under two years old, allegedly from tuberculous meningitis. This sibling is shrouded in mystery. Sidney swore to the certainty of his memory but my mother looked at me in astonishment when I asked about Stephen and said "I only had five children". This may give a clue to her personality; there was much that was unpleasant in her life; she seems conveniently to have forgotten the worst. Perhaps most of us do that.

---

*By chance 44 years before my marriage to Gillian Edwards

The family settled into a living at Sandridge in the Diocese of St Albans where Mr Quin was instituted in October 1919. The vicar was popular and the Church was a thriving, living organisation. The vicar's wife was a personality in the community albeit an impoverished one. But life at home was stormy. My own future wife's grandfather was a financial officer in the Diocese and knew individual incumbents well. It was generally known that part of Mr Quin's piety derived from purgatory at home. Escape to the Lodge must have been welcome. Eventually he took more permanent escape, when he died at the age of 36 on 29th September 1926. My mother always swore it was typhoid fever contracted from drinking from a mountain stream; the evidence, such as it is, suggests acute rheumatic fever. Whatever the cause, Mother was a widow with four children.

Charles, then a boy at Christ's Hospital, remembers being sent for by his housemaster, Mr A.E. Johnson and told of his father's death. Mr Johnson was kind and considerate. Charles was sent to the Dining Hall to be given a meal by himself in that vast room where loneliness added to the melancholy of the occasion. He then walked the half mile to the station to travel alone from Sussex to Hertfordshire. He was not yet twelve years old and it seems hard that a child should have to face such an ordeal alone. He commented to me over sixty years later 'I doubt whether the presence of anyone else would have improved the situation.'

The parish was supportive, one gentleman, grandfather of the girl I was to marry nearly forty years later, being particularly helpful with financial advice. But there was very little to support four children.

Mother left the vicarage moving to a house in Ox Lane in Harpenden where she took in lodgers to help with the rent and the hunger of her children. One of these lodgers was to become my father. Why a bachelor, after a war which had left a huge surplus of single women, took on a woman seven and a half years older than himself with four children is beyond conjecture. Certainly everyone advised her against it particularly my future wife's grandfather.

My father was a strange man but, though I would never have admitted it, I adored him. Edward Hull, born on first of December 1899, was somewhat reclusive, and seemingly without ambition. Looking back at my father with the experience of seventy six years, I still cannot understand him, even though I see his face every time I look in a mirror. He came of what had been a relatively well-to-do Cheshire family. His father, an austere moustached Victorian paterfamilias, who terrified his only grandson, was an interior designer. Before the first World War when a rich man bought a new house, he would employ a firm to furnish it. This implied decoration and the supplying of all the contents from dining table to teaspoons and from antimacassars to aspidistras. This was my grandfather's job and it must have been lucrative. Edward, his eldest child and only son, went to public school at Giggleswick. But Grandfather's business crashed with the war. At the age of sixteen father was abruptly removed from school and his education was over. He started work in Manchester as a clerk in the London Midland and Scottish Railway. He served as a private soldier in a kilted regiment, The London and Scottish, in the last days of the first war when he guarded German prisoners working in the harvest fields. He found this so boring that he laid his rifle down and rolled up his sleeves to help them. Immediately he was confronted by a German soldier pointing his rifle at his breast. The German handed the gun back charging my father never to do that again; there were, he said, no such second chances in Flanders.

When the war ended my father returned to the railway company where he occupied a clerical post until his retirement on health grounds in the 1950's. Just after the first World War, there was a huge pandemic of particularly virulent influenza. This 'flu killed more people throughout the world than died in the war which preceded it. It was associated with severe complications, especially 'heliotrope pneumonia' so-called because of the colour of victims shortly before death. My father contracted this illness when he was living alone in digs just after leaving the army. Nobody came near him and he later lapsed into unconsciousness. Fortunately someone then found him and admitted him to hospital. It seems possible that he had encephalitis and was lucky to survive. This may have had a bearing on subsequent events. In his fifties, he suffered from tuberculosis which led to his premature retirement. In later life, he developed Parkinson's disease which could have been related to an earlier neurological infection. Whether his illnesses affected his personality is largely conjectural but not impossible. Certainly some of his bizarre behaviour in his seventies was attributed to it. He appeared to be completely devoid of ambition preferring walking his dog and observing nature to anything else. He was also profoundly sentimental and this may have led him into the disastrous marriage with my mother. Perhaps he saw himself as the saviour of the family though why he should think that on a railway clerk's salary is also obscure. Eric, when claiming for a grant to augment his Cambridge Scholarship in 1941, ascertained that my father's income at that time was £280 per year (the equivalent of about £9300 in 2006). In addition to his poor income, he appeared to lack ability to manage the little money he had and was likely to spend it on a whim or even give it away. He was always kind except when rowing with my mother and was a never-ending source of interesting ideas and things for a boy to do. He had endless patience and came to love the fishing I introduced him to.

Charles, Sidney & Eric at Sidney's Wedding, May 1940

Once, when fishing for tench (which requires patience and extreme quiet) a kingfisher sat a few feet from him on his rod giving him a moment that he cherished more than the success that other men strive after. He smoked heavily which drained family funds and was a bone of contention with my mother.

My parents married at St Pancras Parish Church in Euston Road in London in 1929. Sidney and Charles in their teens were less impressed than Eric and Pat who still speak of him as a marvellous companion and teacher as they grew up. There were strained relations between the eldest stepson aged 16 and Mother's new man who was not yet thirty.

I remember the most violent arguments between my parents as a young child and had a distinct feeling that Mother always came off best. I cannot conceive of what their sexual relationship could have been like. My mother once remarked that the only good thing about sex was the babies it brought–hardly a view which would appeal to many women today. Otherwise I only remember one incident that suggested that there was a sexual relationship between them other than my own conception. As a small boy, I was playing in the bath where I found a new plaything. It was a little rubber boat like a coracle which nicely transported cargoes of soap and pumice from the square end of the bath to the round. Suddenly a furious mother stormed into the bathroom seized my boat with a cry of "That's mine" and withdrew leaving a startled, but fascinated, little boy puzzled that somehow he had been near to discovering something fantastically interesting.

The strangeness of the relationship between my parents possibly accounts for the peculiarly disrespectful attitude towards my father revealed in some of my boyhood letters which were always addressed to my mother. I referred to him as 'The Walrus' because of his Crippen-like moustache. Yet I adored him, as did Eric and Pat to whom he was almost a father. Sidney, who as eldest son had difficulty coming to terms with mother's second marriage, also found it impossible to know how to address my father, who eventually and pompously became known to all by the Victorian title of Pater. This title was suggested by a family of spinster sisters who had been members of Mr Quin's congregation and who had become Godmothers to Eric and Pat. The name became so established that more distant relatives even referred to him as 'Uncle Pater'. We all look back on a kindly, gentle man who taught us to observe and to love the countryside. My mother once made the mistake of asking me which of my parents I loved most and told me that my reply was immediate: "You... but Daddy's more interesting."

Sidney went to school at St John's, Leatherhead which catered for sons of the clergy. But the problem of education for the others must have been a prodigious burden. Then my mother heard of Christ's Hospital. 'CH', or 'Housey', as it was known to generations of boys and their parents, was founded by Edward VI. On 15th June 1553, a few days before the boy King died (probably of syphilis inherited from his father Henry VIII) he laid down his pen and observed "Lord, I yield Thee most hearty thanks, that Thou hast given me life thus long to finish this task to the glory of Thy name". Edward VI in 1553 did my family a great service.

The school, whose charter refers to it as "the Religious, Royal and Ancient Foundation of Christ's Hospital," was founded for paupers of both sexes. The original school was in Newgate Street in the City of London where both boys and girls were admitted. From the start, thanks to the school's prodigious endowments, it was only possible to get into Christ's Hospital if one was without means. Entry was far from easy; there were many whose genteel poverty qualified them for admission and it was necessary to be presented by a Governor of the school. My Mother, an indefatigable letter writer, obtained a list of Governors of the school and laid her case before each of them. In turn, Charles, Eric and, much later, 'Wee Robin' donned the long blue coat, knee breeches and yellow stockings of the Housey uniform.

The experience of the three boys at Christ's Hospital seems to have been very different. Charles disliked it and spoke of many trials there. Perhaps, as the least athletic of the three, the physical hardships were less endurable. He tells a story of rugger which reflects the Spartan attitudes of the school. On a bitterly cold

February day, he had donned two jerseys when, being comfortable, he played well. The master who was the referee, noticing his rather bulky appearance exploded saying 'Are you wearing two jerseys?' and when being told that the boy was so clad, he added: "No wonder you are playing so well–take one off at once."

Another master who was Charles' junior housemaster in Middleton A and taught maths, was rather eccentric. He had no interest in games and was somewhat cerebral. He often said to his classes 'It does not matter if you have no food, it does not matter if you have no clothes to put on as long as you have intellect.' His audience was not impressed feeling that the possession of intellect was no compensation for hunger.

By the middle 1930s, Sidney and Charles had been away from school for several years, the former to work in the Westminster Bank and the latter as an insurance salesman. Sidney rose to become Assistant General Manager of the Bank. The difference between us in age made Sidney more like an uncle than a brother to me and we disagreed on many things. Charles' career looked less exciting but I had enormous respect for him especially when he read to me in bed. He always chose Tolstoy or Chekhov for his little brother; I loved it but wonder how much I understood of Russian literature at the age of seven. Charles was a quiet, unassuming, unathletic boy who hated Christ's Hospital where he made little mark though he enjoyed singing treble in the choir and playing the clarinet. He left school as a misfit without matriculation and was extremely unhappy working in insurance. Through the kindness of Eric's Godmother, who helped him to obtain a loan from the Society for the Propagation of the Gospel, financial help from Christ's Hospital and by dint of exceptionally hard work, he gained sufficient funds and qualifications to enter Charing Cross Medical School to read medicine. Originally he had intended to become a medical missionary but subsequently he became a consultant physician in Brighton. As a medical student he was my most interesting brother and once, shaving while I was lying in the bath, regaled me with a lecture on my anatomy. Even better was the plain wooden box under his bed that contained a human skeleton. On special occasions I was allowed to play with the skull which, for reasons I did not then understand, he called Yorick.

For much of the time, holidays away from home were too much of a luxury for the household budget but one of the privileges of being a railwayman permitted free, or at least heavily subsidised, travel within Britain. I have vague memories of interminable journeys to Cheshire to visit my adored Irish grandmother and my feared Victorian grandfather. Probably he would have been kinder had he not suffered painful sequelae of diabetes*. There were even longer journeys to a hideous place called Glasgow where I have nightmare memories of watching street people picking over the dustbins and eating what they found; there was never plenty at home but at least we were spared that indignity. But the Glasgow uncles were kind, one made scale working models of the Clyde steamers which fascinated a small boy. Other relatives lived in Rothesay which involved a trip 'doon the watter' in a real steamer to Bute. I returned there nearly seventy years later and recognised the house; seeing it brought back a memory of a smell I have always associated with elderly spinsters.

Those steamers were wonderful with great polished brass pistons which hissed and clanked as they drove the paddles. One memory of that trip persists as the steamer entered the broad estuary of the Clyde my father pointed at small dark birds flitting over the surface of the sea. "Look, Robin," he said, "those are Mother Carey's Chickens." Those were the first Storm Petrels I saw and it must have been many decades before I saw them again.

Not far away from us in Harpenden was another Scottish mother who visited and blethered with mine. This lady, Dédé Bailey, was a gipsy-like Glaswegian who 'read teacups' seeing dark strangers and long journeys in their leafy dregs. In an earlier century she would probably have burned at the stake. She was married to a wreck of a man, gassed in the trenches who seemed to spend his time coughing and listening to endless Scottish football results. More to the point the couple had a daughter slightly younger than I was. Pauline and I were inseparable even at bath time when we observed, and wondered at, 'The Difference'. The stairs up to

---

*Whose genes, unfortunately, I inherited.

Pauline's 'nursery' were decorated with swords that played a large part in the adventures we had together as we sailed on those stairs across the seas to Coral Island and the Never-never-land. Together we adventured in the garden, making mud pies, finding woodlice and the terrifying beetles my father called Devil's coachmen that, scorpion-like, raised their tails in an exhilarating manner. There was a small pond where we guddled for tadpoles to the alarm of brother Charles who focussed his microscope for me to see a new world of life in a tiny drop of pond water. He alleged it was lethal but spoiled the effect by showing me a piece of cheese from the kitchen table which was far more terrifying in its creepie-crawlies.

In those days Hertfordshire was an intensely rural county with very little traffic and, if paederasty existed (as it must have done), it did not seem to worry either of our mothers: so, as we grew, Pauline and I wandered freely. Not far away was the River Lea, where many shallow beds had been constructed for cultivating watercress. These beds were much more fun than the garden pond and yielded trophies like fresh-water shrimps and 'tiddlers'. Once, glistening in my net, was a flapping inch-long bar of silver and in that moment a life-long fisherman was created. Pauline cut her foot on broken glass in the stream and, wishing to emulate brother Charles, I emptied a whole bottle of iodine over it. Surprisingly, despite her screams, we remained friends and I still have a book (Frances Pitt's *How to see Nature*) which bears the inscription 'To Robin From Pauline April 1941'; it cost 3/6d too.

Not far from Ox Lane, where Pauline and I lived, was a mysterious place called Rothamstead. At that time I had little idea what happened there but clearly it was important because it attracted the attention of two science masters from Christ's Hospital where Eric was a junior in a house called Middleton A. These masters were Dr. van Praagh, a chemist, and Mr. Kirby, a biologist, and mother invited them to stay with us. Charles did not like this invasion from a school he had hated, Eric tolerated it in the embarrassed way of teenagers but I loved it. Kirby had an old van in which he and 'VP' commuted to Rothamstead. On occasions I would be taken for rides by this eccentric biologist and once was made to remove

31

my Wellingtons to provide a receptacle to convey a captured frog home to be put in the garden pond.

Mother looked after them well serving Kirby's insatiable appetite for cold almost raw beef , which he called 'cold bloody cow'. Little did I know that this was all part of Mother's master plan for my future.

Chapter 2 Arran and Housey 1939 to 1950

It was Dédé Bailey's suggestion that my mother visit Arran, an island she had viewed often enough across the great Firth of the Clyde but had never been to. So in the summer of 1939 the Hull family with Eric and Pat set out for Arran as war clouds gathered in that glorious last August of peace.

I was seven and it is the first holiday I remember with clarity; the sea and mountains were to have a lifelong effect on me. We crossed the Clyde by ferry which was exciting with its huge and terrifying, highly polished pistons which clanked up and down to drive the paddles and its luxurious saloons full of marvellous highly carbohydrate Scottish food. Clyde steamers before the war were wonderful ships; the people-moving, roll-on-and-off vessels of today are poor shadows in comparison.

We arrived at Lamlash pier, where the steamers called before the war, on the way to the 'nob's resort' of Whiting Bay where shorts were disapproved of and ties *de rigeur*. We got off at Lamlash with no idea that this was to be our home for several months. Pater arranged a limousine of seemingly enormous length which whisked the family along the shore to turn through woods over a humped bridge spanning a crystal burn and up the hill to Gortonalastair. White Rock cottage is still there commanding a fine view over Lamlash Bay and Holy Island. Far away the peak of Goatfell beckoned and there was a mysterious little hut at the bottom of the garden. This was the first long drop privy I had met, I viewed it with delight and disgust. From the cottage a magical footpath, called the Cuddy Dook, ran steeply down through hazel woods, where the first red squirrels I had seen flirted in the canopy, to a rocky shore where I could be out-'de-Lessepping' other canal builders draining rock pools. Eric, at the superior age of sixteen, even deigned to help his little brother. Old photograph albums reveal him in the striped rugger jersey of Middleton A, his house at Christ's Hospital, and of me in shorts standing on a rock with bucket and spade. It was September 3rd, 1939 and my mother observed at 11 o'clock that it was odd that the church bells were

ringing for there was no service at that hour on a Sunday morning.
Britain was at war.

My parents were concerned at war but kept their fears from us.
Mother, with two sons in their twenties feared for their lives. Eric,
she hoped would be too young. Her only concern for me was that
of upbringing, difficult enough financially already but with war,
doubtless even more problematical. Harpenden, 25 miles north of
London, was likely to be a target for bombs, possibly even gas.
To travel South seemed foolish and Mother was on the river of
her childhood, remote on a safe island. It was decided we should
stay in Arran. To a young boy experiencing the wildness of that
glorious place, the war was heaven-sent even if it did mean going
to the village school in Lamlash. Pater found a smaller, cheaper
cottage near the harbour to house my Mother, Pat and me. This
tiny, two-up-and-down house, Myrtle Bank, was lit by candles
and had a built in bed in the kitchen wall in the manner of many
small Scottish homes. The box bed gave a child a privacy for
dreaming and playing and made a wonderful theatre where a boy
could experiment with pantomime. Myrtle Bank was heaven and
only minutes from the shore where a tiny burn entered the sea.
The cottage was owned by Mr Kerr who kept the shop by the
pier which sold everything from paint to potatoes. Mr Kerr was
a romantic figure concealing a kindly personality behind a gruff
one-armed exterior (he lost his right at Gallipoli). Myrtle Bank is
still there too. I visited in the autumn of 2006 to find it lived in by
a woman I had been to school with 66 years before.

Actually there were 'three up' for in the middle was a tiny room
large enough to take a small bed. This was my bedroom; though
later, when it grew cold, I was moved to the warmth of the kitchen's
box-bed. The ceiling of the small room sloped and was lit through
a skylight by day and by a candle at night. Through the skylight,
by standing on the bed, I could see the bay and the great swathe of
the Clyde behind the bulk of Holy Island in the bay.

Below there was a rarely used parlour in addition to the kitchen;
there was an outside privy but no bathroom. Beside the house a

burn trickled down to the bay. Here there were flounders and elvers to fish for and dams to be built. Once I met a Glaswegian evacuee there. We had no common language and soon strife broke out and the young Robin ran home sobbing with a black eye. I have viewed Glasgow and its inhabitants with distrust ever since.

My father returned to work in London and Eric to boarding School, expecting to be bombed at any moment. I started school which, among evacuees from central Glasgow, was an eye-opener. With my Sassenach accent and my ignorance of basic Scottish educational attainment, I puzzled staff and fellow pupils. Slowly by dint of homework and frequent application of the tawes spelling improved. The school taught Gaelic and I learned a poem about the cuckoo, now long forgotten, but an atavistic memory causes interest in the old language of Scotland and some words, most derived from place names, survive to this day.

Despite school, our sojourn in Arran was superb. For years afterwards, when art-masters made me paint the result was always the same; the twin headlands of Clauchland's and Kingscross Points embracing the mountain of Holy Isle in the centre of Lamlash Bay. Near Clauchland's point, the northern arm of the bay, there was a big house taken by an Edinburgh solicitor as a haven for his two boys who became my firm friends. I remember teas there when we had wonderful wooden-sword-fights among the rhododendron bushes. We got up to much mischief hurling bombs, made by sticking gull's feathers into tatties, which circled magnificently as they descended. We 'smoked' cigarettes made by peeling the pith out of elder stems and thought ourselves swells. One disreputable friend found a clutch of hen's eggs which he threw at the corrugated iron roof of a Dutch barn. I was horrified, my upbringing made me regard food wastage as anathema; hadn't he heard there was a war on? However the war was remote apart from the blackout and the coming and going of Coastal Defence vessels in Lamlash Bay. One morning I was woken early to see the British Battle fleet sailing from the Clyde. I saw the great capital ships HMS Hood and Renown which were sunk not long after.

Once, mother got into trouble with the air raid wardens. She had banked the fire up in the late afternoon while we went out. It was dark when we returned, and the fire was burning brightly acting as a beacon to any enemy bomber in the vicinity. Mother, distrusted as a foreigner, despite having been born on the Clyde, was probably a German spy! The fact that there had never been any bombers over Arran, only a couple of minesweepers were in harbour and Mother was every bit as Scottish as the warden, made no difference. In those days, there was much paranoia and tempers were short.

Pat got work nursing at Lamlash War Memorial Hospital. There, she learned of the need for sphagnum moss which was dried, sterilised and used as an absorbent wound dressing. Everyone had to do his bit and, for us, this meant collecting moss. We spent many hours gathering quantities of sphagnum, which filled every ditch in the island. The dreary job was made exciting by thoughts of battles and blood.

Mother was faced with the last of her education problems. She had had a promise of a presentation to Christ's Hospital for me from a Governor who died suddenly a year before I was due to enter the school; his presentation died with him. Frantically, Mother started writing letters to try to find another Governor who would present me. By chance, the lead came through my sister Pat. At Lamlash Hospital, she met the local landowner, the Duchess of Montrose who lived in Brodick Castle. Somehow Pat persuaded this lady to visit our cottage for tea. I remember a big, friendly, smiling woman with a long tear in her rather grubby mackintosh. She had a relative who might be able to help and Mother's writing paper came out again.

At Christmas Pater came from London bearing the last box of mandarin oranges we were to see for many years. Eric returned from Christ's Hospital and Pat had time off from the hospital. Arran is bathed by the Gulf Stream and Christmas day was so mild we sat in the garden in shirt sleeves. Then the weather broke in time for us to journey away from the magic island on a snowy January day with a pile of dead stags on the deck of the steamer as it took us back to reality, to war and England. Brought up on JM Barrie's *Peter Pan* and *Mary Rose* Arran became a dream to me during the long years of war; a hallucination that only became real when I was there myself.

Harpenden had changed, there were troops everywhere and the military activity puzzled me considerably as camouflaged trucks passed along our lane. I asked my father the question that worried me.

"Why do they paint the trucks those funny colours?"
He explained that it made them more difficult to see.
"But", I expostulated, "it doesn't, it makes them easier to see".

I was told not to be silly and the unreasonableness of this rebuke rankled for many years until at the age of seventeen I discovered that I was severely red-green colour blind. Defective colour vision, like haemophilia, is inherited through a sex linked recessive gene. Mother had given all four of her sons varying degrees of colour blindness.*

Mother's efforts on my behalf at last paid off. Years later she wrote to me: 'I found the enclosed when cleaning out a drawer. I thought it might interest you as it concerned you. I know I got a great thrill when I received it as I had nearly given up hope of getting a CH presentation.'

The letter from Harewood House Leeds dated 10th April 1940 read: 'Lord Harewood has heard from the Duchess of Montrose asking if he could present your son to Christ's Hospital. He is likely to have a presentation available in the near future, and he will be obliged if you will let him know your son's age. As you are probably aware children must be not under 9 nor over 11 years of age at the time of admission. Yours faithfully, C. Bliss Secretary

A second letter three days later acknowledged mother's reply and enclosed an application form. The voyage of my education was launched; it was to be a stormy passage.

---

*At the time of writing three of my grandsons, born to my three daughters have inherited my defective colour vision; the other one is too young to be tested.

On a dreary Saturday, in January 1941, just after my ninth birthday, I travelled to Sussex with mother who exhorted me to do my best though I was far from sure what the long slow journey in poorly heated trains was all about. The enormous buildings of the school near Horsham, designed by Aston Webb, who built Birmingham University, completely overawed me. The Avenue, the school's aorta, was lined by huge lime trees which presented skeletal arms to a grey and frigid sky. The sixteen Houses, each accommodating fifty or more boys, towered in an architectural style I later came to associate with hospitals or prisons. Life at Christ's Hospital, always Spartan, was doubly so in wartime. Years later, when I read Solzhenitsyn's 'One Day in the Life of Ivan Denisovitch', I found the description of the Siberian gulag mirrored Christ's Hospital. I

Robin with wild Dafodils and in Housey Uniform, Spring 1941

was cold, I was hungry and frequently frightened; often I walked round three sides of a quadrangle rather than pass a boy who presented a threat.

After exploring the school with mother and Eric there was an entrance examination which was quite enjoyable; perhaps the tawse in Arran had instilled something into me despite the low level of achievement accepted by my English prep school. Whether it was I who passed the examination or mother is open to question; probably it was she. Mrs Quin, Mother of Eric and of the now largely-forgotten Charles, was well known as a determined lady. Now, as Mrs Hull, she was all the more formidable. Eric's Housemaster, Dr. van Praagh, supervised the test. At that time, Eric was at the peak of his school career; a Grecian*, House Captain and Swimming Captain and accepted for Cambridge. van Praagh looked at the unprepossessing little boy who was his House Captain's half-brother and suspected that there must be some good in him somewhere.

I was sent to be equipped with the fancy dress which was the Housey uniform. Used to soft shirts and underwear, the coarse white cotton of the button-less shirts and stiff underpants chafed my skin. The collar, referred to as 'bands', served up with two large safety pins was a mystery. The breeches with their three smart buttons at the knee were like riding breeches and the bright yellow stockings slid quickly down my tiny shanks. The whole ensemble was covered by the navy blue, ankle length, coat pleated and flared from the waist, where it was gathered by a loose fitting leather girdle. The front of the coat boasted seven buttons; the lowest was twice the size of the other buttons hinting at undreamt of future glory, for every newcomer was a potential Grecian who wore the finery of better cloth, velvet cuffs and fourteen big buttons in a vertical median over his exalted breast.

I was admitted to Christ's Hospital; soon afterwards, mother, her work done, and ambition realised, returned home while the full awfulness hit me. I was attached to a lordly senior with a term's experience of the 'Prep' whose task it was to show the 'newsquit' round and

---

*At CH the most senior boys were called Grecians, from the days when Greek was the common classical language taught at school and prerequisite for university entrance.

indoctrinate him in its language and custom. In the dormitories the beds seemed designed for torture; a hard mattress was supported by boards across an iron bedstead of unyielding rigidity.

The dormitories were heated by single round radiators which produced a tepid warmth. This was comfortable to sit on if one were lucky enough to arrive first and hold the seat against competitors. Stringent black-out precautions decreed all bulbs were painted purple to reduce what little light their low wattage emitted. At each end of the dormitory, there were 'lav ends' with door-less loos. Washing in dark, freezing 'ends' discouraged cleanliness and everyone suffered from chaps and chilblains throughout the winter. To this discomfort was added the humiliation of queuing, stripped to the shivering waist, for inspection by matron when those deemed unclean were sent to freeze again in the 'lav ends.'

Even stranger on the first night in the dorm, (after routine inspection for circumcision which would automatically relegate each new arrival into the categories 'The Roundheads' or 'The Cavaliers') a senior boy of about eleven, decided to give one of the new boys an enema. The naked victim was bent over the bath where his buttocks were separated while soapy water was poured onto an anus in tight spasm. To me, watching, this was a spectacle of extreme fascination tinged with fear; would I be next? Fortunately, authority appeared and the victim, who seemed unconcerned, even apparently enjoying the experience, was released before awkward questions were asked. Release from fear came at lights-out only to be replaced by waves of homesickness and racking sobs.

We rose at seven, to march the quarter mile to what I thought must be the biggest building in the World: the Dining Hall. The food, by tradition, was execrable and wartime shortage made it worse but given a growing boy's appetite it was surprising what could be forced down. 'Housey stew' consisted of tough gristle floating in a sea of fat, yellow haddock came stewed in a thin milky fluid and there was the ultimate horror of 'worms in carbolic' as the boys called spaghetti. Years later, I had nightmares about tearful sessions when I was made to eat this awful food. I learnt to do so;

the alternative was hunger. Less awful were endless supplies of kippers and herrings and sausages were such a luxury the standard school wager was 'half a sausage on it!' Like many others who spent the war at Christ's Hospital, I was thereafter able to cope with any culinary disaster.

Eric, House Captain of Middleton A, was on nodding acquaintance with God and even the Headmaster. On my first morning at breakfast, awe touched the long table where we ate our meals when Eric visited the Prep to see how little brother was coping. A visit from such an exalted personage caused a momentary stir. My prestige surged before, within seconds, interest was lost at my presumption at being related to a Grecian. From hall, everyone marched back to the Houses and made their beds before prayers. Not for nothing was Christ's Hospital a religious foundation. In the senior school, there was daily chapel, twice on Sundays with an optional early morning communion for the confirmed. There were always evening prayers, called 'Duty', read in the Houses and many boys knelt at their bedsides before sleep. This was accepted and tolerated to such an extent that prayer was a splendid refuge against bullying. Fear, rather than devotion, often prolonged bedside orisons.

There were lessons till the lunchtime march back to dinner. In the afternoon the boys were made to don games clothes and run across country or play that barbaric and traumatic, utterly incomprehensible game called rugger which was supposed to make men of them. At these times home seemed a long way away and the prospect of becoming 'a man' extremely unattractive. After that there were more lessons, tea, evening prep, and then the horrors of the dorm with more tortures of Chinese burns or arm twists before the solace of a damp pillow.

Every Sunday throughout the school, there was a time set aside for letter-writing when each boy had to write home. Doubtless without such coercion, parents would never have known their offspring were still alive. All boys hated letter writing; it was another of those mindless, pointless chores thrust upon them by authority whose sole function was to thwart the unspeakable things that boys always want to do. Mother saved many of these letters* which never mentioned the horrors: the boys' fascination with their own and others' genitalia, the bullying or even the awful food. Only rarely were there references to the war, which hardly obtruded in the rural peace of Sussex; when it did it was of little concern compared with the conflict of everyday life. Far more important was the collection of butterflies and birds' eggs: the Natural History Society was a thriving affair at all levels of the school.

Christ's Hospital started four centuries before as an intensely urban establishment, but had become rural with its move to Sussex in 1902. Two miles from Horsham it was set on the heavy clay of the Weald with distant views of the South Downs. Not far away the small but attractive River Arun managed to cope with the effluent of Horsham as it meandered south to the English Channel at Littlehampton. The countryside was well wooded with the remnants of ancient oak forest, which provided excellent habitats for wildflowers, birds and butterflies so letters home were full of bug-hunting and bird quests such as : 'several crysalids have hatched out. No more news except a Newt has come to live with the fish.' Newts, fish and 'crysalids' were naturally of far greater import than the remote affairs of war.

During the first few days of January 1943 the Hull family moved house. I was not sure that this was a good thing. The house in Ox Lane, Harpenden was large and comfortable and the only home I could remember apart from the idyllic Myrtle Bank in Lamlash. The new home was tiny, poky even, and without electricity. The lighting was by gas with the mystery of mantles which crumbled to dust if touched. The wireless, essential in wartime Britain, worked on huge batteries and heavy glass accumulators filled with acid that had to be taken to a nearby garage for recharging at sixpence a time.

Return to Housey revealed that after two year in 'Prep' the expected metamorphosis to the Upper School had taken place. I, along with two other boys, Fatty Davidson and Ally Parker, was in Middleton A, where two brothers had preceded me. We were three excited but frightened little boys all aged 11. Bullying has always been present

---

*My mother saved many of these execrable epistles which I later used as a basis of a book about CH called *A Shoolboy's War*, published by Limited Edition Press in 1994.

in boarding schools. Certainly it existed at Christ's Hospital as the prep had shown me. But in the prep all the inmates were much of an age, the senior school, with an age range of 11 to 19, meant some boys had tremendous advantages of size and strength. A few took advantage of this in establishing their position in the ecological pecking order. Sexual abuse occurred both between boys and between masters and boys though the latter either rarely came to light or was very unusual. In Middleton A, there was continual harassment of the young by the older boys. The most senior boys of the House were the House captain and five monitors. The next most senior was the 'Trades Monitor' whose function was to organise the refectory chores. The 'top table', next in seniority, were boys of about sixteen including many in their last year at school because it was deemed they lacked the intellectual equipment to progress to University. This group included some of the worst bullies. Those who reached the Olympian heights of Grecian-hood were, though men of considerable authority, rarely unkind. Nevertheless, a small boy's life could be made unbearable.

Monitors were allowed to issue punishments and did so frequently. The two most commonly awarded were 'changes' and 'Post Offices'. A change meant removing everyday clothes and donning rugby kit and then back again in five minutes. One had to parade before a monitor for inspection to see that there was no cheating and that each change was accomplished tidily. This was a soul-destroying punishment and a boy might spend most of a precious Saturday evening doing changes. 'Post Offices' were even worse. A tarmac cycleway ran to the school Post Office, a little over quarter of a mile from Middleton A. To do a 'Post Office', a boy had to run to the Office and back in five minutes and report to the timekeeping monitor. This was not difficult to do the first time but six post offices were an awful punishment. The only advantage of this was that monitors found supervising these punishments extremely boring so it was possible to avoid running the whole distance. Beating was supposedly administered only by masters but the rule was more honoured in the breech (sic) than the observance. Some monitors used their plaited girdles which made excellent whips. Some masters had ferocious reputations: one liked to bend his victim over under a door handle. Invariably, the gluteal pain made the boy forget the risk to his head which, after being hit on the doorknob as he straightened up, was as painful as his bottom.

The Sussex woods were prolific in wild daffodils and primroses which were both sparse in Hertfordshire. I used to watch for the first spring flowers and, when Pater visited the school there were expeditions to find them. Sharpenhurst was 'a green hill far away' on the western side of the huge playing fields that made up half of the school's 1200 acres. There were two paths up Sharpenhurst, one across two railway cuttings whose banks were rich in wild strawberries. The other lay through Shelley Wood which was named for the poet who is reputed to have listened to nightingales there. He may well have done so–they were plentiful in the 1940's.

The spring holiday of 1943 was magnificent. Ally Parker stayed with me in Harpenden where we birds-nested on the common. In the tiny garden Pater had made a pond in which we kept stickleback and remarkable little fish called Miller's Thumbs, caught in the watercress beds by the River Ver. But the real excitement was Tigger. Tigger was to be the name of the new dog who was coming to replace Toby, a deceased unbeautiful mongrel. Eric, now in the uniform of a tank corps second lieutenant, seemed to have one beautiful girlfriend after another and I fell in love with them all. One of these ladies was Doreen Terry whose father farmed in Kent. The Terrys owned a labrador bitch who had just whelped. In that holiday I visited the farm where Doreen's sister June was my junior by a year or two. June introduced me to the litter of pups. There are few creatures more irresistible than Labrador puppies; but June made matters even more interesting. Crouching beside the litter with her knees parted to reveal her own scantily knickered crutch she delivered a fascinating lecture on the difference between a penis and a vulva while turning over the still blind whelps. It was love at first sight, mostly for the pup but quite a bit for this girl who knew such interesting things. Tigger was the Terry's name for the dog that was destined to be ours when old enough to leave his dam and after my return to school.

Tigger was renamed Terry in honour of the family who bred him and I longed to see him. Meanwhile, a new craze was entering my life. Fishing had graduated from Stickleback and Miller's Thumbs to the pursuit of proper trophies such as Gudgeon, Roach and even Carp. A new heaven was revealed in the turgid waters of the duckpond at the school farm. Fishing was all-absorbing, every moment of spare time was spent at the duckpond, which could be reached in five minutes from Middleton A. It was just beyond the Post Office and, armed with my rod, I covered the distance faster than I ever did for punishment. One week, I determined to fish every day no matter for how short a time. On some weekdays, that meant just half an hour between the end of morning school and lunch. So many tiresome distractions such as lessons crowded in on a busy life that economy of time became paramount. My life became a time and motion study so that every free minute could be put to maximum use. Lessons provided time for rest, relaxation and recovery.

I still had to see Terry whom I had not met since the pup's eyes had opened. Every letter from home must have been telling stories of the whelp's development. It was not until June that my parents visited Housey with Terry. Pater said that when they met me with the fat, squirming, ten week old puppy, I did not even speak to them in greeting. I only had eyes for my pet: No such dog ever existed, or ever will exist, and he grew to be a model Labrador–the first of many throughout my life. He was patient, loving, courageous and my closest companion. Terry was the ever willing playmate of holidays and he was a perennial supplier of food since in a team with Pater and me, he became a splendid rabbiter. Terry taught me to poach; soon another major occupation at school.

On that idyllic weekend, I took my parents and my dog round the school. The pup careered across a pond covered with duckweed, sank in a surprised splash to emerge with green measles and a newly discovered love of swimming The long summer afternoon was spent collecting enough pungent, bittersweet wild strawberries on the railway embankment, for tea.

In that hot summer, the Arun attracted me like a magnet. It abounded in fish particularly dace which I found difficult to catch but which were fun to watch as they rose like trout. Guthrie, a friend in a neighbouring house, Thornton B, could catch them on a fly. It was forbidden to swim in the Arun but we ignored this injunction, braving its murky water redolent of methane. A mile upstream, Horsham sewage works discharged its effluent into the river; there was good reason to avoid swimming. A case of poliomyelitis at the school underlined this but it was hot and the temptation was too great especially when the fish would not bite. There were kingfishers and herons to watch and the moorhens of the Arun yielded many a spotted egg to supplement my tea. This amazed many of my more urban fellows, but Pater had taught me that moorhens' eggs are good to eat.

After Christmas, things in London seemed quiet and in January for a treat, I was taken to see Agatha Christie's 'Ten Little Niggers', in the West End. Travel home in a crowded, cold, blacked-out train was tiring and it was midnight when we got to bed. There was a knock at the door; a call that late that meant trouble and I heard Pater go down to investigate. There was a mutter of voices then my father called up the stairs.

"It's the police, they are looking for a Mrs Maxwell, do you know anyone by that name?"

Mother's voice, full of strain, said; "That's my second Christian name" and she went down too, shutting the door so I heard no more.

Eric had been involved in an accident and had severe injuries. His identification papers were illegible with blood. The only readable part of his Mother's name, given as next-of-kin, was Mrs Charlotte Maxwell. The next day, she travelled to Newmarket and found her third son in desperate straits with his life in balance. Apart from a serious head injury, he had a fracture dislocation of his shoulder. Eric had made a detour from the tank convoy he was escorting by motorbike to visit a Cambridge friend. Leaving the college late, his driver had to hurry. It was wet; they skidded on a curve and had a head on collision. The driver fractured both femora but the bulk of the force fell on Eric. But he was young and tough so he survived. A few months later, many of his regiment, including the man succeeding him as troop commander, were killed in Normandy. Ironically his near fatal accident saved his life.

At last war came to Housey with Hitler's V1 flying-bomb, but even they did not prevent fishing. I had my biggest fright by the Arun. In the middle of a Sunday afternoon I was near the weir where the river ran through a deep cleft in the clay banks of the Weald. Above the fall, it was sluggish and poor fishing. At the weir, there was a fall of about six feet into a large pool where pike could be caught. The river then meandered but had a brisk current where there were good dace and roach. I was intent on fishing when suddenly I heard the throbbing engine of a 'doodlebug'. The device was flying slowly at low altitude and coming straight for me. As it cleared the top of a wood, I saw it a hundred feet above me. I knew it was safe with the engine running and I willed it to keep going. Right overhead, the engine cut out and I dropped my rod and rolled down the steep riverbank. The bomb dived as I lay half in the river and waited, wondering if this was my end. The bang, when it came, was accompanied by a sudden blast of wind pressing me into the muddy river bank. The bomb had exploded harmlessly a field away. I abandoned fishing and returned to school shaken but proud of the tale I had to tell.

The Summer holidays that followed were superb but I worried about rationing. There was a big estate near Harpenden which was kept for shooting and the river Ver was stocked with trout. As a boy, I explored the estate while gamekeepers were busy at war. It was here that I learned about living off the land with Pater and Terry. Each weekend we walked miles to a working watermill. I loved this mill whose creaking oaken cogs were powered by the Ver, which, unlike the Arun, ran gin clear in summer since it rose in the chalk of the Chilterns. Above the great iron millwheel the water stood six feet deep, where shoals of large red-finned roach cruised amongst water crowfoot. An overflow carried excess water away to join the main river further downstream and was spanned by a small footbridge. Below the footbridge there were many miller's thumbs which could, with patience, be caught by the hand as I lay flat on the bridge. I caught lampreys in my hands and saw their suckers clamped onto the glass of my collecting jar; the only time I have ever seen these strange parasitic fish. The best places for trout were in the deep water by the overflow and under the great wheel itself. Once, Pater and I tiptoed to the overflow and surprised the miller lying flat by the edge of the wall above the stream. Suddenly he jerked upright rolling onto his back hauling up a long garden cane. Wriggling on the end of the cane lassoed by a rabbit snare was a fine fat brown trout. I had never seen a trout close to and was captivated by the beautiful combination of gold, black and red. The miller was poaching and though snaring trout is hardly sportsmanlike, it is very difficult and I thought him wonderful. I longed to catch a trout but meanwhile Pater taught me how to use a snare for rabbits.

Some time before, Pater had purchased a tent in the hope that, as the pressures of the war eased, it might be possible to think of holidays again. After trials on Harpenden Common, it was decided that we would try an experimental camping holiday during Pater's week's summer break. It could only be local since, as a subaltern in the Home Guard, duty came first. Camp was pitched in a field near the River Ver where all the gear could be transported by bicycle. This camping venture was to establish a new relationship between Pater and me which was to develop over the next five years.

Another way of getting rabbits for the pot was much more fun and depended on co-operation between Terry and me. Combine harvesters of today, whilst efficient, have spoiled the sport of harvest time. Those marvellous machines called 'reapers and binders', which clicked their way round the wheat-fields of the 1940s, could be heard fields away. The reaper cut the wheat only an inch or two above the ground, clumped it into bundles which were knotted together into sheaves. The sheaves were thrown clear of the machine to be left lying; the cornfield was covered in sheaves presenting an obstacle course to creatures running from the diminishing island of uncut corn. This presented great sport for the few gentry who were at the big house who came to the harvest fields with their shotguns. It was too early for pheasants though if cutting were delayed till after the beginning of September there might be a chance at partridge. But there were rabbits galore. The excitement, as the lessening cover given by the island of standing wheat reduced with each circuit of the reaper, became intense. The boys, armed with sticks, simply ran the rabbits down as the animals dodged through the obstacle course of sheaves. Terry and I learned to work as a team the dog flanking the rabbit turning it back to me. Many escaped but the dog got some and I a few more. Those summer evenings running hard with my dog remain some of the happiest memories of boyhood.

The guns were amused to see boy and dog work together and left one side of the field to us. They picked off far more rabbits than the athletic canine and human pair but I doubt they had such fun. Once a brown, partridge-sized, bird with a weak fluttering flight got up and was immediately shot. It was a corncrake, then often heard in the south of England though vanished now. Like the reaper and binder, it is gone. That harvest finished in a blaze of Indian summer glory. We had found a new place to fish in a pond full of small perch beyond St. Albans. I was captivated by the spines and the vertical black bands of the little fish. Armed with cheese and marmite sandwiches, we angled in sunshine ignoring the aircraft overhead, taking reinforcements to the battle at Arnhem, across the Channel.

Christmas 1944 was the last of the war. Though the doodlebugs stopped when the allies overran the launch sites the even more frightening V2 rockets continued, killing or injuring many. By February the war was all but over and all the family were safe. Eric had made a spectacular recovery but was still convalescing. At Christ's Hospital, my interests turned, as usual, to food and rabbits. I caught one in Shelley Wood which I took to Mr Kirby as he wanted one for a lesson. That rabbit marked, if not a turning point, at least a significant bend in my progress at school. I was due to have an English lesson from my form-master 'Gaff' Malins who regarded me as a hopeless case. I applied for permission to miss the

English lesson and go to Kirby's lab to watch the dissection which was to take place before Biology Grecians studying for medicine. Malins said I might as well since it could not do me any less good than the scheduled English lesson.

Nothing in the subsequent dissection, not even five embryos, impressed me as much as that brilliant anatomical concept with which Kirby explained the structure of the peritoneal cavity. It was fun, it was stimulating and it was the same sort of lateral thinking I was beginning to appreciate in the Daily Telegraph Crossword. 'Gaff' Malins' lesson was well missed. Not only did I start a new interest in anatomy but I began that day to develop a new concept of schoolmasters. Clearly, they were not all bent on thwarting my natural interests and some could actually be quite stimulating.

Meanwhile, friendship was developing with a boy called Miller who lived near Harpenden and who, at school, was in the neighbouring house of Thornton A. Miller was a close friend of Guthrie, the butterfly-collecting friend in the Prep of some years before. These three boys together formed an inseparable group, an unusual relationship between boys of different Houses. The link was natural history. Miller was a fisherman and Guthrie was by now a knowledgeable butterfly man. One day we were on a long Sunday walk when we came to a pond we had never seen before, miles from the school. It looked eminently fishy. Turning out our pockets Miller had a hook attached to a piece of gut (that's how one bought them then). I had a knife and a good length of string and Guthrie had some lead shot. While I cut a 'rod' from a hazel bush the other two found a large pheasant-feather to make a float and we all turned over soil for worms. Within a few minutes we caught a tench–it wasn't very big but it was satisfying to prove we could fish just from our pockets.

It was in the summer term of 1945 that the rabbit business started with Guthrie and Miller. By now, the technique of snaring rabbits had been mastered; the only difficulty was getting time to harvest the catch. The route to Sharpenhurst or Shelley Wood took time and we organised a rota for visiting the snares. When rabbits were caught, it was a simple matter to 'leg' them so that as many as four could be carried slung from one's braces invisible under the folds of a Housey coat. Thus armed with merchandise, it was necessary to establish the market. In those days of meat rationing, rabbits were a welcome addition to protein-deficient diets. We watched the masters' homes till the master left, then his wife would gladly part with half-a-crown (12.5p) for a nice fresh rabbit at the back door. One of the best customers was none other than Mrs Malins, the wife of my form master. There must have been some interesting ethical discussions over dinner tables where rabbit stew was enjoyed by a master sworn to secrecy by his wife.

Suddenly it was over: At Luneberg Heath the German High Command signed unconditional surrender: May 5th 1945 was a sudden and unannounced half-holiday. I spent the day in the field adding a Bullfinch's egg to my collection. However the lack of evidence of my scholastic progress was causing concern at home where it was decided that I might make a serviceable agricultural labourer. Brother Charles, back from the RAMC, suggested a career in forestry. On a day when a still-convalescent Eric was sent to the school and to make enquiries about my future I had volunteered to work in Kirby's garden rather than endure the tedium of the cricket pitch. Just before Eric visited, I was sent to cut grass with a sickle. Having got a really good edge on the blade, I hit my left hand opening up a large laceration. Staring at the damage in surprise, I saw the extensor tendons of my index and ring fingers beautifully dissected. By the time I got to Kirby I was bleeding profusely. Kirby applied pressure to my brachial artery and drove me to the infirmary where Dr. Scott sutured the cut while I stood watching. Perhaps it was then that the old ambition to become a doctor resurged in me. The accident somehow had impressed Kirby. When Eric visited Housie, I was wearing a splendid sling and Kirby was slightly less damning about me than he might otherwise have been. With Gaff Malins, it was different. He told Eric: "I have never been so certain of anything in my life as I am when I say young Hull will never, never, never become a doctor."

With the end of the war in Europe, Pater decided that it was time again to take advantage of his railwayman's travel privileges with a summer holiday. Where else but Arran where the last family holiday had been nearly six years before. By now, Pat and I and even Mother were getting used to holidays under canvas; Terry was happy anywhere. August saw the family disembark at Brodick whence a taxi took us the ten miles to a camp site in North Glen Sannox. The journey was magical. The coastline of Arran is dramatic with igneous mountains rising nearly 3000' from the sea. Recurring fluctuations in sea level over the millennia had left a series of vestigial beaches at different levels. Huge accidental rocks littered these beaches and strange twisted and gnarled oaks formed a coastal wood filled with red squirrels. The sea was alive with unfamiliar duck* and seals basked on the rocks. I could hardly believe this wonderland, of geological and avian novelty. The campsite was where the North Sannox Burn ran into the sea, above which the tiger's tooth of *Cioch na h'Oighe*† towered above a great corrie, The Devil's Punchbowl or Cauldron. The place was deserted, incredibly and magnificently beautiful. Terry and I adored it and were in the sea as much as out of it. There were elusive trout in the burn and, at high tide, the estuary was filled with small coalfish which I caught for Terry's supper: he probably fed better than us. Food was very short and the main staple was marmalade sandwiches until we met Mr Work, who was almost as wonderful as Pater.

'Old Work', as Pater called him was an Orcadian, a retired Glasgow CID sergeant who owned a boat. For some reason, he took to us and we spent hours in his boat fishing the bay to supplement our diet. My camp-duty was the daily visit to Mid Sannox farm for milk. One day in August, Mr Work elected to take his wife and the Hull family 'for the messages' in Corrie by boat. I was landed on the Sannox jetty by the farm to collect the milk. There was quite a delay waiting for the shoppers to return. I was happy sitting in the sun drinking milk and watching a family fish from the jetty. The father of the family ran up in great excitement. He had just heard a news bulletin that the Japanese war was over after the use

---

*Later identified as Eider and Red-breasted Merganser.

†The Maiden's Breast.

of a new sort of bomb. But important things were happening with fish and none of the children took much notice. Eventually, the shoppers returned. I embarked with what was left of the milk and after several minutes said: "By the way the war's over". I thought all the adults had gone mad and their excitement jeopardised the stability of the boat, but then adults always were unpredictable.

So the war which, for me, had begun in Arran ended there too. There was a tremendous celebration with a bonfire on the point near Sannox Kirk where the family gave thanks.

That holiday proved to me that each day could show a newer and better heaven. Once, looking at the summit of *Cioch na h'Oighe*, I announced that I wanted to get up there. The next day, father, son and dog, none of whom had ever been on a mountain, made the attempt. We failed but not before learning of the magic of high, wild places where golden eagle and merlin hunted among grouse and ptarmigan. We reached a point from which progress was impossible and sat looking at the view. Out to sea, the dorsal fin of a cruising basking shark was clearly visible and, as we watched it, we saw that Terry, his ears streaming out behind him in the updraft, was staring fixedly at something far below. He had spotted a herd of red deer, the first that any of us had ever seen in the wild.

Other new creatures spiced the island with danger; the machair swarmed with adders and terrifying, but actually, harmless wood wasps, *uroceros*, hovered round the campfire wood pile probing the logs with sinister ovipositors like enormous stings. Arran, had us all enthralled; for me, it seemed incredible that any place on Earth could be so perfect.

The transition from war to peace occurred as my own manhood began to stir and I was worried that peace might be more troublesome to me than ever war had been. There were hints of new challenges and responsibilities which might interfere with the tranquillity of a boyhood of war. That Christmas, Eric gave me a present that was to be cherished for years. The 'Fisherman's Bedside Book' was edited by a man identified by the initials 'BB'*. It included essays on fish and the natural history of the

*The nom-de-plume of Denys Watkins-Pitchford [1905-1990] writer and illustrator whose writing influenced me for life. 'BB' was the size of shot used for geese.   53

waterside by people such as Thoreau, Isaak Walton, and Richard Jeffries. These writers captivated me and sent me to the library to find and read more. Jefferies particularly became a favourite and 'The Amateur Poacher' was read and re-read. But Eric's gift also introduced me to fly-fishing, suggesting that with such skills the trout of the Arran burns might be more co-operative.

At school, the flourishing rabbit business became eclipsed by farming. The Young Farmers Club had raised funds to buy four piglets which were kept at the school sties. This involved a lot of work; the pigs had to be fed every day and mucked out at the weekend. Time was short since much had to be fitted into the short free minutes the school allowed. There was half an hour between breakfast and morning chapel which was supposed to be used for bed-making. I found if I got up immediately the bell went at 7am and made my bed before breakfast, I could have this half hour to myself. It took only a few minutes to run the half-mile from breakfast to the pigsties where swill from the kitchen-waste seethed in cauldrons almost as devilish as that in Arran. The pigs loved this concoction of discarded meat, bones, fish heads and old vegetables. The trouble was that many foreign bodies, including broken crockery and sharp bones, got into the waste bins which could cause the pigs harm. It took but a moment to slip my Housey coat off and plunge my arm into a bucket of swill to check there were no hurtful sharps in the feed for my charges. There was no means of washing and the congealed stinking grease of the swill was roughly wiped off the forearm while the pigs' breakfast was served. Then I ran back to the cloisters where I could slip into the marching column of my house as it arrived for chapel. The pews were crowded but I always had plenty of space; pig-swill never smells sweet. There were spin-offs from this morning routine: I became a passable middle distance runner for the school and learned a lifelong hatred of wasting time, which my family call impatience!

In the summer of 1946 Pater and I returned to Arran to camp in North Sannox. Mr Work again took us out in his boat but more excitingly, he took us poaching sea trout at night and after deer with a .22 rifle. Splash netting, an illegal way of taking game fish in the estuary, involved circling with a net drawn behind the boat while splashing on the shore supposedly drove the fish into the trap. The excitement of this nocturnal poaching heightened the fun especially when the distant putter of the bailiff's outboard engine became audible. Both these poaching expeditions were fruitless but very exciting.

So time passed inexorably towards the dreaded School Certificate. School work was frankly a disaster but I was an insatiable reader and was by far the best person at crosswords in the House. Like most at the 'Religious Foundation', I was by this time devoutly Christian. I had been confirmed in 1946 and regularly sought divine intercession with the School Certificate Examiners so that I might pass. If any boy needed such intervention it was me.

That summer Miller and Guthrie camped with me in Harpenden while we harvested apples. When we finished work in the orchards, we cycled to the River Ver where we had permission to fish for pike to the delight of those who stocked the river with trout. Food was still short and the pike were turned into delicious fishcakes by Mother*. Again, in that wonderful summer Pater and I went to Arran. By this time I had a small .410 shotgun. I discovered how to catch sea trout and Pater and I had an excellent daily diet of delicious fish followed by rabbit stew. Neither could remember when we had last had such protein rich meals. That summer my life was nearly abruptly ended. Hunting rabbits among fallen rocks I fell backwards; the muzzle of the cocked and loaded .410 pointed up just below my chin. God, it seemed, did not want me.

By now, I was working rather haphazardly. Maths, a subject I did not care for, was essential and I prevailed on a somewhat reserved Master, Mr McConell, to give me extra tuition. Suddenly, in one to one teaching, I began to realise that masters, whose sole function had seemed to be the discouragement of all I wanted to do, were not only helpful but quite interesting. German was another impossible subject in which a credit had to be achieved. I could never grasp declensions nor understand the difference between

*From a recipe given by 'BB' in the Fisherman's Bedside Book.

'*den*' and '*dem*'. Another master, Mr Dean, taught me to read the lips of speakers when it is easy to distinguish between 'n' and 'm'. I am sure this trick made all the difference when taking German dictation. Other subjects such as Macbeth and Shaw's 'St. Joan' presented much less problem for I knew most of both by heart and often declaimed them while fishing.

I sat School Certificate at Christmas 1947 because it was thought that the extra term's preparation might just give me the chance of passing one or two of the seven subjects. I actually enjoyed it, treating the whole test as an enormous crossword puzzle, I used every trick of lateral thinking I knew. The English literature paper was the best fun. I returned in January to find that I had not only passed all seven subjects with credits and had matriculated but had also attained distinction in English Literature. Maths I had done quite well in but to this day the credit in German is a mystery though it was significant that my highest mark came in the dictation.

Those results were something of a nine-day wonder; instead of having to leave in the summer of 1948, I was put into an upper form to study for Higher School Certificate and there was a lot of catching up to do. Suddenly, instead of being a dunce of little interest to masters, I found myself getting attention from some of the most able teachers at a highly achieving school. Kirby, with no comment about the seeming miracle said "I shall try and teach you to think." He gave me a spade and made me dig out a huge patch of ground elder hovering round me repeating 'By the time you've done that, you'll know all about vegetative reproduction'. Someone must have succeeded in that process of inducing ability to think, though whether it was God, my father, Kirby, or the compilers of the Daily Telegraph crossword I do not know.

One subject that Housey was to cultivate in me was a love of drama. I took every opportunity to act and at school there were frequent productions. My debut came in a Speech Day production of a play by 'Old Blue'* George Peele [1556-96] called The Old Wives Tale in which I played the part of Zantippe, a love struck maiden, in the huge theatre of Big School. I had the whole stage to myself and

---

*Old boys of CH are called 'Old Blues'.

for the first time savoured the heady experience of having a captive audience silent before me. It probably had a lasting, and possibly damaging, effect upon me. Strangely the producer of that play was none other than Gaff Malins

Higher School Certificate in chemistry and biology were easy though how I ever scraped physics is another mystery. Another great teacher was Mr. Archbold. 'Archy' as he was known, was remarkably tolerant because I regularly fell asleep in his late afternoon lessons after playing rugby at which I had improved considerably. Archy taught imaginatively but he and I had a disagreement over a microscopic organism called *Chlamydomonas*. This green creature has, so I am told, a red eye spot. I disputed this and Archy tried with drawings to show me where it was. Eventually, he said: 'I believe you are colour blind, go and see the doctor'. He was right and suddenly I realised the reason behind the dispute I had had with my father over camouflaged vehicles at the outset of the war.

In 1949-50, my last year at Christ's Hospital, I was a Grecian, House Captain, playing rugby and running for the school; never before or since have I been so important. By then, having decided on medicine, I was invited to St Mary's Hospital for a competitive

Eric's Wedding to Doris with Pat and Doris' friend as bridesmaids.
Robin in a Grecian's Coat. Summer 1950

57

scholarship interview. Dr Tommy Scott, the school doctor, was an ex-Mary's man and he wrote a letter of support. Denis Brinton, a neurologist, was Dean of St Mary's at that time. He asked me a lot of questions about natural history and field sports before startling me by asking if I had ever been deer stalking. Despite evading this question, I seem to have impressed him. It must help attending an interview in Housie uniform; certainly, the yellow stockings made one as memorable as Malvolio. Perhaps it was that, or the letter from Dr Scott, perhaps they just needed a new hooker in the scrum; I was not only accepted but I was awarded the scholarship without which I doubt if medical school would have been financially possible. Returning to school with a university scholarship elevated me to the dizziest, topmost ranks of Christ's Hospital's hierarchy: a First Parting Grecian, a scholar about to depart for university. Just before I left school I played in *The Happiest Days of Their Lives* as a woman. My makeup was sufficiently adequate for me to have an interview with a master I knew well posing as the mother of a boy in his house. I began to see play-acting had enormous potential!

In 1950 I spent a last holiday in the Arran hills - walking with my father and much later recalled reaching the island's summit.*

'Goatfell, a perfect cone of a peak, rises Fujiyama-like out of a broad bay. Its lowest slopes are wooded with rhododendron, oak and pine from which red squirrels swear at walkers. Higher, the moors are quartered by hen harriers where fierce merlins harry the meadow pipits. The summit is a scramble amidst cyclopaeian walls of fissured basalt sparkling with quartz and far below, the sun-speckled sea reflects the changing cloudscape. But the glory of this summit lies in crossing to its eastern face where the deep cleft of Glen Rosa gapes before as crenellated a skyline as any in Scotland. The sun broke through as I paused at that view. And then I saw him. Perched on an overhang not twenty feet below me, with the vernal sun lighting his full glory, he contemplated his kingdom. A pebble moved; he glanced up, and, for a moment, eagle and boy looked each other in the eye. With unhurried disdain at a trespasser in his mountains, he eased forward till gravity caught him and he fell crook-winged into space The great bird plunged till, finding

*For the British Medical Journal, 18th October 1973.

a thermal, the perfect pinions opened and he wheeled so that the sun reflected on his majestic copper red back. For a mile he soared without a wing-beat, first down past Cir Mhor's jagged crest, then as a cross breeze caught him up and up over the shoulder of Beinn a' Chliabhain till he crested A'Chir to leave the boy, breathless with wonder, staring after the wildest being in the air and pinching himself in disbelief.'

At the end of that twenty mile walk Pater was in severe pain and bleeding rectally. That was the first indication of a tuberculous ischio-rectal abscess which was to trouble him for the rest of his life. Characteristically, though he walked very slowly, his only comment was that he had to keep up with me because lunch was in my rucksack! In that last summer holiday with Pater, my deer stalking at last paid off. With 'Old Work's' stolen Lee-Enfield Army rifle, I bagged a stag under the tutelage of that retired Glasgow CID Sergeant! Life in Scotland's remote places was still fairly casual but my poaching days were almost over. Not long before that, I had attended the tear-jerking school leaving service for the last time to be presented with Bible and a Prayer-book, as memories of Christ's Hospital.

Within months I was a newsquit again at St Mary's Hospital... but that's another tale.

Part II Medicine

Chapter 3 St. Mary's

In the October of 1950 I started at St Mary's. This was exciting but posed a number of problems not least of which was where I should live. Charles, when a medical student, had lived in Harpenden and commuted to Charing Cross Hospital and I assumed I would have to do the same. Dédé Bailey came to the rescue for she knew a Dr. and Mrs. Barton-Wright who were about to move to London and it was arranged that they would offer me digs in Earl's Court from where I could cycle to St Mary's. Barton-Wright was a biochemist working at Whitbread's research laboratory in the city. They were very good to me, housing and feeding me two meals a day for what seems now to be the ridiculously small rent of two guineas a week. I got my lunch and a cup of tea in the afternoon each weekday at the medical school restaurant for ten shillings a week and this even left a little over for a pint after Saturday's rugby. I went home on Saturday night and took an early London train on Monday.

My arrival at Mary's was to be greeted by extreme disappointment. My Higher School Certificate was not accepted as exemption from first MB and I was told I had to repeat all that physics, chemistry and biology. Five weeks into this course, on a return visit to Christ's Hospital, I mentioned this to Mr. Archbold, my biology master, who questioned the ruling of the St Mary's Secretary and suggested that I take the matter up with London University authorities at Senate House. I did so and the Medical School decision was reversed. That meant immediate promotion to the second year but in the interim I had lost six weeks and missed the whole of the dissection of the arm and a great deal of physiology and biochemistry. Already worried by the immensity of the work confronting me it was a devastating blow to find I was so far behind. Worse still the year into which I was thrown had settled, made their friendship groups and I was an outsider. In consequence I have never been so frightened as when I first entered the dissecting room to join the second year. I was told to report to a student called Peter Barnard, who later became a life-long friend. I did so, taking great care not to look down at the cadaver which lay on the table between us. I was never to forget the trauma of coming to terms with the first dead person that I had ever seen, whose body, after six weeks dissection, was somewhat ravaged. This incident was to influence research I carried out 40 years later on attitudes of medical students to death and dying*. Nothing was done in the fifties to address problems students might have on meeting death for the first time and that had hardly changed by the 1990s. We had to hide feelings and grow a carapace of insensitivity to protect ourselves; hardly a good start for members of a caring profession.

Catching up was difficult and I spent most of the following summer vacation alone in the dissection room with a whole arm to myself as well as working for Barton-Wright in the laboratory at Whitbread's to boost my grant. Despite initial squeamishness I found anatomy exciting, incredibly complicated but more challenging than anything I had met before. The understanding of the structure and function of the body was to me just an extension of the natural history I had always loved. During that summer vacation working in the vast, empty dissecting room surrounded by shrouded cadavers, exploring the complex, yet logically simple, relations of muscles and tendons, arteries and nerves I became fascinated by anatomy, my late entry to the second year turned from disaster to advantage and I began to plan a career in surgery. But it was hard graft and wonder at the subject's complexity combined with the awe at the amount of knowledge I must absorb seemed overwhelming. I remember describing to Peter Barnard how I felt. "It is like climbing from the bottom of deep well; at first everything is darkness, then there is a chink of light; it grows bigger as one climbs and one begins to feel hope of ultimate success. Finally one realises that as the circle of light grows bigger so the perimeter of dark ignorance grows geometrically."

Medical school has many distractions especially for a nineteen year old fresh from the monasticism of Christ's Hospital. There was rugby, there was beer, there were girls. The Student Union had many clubs and societies tempting me away from work but I was so terrified of failure, especially after my false start, that for the

*Death. dying and the medical student. Medical Education 1991, 25, 491-496.

first eighteen months I did little but work. Nevertheless messages were seeping home about my indolence. Poor Charles was sent to convince me that medicine meant a lot of hard work with nose on grindstone. He bought me a beer in the Fountains Abbey, the student pub across Praed Street, and read me a little homily. A week later it gave me great pleasure to ring him to say I had won prizes in anatomy and physiology and soon afterwards I passed the preclinical exam, the dreaded second MB, the biggest single hurdle of the medical undergraduate's life.

Clinical work as a student was even more exciting and there were two and a half exam-free years until the first part of finals. I was soon involved in dramatics, music and mountaineering. I played in Ian Hay's Housemaster, in Ruddigore and took the part of King Gama in Pincess Ida. Whenever possible I hitch-hiked the 200 miles to Snowdonia and learnt rock-climbing on Tryfan. Above all, there was bridge played for anything up to two hours every day. I loved it. One of the bridge fanatics was a rather bumptious Yorkshireman who got up everyone's nose. To make matters worse he was well off and that set him aside from the rest of us. Once, at a party, he became very obnoxious and clearly needed taking down. We got him very drunk, carried him to casualty and put a plaster cast on his arm. He appeared next day very sorry for himself and we all sympathised about his 'fracture', which he described as extremely painful. We left that plaster on for three weeks before we told him what had happened. After initial wrath he became a changed man.

By now the Barton-Wrights had moved to Paddington to a small mews flat where there was still room for me. This gave me such proximity to the hospital that I spent long hours in casualty most evenings, not just for the clinical experience but also for the sheer human drama. One night I spent an hour sewing up the multiple lacerations of a battered wife. In those days we did little but repair the physical damage; there was nothing in the way of social support. When I finished I let her go home only to hear from an irate casualty sister that she had taken our heavy duty torch as she left. An hour later her husband attended with a six inch scalp laceration; more practice for a keen student. When I finished suturing him he fished in a bag saying 'my wife said I was to give you this' It was our torch, badly dented from the blow to the man's head, but still working.

I loved the people of Paddington and found a new aspect of natural history in the study of people such as I had never come into contact with. One lady I got to know well; her heart was failing as a result of rheumatic fever as a child. I discovered she had had seven children and when I asked conversationally what her husband did she said " 'e's not me 'usband; the one thing my doctor told me was that I should never get married, not wiv my 'eart!"

Another old crone gave me an escorted tour of the surgical battlefield that was her abdomen: "This," she said, pointing to an epigastric scar " was me doodenal, this me gall, this 'ere in my side was me benedict* this one were where it were all took away†," then, pausing to add gravitas to her gesture, she pulled down calico knickers revealing a silver-haired pubis and a hairline scar in her groin "and this was me operation for rapture."

Praed Street was paraded by ladies of the night. A friend, rather nervous at his first attempt to take blood, approached one in a hospital ward with the time honoured "just a little prick" and was discomforted at her reply "that's all right duckie, I likes little pricks." A similar lady had a tattoo on her thigh of an arrow pointing inwards and upwards with a scroll below reading 'here's mine, where's yours?' I always thought it ecologically apt that Fleming's discovery of penicillin, which so readily cured gonorrhoea, should have floated in from Praed Street where the oldest profession encouraged venereal disease as it was called in those politically incorrect days..

There was little time for natural history but most days I took a lunchtime walk in Hyde Park where I listed the bird life of central London. I escaped from the city whenever possible for Capel Curig where the mountaineering club had a hut. There I spent my

*Appendix.

†Hysterectomy.

time walking, rock climbing and studying the flora which included masses of purple saxifrage, which I was not to see again until I came to live near Ben Lawers. I also saw my first ring ousels breeding in the gullies of Glyder Fach.

The president of the mountaineering club was Charles Rob, the Professor of Surgery, and we got to know each other quite well.

Learning to climb. Little Tryfarm, Snowdonia. Summer 1952.

65

Once when we were rock climbing together he fell while leading. He was only a dozen feet above me but as he fell he staggered backwards across the narrow ledge which separated us from a cliff. I threw myself at him pushing him back on to the rock face restoring his balance. He was winded but soon had enough breath to mutter: 'Thank you, Robin' before leading the climb again. Cynics said that had much to do with me subsequently getting, as my first job after qualifying, the prestigious professorial house surgeon's post at St Mary's under Professor Rob.

I look back on great names among my teachers: George Pickering was my Professor of Medicine before he was stolen away to become Regius Professor at Oxford. He was physically quite small but a giant among doctors. He was untidy, often with wisps of cotton wool on his face where he had cut himself shaving. Once he met his daughter's visiting boyfriend at the station. The boyfriend, assuming the dishevelled man who greeted him was the gardener, addressed him as such only to discover later who he really was. Another story was told of a patient whose relatives asked about the Professor Pickering whose name appeared above her bed. "He's such a nice young man," she said "he's always in the ward day and night, but what I like best about him is he's so kind to that untidy old man who sometimes comes round with him." The house physician was duly flattered.

When Pickering left he was replaced by a young Professor called William Stanley Peart who was a brilliant teacher and whom I remember with affection. While Pickering frightened us Peart almost treated us as equals and invited our naïve comments; his teaching rounds were a joy. Another great name was that of Sir Alexander Fleming, who sometimes passed us in the corridors. He was a bow-tied, broken nosed, diminutive Scotsman whose medical stature was enormous and international, but he was a terrible lecturer.

Perhaps my favourite subject was pathology taught by the avuncular, entertaining Professor Newcombe. Each student was supposed to carry out a dozen post-mortem examinations. Some of my friends hated this and did their best to avoid the PM room. Under Newcombe's tuition I did at least twenty, and though I found the first incision required all my courage once begun the mystery of finding the cause of death became so riveting that I enjoyed the gruesome task. Ryle*, who stressed the importance of natural history in medicine and particularly urged students to study post-mortem findings, would have approved.

My lasting memory of Newcombe was one of his autopsy demonstrations. There must have been ten or more students present. I was telling a friend a story. Suddenly the professor threw the organ he was teaching on at me with the cry "What's that, Hull?"

I caught the missile, which resembled a rugby ball, and threw it back at him answering correctly "A cricket ball spleen, Sir."

The immaculate white coat was splattered but the great man had little choice but to laugh.

Surgery was taught by a flamboyant individual called Handfield-Jones who always addressed male students as "Dear Boy". He was witty and acerbic but a great teacher. He shared his wards with Sir Arthur Porritt, a quiet athletic man who had been an Olympic runner and whose teaching, like that of Peart, made students use their eyes and think as if they were natural historians. Many of my contemporaries found that even more terrifying than HJ's biting sarcasm; I loved it.

Another teacher was Dr Carmichael Young, always known as Car. I was a medical clerk under Car and so enjoyed his teaching that I subsequently became his house physician at the nearby Paddington General Hospital where we students had much of our clinical teaching. As a student I had a male patient, a Mr. Birdseye, who presented with bloody urine and enlarged kidneys. I liked the man and was fascinated by his disease, perhaps because like my own problem of colour blindness it was genetically determined. After he left the ward I visited him at home in the back streets of Paddington and got to know his family well. This was my first

*See Preface.

'home visit': it was pure natural history and most exciting to see a patient in his own environment. Partly because of his unusual name I was able to work out his family history and published my first scientific paper* as a student.

In those days there were no elective periods which today allow students opportunities to travel and to gain wider wisdom and knowledge than the purely medical. Through serendipity I was fortunate to get such a chance that established many interests and probably determined much of the rest of my life. It happened that in November 1954 I was still suffering from post-exam lethargy following passing first part of finals, in Pathology and Bacteriology. There was now six months before the major hurdle of Medicine, Surgery and Obstetrics and Gynaecology in part II of finals. One foggy, damp night in November I was supping with the Barton-Wrights when suddenly my host asked, "Would you like to go to Ecuador." Not knowing where Ecuador was, I said, "Yes." And this is how I went.

A company in Belgium imported bananas from Ecuador but much of it was too ripe for sale. A very large claim was submitted to a London insurance firm who sought scientific advice from consultant microbiologist Dr. Barton-Wright who identified the trouble to be due to a fungus called *Thielaviopsis paradoxa*. The question from the insurance point of view was: are the bananas infected before loading (when the exporters would be liable) or on the ship (where it was the responsibility of the shippers)? So someone should go to see. It was suggested that I should be that person

Though it seemed impossible just before finals I determined to try and made an appointment to see the Dean of the Medical School, ophthalmologist Mr. Alexander Cross. To my surprise he seemed to know all about me as if he personally had followed my progress at the medical school. He probably had been given my record to look over before he interviewed me but at the time I was most impressed. He listened kindly to my request and astonished me by saying; "You must go, but I warn you, if you fail finals I shall personally have your guts." What a splendid Dean! My six weeks

*Polycystic Kidney Disease, Postgraduate Journal. 1954.

at sea with all my text books probably contributed more to my qualification than the same time working in London. My record of that trip comes from articles written on my return for the St Mary's Hospital Gazette* delightfully illustrated by my friend, a French student, Jean Boucherat. Rereading them more than fifty years later it is strange to reflect on the naïvety of my younger self. They were my first non-medical publications.

In early December I joined *MS Frubell Monica* at Antwerp. The day before, I had heard there were to be two other passengers: a Roman Catholic priest, and a Dutch girl of twenty-one. News of the latter interested me considerably but when I found her in the saloon my interest was instantly dashed: she was ample, almost

'Banana Doc' by Jean Boucherat, December 1954

*Hull, R. Banana Boat. St Mary's Hospital Gazette 1955 Vol. LXI No. 2, 35-38 and Vol. LXI No. 3 78-84.

to corpulence; horribly myopic and had a congenital nystagmus. As it turned out, Father Goovaerts was better company. He was a grand chap and though he hardly spoke any English we played chess together in the evenings. The Dutch girl lived in Curaçao and promised to show me the island. Life aboard was pleasant, the food excellent, drink abundant and cheap, and the company amusing. In my spare time, I even managed to do some work. After ten days at sea it became hot and my books were forgotten. My cabin was next to the Captain's, and though small was comfortable. I was provided with a Dutch wife, a bolster about eight inches in diameter and four feet long. Not knowing what to do with her, I slept with her for a few nights and then threw her on the floor. However, when the wind changed and the sea came athwart the ship, I learnt her function. By placing her under the mattress, I could prevent myself falling out of bed when the ship rolled. The Dutch girl complained to me that she could not sleep because of the rolling, so I explained the qualities of the Dutch wife. After lunch she tried it out, apparently with success, for that evening at dinner, during a painful pause in the conversation, she suddenly exclaimed: "It's wonderful sleeping with a Dutch woman." Fr. Goovaerts nearly choked on his soup.

When we reached the Lesser Antilles, it was getting hot but I enjoyed leaning over the side of the ship, beer in hand, watching flying fish. The sea was unbelievably blue and against it the white flashes of the fish as they skimmed over the water were like flocks of finches rising out of stubble. 'There are hundreds of them - some so tiny they looked like moths skimming over the waves, the biggest about the size of herrings.' Occasionally they would land on board whence they found their way to the galley! I also saw my first dolphin which was bow-riding the ship for hours at a time.

After thirteen days at sea, we reached Curaçao where the Dutch girl's mother showed me an island of dry rock kept alive by Venezuelan oil and covered by a dense pall of black smoke from the refinery. The people seemed to have oil in their blood, for they spoke and thought of little else. They even depend on oil for drinking: the fresh water is made by distilling sea water and is very expensive.

At the Panama Canal Fr. Goovaerts and I had to leave the ship at Cristobal to cross the isthmus by train. Cristobal lay in the narrow strip of Panamanian territory, only five miles on either side of the canal, which belongs to the USA. It was a dirty, picturesque city where native houses were built of wood and stood two stories high with the second storey overhanging the lower by about six feet so that they nearly met over noisome alleys between the houses. They all look dilapidated and some leant at a dangerous angle. The people were largely coloured people–negroes, Indians and a few Chinamen, the few whites were nearly all Americans.

We visited the Catholic Cathedral which was more ornate than any I have seen in Europe. There was much evidence of wealth contrasting with the poverty of the people. 'Fr. Goovaerts tells me that all over South America it is the same, the people are almost fanatical about their God but have no respect for man. Two things do not seem to exist here: they are time and morals. The only thing that really matters is money.'

The noon train across the isthmus to Balboa left, as usual, at 12.30, but once off it did the 48 miles in 80 minutes. 'The line follows the canal for part of the way, but when the lakes are reached, it dives into the jungle, so that on either side there is an impenetrable wall of green. Then suddenly it comes out to pass between shallow lakes, studded with the gaunt skeletons of trees where the rising water had invaded the forest.'

Occasionally we had a glimpse of ships passing through the Canal but apart from small towns at the locks we saw no sign of man: just jungle, water and a few colourful birds. It was incredibly beautiful. Only a hundred miles from Panama on the Southern side there are places no white man has ever visited–or if he has he has never been back to say so–and after seeing the country this was not surprising.

At Panama City we were met by the Panamanian agent. He took us out to a delicious lunch of ripe pineapple filled with tuna. Over this meal he told us his financial troubles: again money was the only thing that mattered. However he was quite good company and told me a lot about Panama. The agent had told us to be back in his office at 5.15 to meet him to go back to the ship. We arrived on time where a negro met us and said "wait". We duly did until 6 when the agent turned up without a word of apology and took us back on board. It was a strange but pleasant Christmas eve.

Christmas Day was marked with a great Belgian lunch; we spent a pleasant two hours consuming the meal before retiring to bed to sleep it off. We were due to cross the Line and I suffered much leg-pulling about my initiation to Neptune however I was left in peace.

We arrived in Guayaquil, 2° south of the Equator, where Fr. Goovaerts left us next day. In the Guayaquil river it was chilly at 7.30 a.m. and I enjoyed my first sight of frigate birds feeding from its murky water. The shipping agent came aboard, laid his revolver on the table before sitting down and remarked that a weapon was essential in Guayaquil. He went on to recount horrifying homicide statistics; in a catholic country divorce was not permitted so murder was the common substitute.

Before long the heat became unbearable and I developed a considerable thirst. Choosing one of the cleaner cafes I sat down so signalling to street hawkers of all descriptions to pounce on me with offers of shoeshines, lottery tickets, cigarettes and the like. One oversexed young woman was obviously not offering me any of these. My fluid balance restored, I had a new quest: to investigate the bananas. I walked along the river to the warehouses I had seen from the ship. There were a lot of ugly-looking individuals around the place and although, compared with them, I was quite big it was not a comfortable spot to be in. However I summoned up courage and wandered straight into the warehouse, trying to look like a disembodied spirit. It was not long before all eyes in the place were turned on me, several whispered conversations started, and it was clear that the consensus of opinion was for my leaving. Remembering the agent's warning and trying to look unconcerned, I sauntered past knots of men who examined me with an unpleasant curiosity. I had a feeling of uncomfortable expectancy between my shoulders and a desire to run. All was well, however, and even in those few moments I gained information which proved of interest to my boss in Antwerp.

The following morning loading started and was a fine sight. The stevedores, stripped to the waist, were every colour imaginable: black from the negroes, red from the Indians, white from the Europeans and yellow from China; most were a mixture of all four. The fruit was carried on the shoulders of the porters from lighters into the hold. By this time it was really hot and the men were running with stems of fruit weighing about 60 or 70Ibs. and the sweat streamed down their bodies. With working muscles gleaming in the strong sun, they made a remarkably fine sight. As animals, they are fine specimens; as men, it does not do to take your eyes off them. Morals, like time, seem not to exist out here. For the women, only one thing matters, and to judge by their appearance it starts mattering at about twelve, but by thirty they become blousy old hags. For that eighteen years they put all their goods in the window.

Loading finished at about 4.30 next morning and by 7 o'clock we were on the way back down the river. As soon as we dropped the pilot my work started. With the help of some of the crew I took 56 stems out of the hold and started the great controlled experiment. All day I slaved on nearly a ton and a half of fruit, labelling, making notes and infecting them with the cultures I had brought from home. Next day some of them were returned to the hold and some were hung on the beams supporting the awnings on the upper deck, making the ship look like some Covent Garden fruit stall. This was to allow comparison of artificially infected banana stems in the refrigerated hold with those kept at air temperature on deck. Then all I had to do was to wait for results and make notes on the progress of the infected stems.

Now I only had the officers and crew for company and, of course, a host of varied beasts who had elected to journey with the bananas. I never saw a snake in the holds myself, though one was reported in the forward hold, but whenever I was down there

I was acutely conscious of their presence. The captain says they are not venomous but I have my doubts and if I meet one in the hold I shall treat it with the greatest respect–even if they have got anti-snake venom serum on board. I took great care in the holds to watch out for them. Once when I was below making notes on my test bananas someone kicked the flex of my lamp and it went out leaving me in pitch darkness standing still waiting to be bitten by something. It was only seconds before the light came on again, but I was terrified. I had no love for the spiders either. They had bodies about an inch and a half long but I was assured they were quite safe and that I only need be worried by them if they had bodies the size of my fist; fortunately I did not meet anything that big.

We reached Balbao on New Year's Eve, too late to pass through the canal. I joined the captain in his cabin and with other officers we drank champagne and entertained each other with stories till Hogmanay. 1954 was longer by five hours than any other non-leap year because I saw it begin in Europe and end in Central America.

We had picked up only 900 tons of bananas in Ecuador which was only three-quarters of our capacity. Orders from Antwerp instructed us to go to Santa Marta in Columbia to pick up another 300 tons. As we changed course from the Panama Canal the Caribbean, so peaceful and pleasant on the way out, had turned nasty and I again lost my breakfast.

Santa Marta was beautiful; the port was built in a large bottlenecked bay much of which was lined by cliffs. A wonderful beach of white sand was backed by the town and a belt of palm trees. While I was there, I made the acquaintance of the British Consul and his wife. Mrs. Consul was a Scotswoman who accepted me on the strength of my Scottish mother. She was very kind, taking me round the town in her car, showing me the hospital, and the tomb of Simon Bolivar the liberator from Spanish rule. I gazed longingly at the foothills of the *Sierra Nevada de Santa Marta*, a northern spur of the Andes, which rise to nearly 19,000 ft. It was to be forty years before I saw the Andes again.

My hostess talked about the place which she apparently loved, and she suggested that I should learn Spanish and go out there to practice. There was, she said, a need of good doctors for tuberculosis was rife and almost everyone had syphilis. She told me there was to be a party that night at the offices of the fruit exporters and invited me to attend. That sounded fun and a good break from shipboard life. The party was not quite what I had expected. I was greeted by a man with a huge scar on his face; seeing me looking at it he muttered "cougar". He led me into a room where three other men were lounging about. I was offered a whisky and seeing it was a good one, I refused water. This seemed to impress them for they all drank it well diluted. One of the men slowly undressed, remarking that he was going to shower. Naked, he seemed to exhibit himself and I began to wonder what sort of party I had been invited to. There was more whisky and my companions seemed to be getting drunk; I sipped my second neat whisky and remained sober. At length a taxi arrived and we all bundled in. "where are we going?" I asked. "To the brothel, of course" answered cougar-face. "But I have no money," I expostulated, the Vice-consul's wife warnings of venereal disease ringing in my ears. "Be our guest." said cougar-face with a hint of menace; Only my ability to drink neat whisky saved me from being a complete wimp, but I did not want to contract syphilis. By good fortune the taxi was passing my ship and I was able to jump out and flee back on board.

The Columbian bananas were loaded very slowly and it was nearly three days before we left. In Santa Marta itself the weather had remained fine and unbearably hot but the Captain was worried by the cloud formation over the mountains. Within an hour of leaving we received a hurricane warning. The vortex of the storm lay right in our course, about 100 miles away. Orders were given to make everything fast and we kept course, hoping the storm would move elsewhere. Fortunately it did, but it left the sea very rough. From then until we reached the English Channel the ship rolled unmercifully, sometimes as much as 34° each way. Eating became more difficult than before from a mechanical point of view. Nobody who has not tried can imagine how much energy must be expended to eat soup on a ship which is rolling badly. On two occasions I had to drop my spoon to hold on to the table, and on each occasion, the spoon fell, vertically, into the plate of the man sitting next to me.

As we sailed east the bananas on deck soon ripened. There were one and half tons of them hanging from awnings. I ate as many as I could, as did the crew but for the rest of my life I have had a marked distaste for them. At air temperature the classical sign of infection with *Thielaviopsis paradoxa*, a smell of pineapple, was exhibited.

Once I had a narrow escape. Wearing plimsolls I stepped out of my cabin onto the wet linoleum of the passage athwart the ship. My feet slipped as the ship rolled and I was flying at a closed door; it should have been made fast but burst open and I was thrown right across the steeply angled deck and half through the guardrail. Clutching the safety rail I was half overboard in a tumultuous sea where rescue would have been impossible. Glancing up at the wing of the bridge above me I saw the officer of the watch cross himself at my lucky escape. That was the second time God did not want me!

The day before we reached the Channel, the wind reached Beaufort scale 12, hurricane, and we were forced to reduce speed because the ship was becoming unmanageable. The seas were tumultuous but the force of the wind was astern and I actually rather enjoyed it. But I was worried to hear that some officers never took off their life jackets even in bed. The sea broke in two scuttles, made of half inch thick triplex with a rim of cast brass which were battened down with a steel plate. One steel plate was torn off, the glass shattered and the brass twisted; the other was not so bad but still a considerable leak in an officer's cabin flooding the adjacent corridor with hundreds of gallons of sea water.

During the storm I asked for all my hold bananas to be brought on deck. I gave instructions to treat the labels with care since they described the inoculation status of each stem of fruit. The able seaman, whose English was poor, carefully removed each label and presented them to me like a deck of cards. My carefully planned experiment was in ruins. Fortunately observations on the

Columbian and Ecuadorian bananas proved my suspicion that the fruit from Guayaquil was infected on loading.

At last, we reached the English Channel and miraculously it was perfectly calm. I have never felt quite such an affection for England as when I saw the Isle of Wight, a dim smudge on the horizon covered by heavy rain clouds. The movement of the ship was stilled in the calm sea, England was in sight and bananas were very soon to be forgotten.

Early next morning we were in the Scheldt and by noon we were berthed. Almost immediately my boss and his wife came on board and heard my news and were satisfied with my findings. Then came the representative of the insurance company and the solicitor, and they too were pleased: so much so in fact that they gave me a handsome bonus on the spot.

That first international adventure had a profound effect upon me introducing me to global natural history and awakening a thirst for more; it also gave me a liking for ship-board life and a love of travel.

Shortly after I returned to the Medical school my friend Peter Barnard married Joan Gunn, one of the women students in our year. I was his best man and fell in love with his sister Winsland who was their bridesmaid. My life at Mary's, which had begun somewhat misogynistically, had developed after second MB and had blossomed with a number of girl friends and thoughts of marriage. However hard work and poverty precluded permanent relationships. Winsland was different but the affair came to a traumatic end when she, inexplicably, broke it off leaving me heart-broken and doubly shy of women.

In March 1955 finals came and to my astonishment were not as bad as I had feared. Suddenly I was Doctor Hull; if I had thought being a medical student hard work I was in for a terrible surprise. The 'house jobs' that followed were unbelievably arduous; a routine day would be from 9 am until 2 am or later the following day and there were frequent night calls as well. Once I worked solidly for thirty seven consecutive hours during which time I was expected to make life and death decisions. It was drudgery and, in retrospect, rather stupid but accepted as quite normal for the time. I was so chronically short of sleep that I learnt to sleep on the operating table for the two minutes it took to remove one patient and bring in the next. I even could sleep standing up when pulling on retractors while the consultants operated.

On one occasion I was assisting the Prof at a routine removal of a stomach. Sleepy as I was, I noticed a pair of artery forceps applied to a bleeding point in the lesser sac of the peritoneum, behind the stomach. The operation dragged on but at last the surgeon finished. Despite the normal swab and instrument counts I awoke during the following night and could not remember those forceps coming out of the lesser sac. Leaving a foreign body behind is everyone's nightmare, is likely to lead to litigation and stringent checks are made to avoid it. Nevertheless my doubts remained but I resolved to keep them to myself. The following morning I explained to the patient that I wanted an x-ray and tastefully clipped his pyjamas with four of pairs artery forceps ostensibly in the interests of modesty. The young radiographer was furious but I became the heavy House Surgeon and insisted. Later she dismissively flourished the 'useless' x-ray plate which showed five forceps.

I met Prof at the front door of the hospital and told him what had happened. He listened gravely, nodded and said "there's a round this morning, leave it to me".

Professorial ward rounds are a serious business. The whole surgical team comprising a couple of consultants, ward sister, a registrar and a houseman accompany the boss. There are several nurses and as many as twenty students. The procession progresses slowly, almost regally, from bed to bed. As Houseman my job was to note the Professor's detailed orders and see they were carried out for each of thirty or more patients. At last Prof approached the bed of the patient with the forceps. Gravely he studied the wound then he looked the patient in the eye and said. "everything is going splendidly, but do you know I think I could make it even better with a very slight adjustment. I suggest I take you back to theatre this afternoon to do just that. Is that all right?" Without waiting for the patient to reply he added: "Fix it, Hull," and passed to the next bed leaving the round wondering if he had gone mad.

The scene in theatre was extraordinary. Prof reopened the abdomen and inserted his left hand. Looking at me scrubbed up opposite him he gave an almost imperceptible wink. The wound was quite bloodless "Seems to be a lot of bleeding," he remarked "Artery forceps sister," and he clamped a bleeding point that only he could see. "More artery forceps," he demanded and went on doing so until all the instruments from two operating theatres were crammed about the wound. Then he started taking them off as fast a he could, throwing them about the theatre; some went into his boots, some got lodged overhead in the lights, some skidded under the door out of theatre altogether. Meanwhile sister was trying to count them. Then, for the first time he took out his left hand and gave me the missing instrument. His only acknowledgement was a faint smile as he said "Sew up, Hull."

So nobody knew... until today!

After Car Young's house physician job I worked as casualty officer at Paddington General Hospital. This gave me an introduction to the seamy side of Paddington life. I frequently had to repair knife wounds and occasionally dealt with homicides. I, and my fellow Casualty officers, were frequently in court as expert witnesses. Once at the Old Bailey a barrister who had questioned me before made me feel welcome by saying "How nice to see you here again Dr. Hull." But not all legal gentlemen were so pleasant. A colleague was asked his qualifications by a cross-examining counsel and replied "MB, BS London"

"Would you explain those abbreviations to the court?"

"Bachelor of Medicine and of Surgery," replied the doctor.

"Ah, I see you are not a doctor at all."

My friend suppressed his anger, thought for a moment and replied: "That is quite correct but my colleagues refer to me as 'doctor' in the same way that yours speak of you as their 'learned friend'."

During my time as a student my National Service had been deferred. Now that I had completed my obligatory pre-registration House jobs I was officially registered as a medical practitioner and so qualified to practice independently. But now the deferred National Service was looming. After my six weeks at sea with the bananas I had a hankering for the navy and chance was to increase this.

As a casualty officer I was still poorly paid but did get a holiday. I set out to hitchhike round Scotland where I had not been since 1950. I liked hitchhiking and once in a vehicle I repaid the driver's generosity with conversation; most drivers are bored and chat helps pass the time. Doing this I have discussed every conceivable subject and learnt a lot by doing so. Perhaps one of my most illuminating conversations concerned the works of Shakespeare but the truck driver who took me most of the way to Scotland was far better informed than I. On another occasion returning from Snowdonia I was picked up by a full car of Welshmen as darkness was falling. There was hardly room for me and my bulky rucksack, rope and ice axe. I was very surprised they had stopped at all. There were three of them; a father and two sons. They had just come from identifying the body of the third son who had been killed hitching-hiking home after a climbing holiday in the Lake District. Like me he was young, unshaven and unkempt and hampered by rucksack, rope and ice axe. The boys had not wanted to stop for me, but their father insisted and for two hundred miles he showered me with cigarettes, bought me a meal and called me by his dead son's name. When he dropped me near my home he hugged me and his tears wet my face as he kissed me. At twenty this was my first experience of grief; I was to remember it all my life.

In that summer of 1956 I got further north in Scotland than I had yet been. I visited Skye and then headed for Torridon. At Ullapool there was a destroyer in Loch Broom and, driven by midges into a pub, I met up with a group of naval officers. Chatting to one

I found we shared the same surname and that swiftly led to an invitation to the wardroom. I was captivated by what I saw of the warship and undertook to show Lieutenant Hull RN and a group of ratings some of the local mountains. Next day I took them to *Stac Pollaidh*, one of Scotland's most bizarre mountains. I liked the sailors and admired the easy but formal relationship with their officer. The Royal Navy seemed even more attractive.

National Service had hung over me all my student and pre-registration years. It had been deferred again to allow me to complete six months as Casualty Officer at Paddington. This deferment was not entirely altruistic; the services were short of medical officers and the more experience they had the greater their value. But by 1957 the patience of recruiting authorities was wearing thin. My friend Peter Barnard had decided to enlist for a three year short service commission in the Royal Navy. He pointed out to me that as we had to do two years anyway by joining for a third we became entitled to a handsome gratuity when we left. I decided to do the same. In many ways the services were to prove one of the most educational periods of my life. What those years did do was to make me realise how little I knew of the world outside the places where I had grown up and increased the yearning for travel born of my visit to Ecuador.

I was to be disillusioned at first as my colour vision was so severe that I was medically unfit, even as a doctor, for the navy. At the time the service was so short of doctors that my disability was ignored. I was suddenly Surgeon-Lieutenant Hull Royal Navy and another important phase of my education was begun.

Chapter 4 Naval Interlude

Periodically the military, as if to remind me of my unfulfilled duty to Britain, sent for me to have a medical examination. As a houseman I worked round the clock and I smoked heavily. Winter brought chest infections to the smog bound denizens of Paddington and I was amongst them. Coughing hard one day there was a sudden gush of blood but the chief's ward round was starting and there was time only to put the bloody handkerchief away and get working. By chance a few days later I was bidden by the RAMC to have a chest x-ray. The following morning I received a call from an apologetic Colonel "they had", he said, "made a pig's ear of the x-ray and would I return today for a repeat?" I remembered having said the same to patients when something alarming was observed on x-ray films. Then there had been that blood.....

In some concern I attended for my x-ray at the squeezed in time of 13.45 when everyone was out to lunch. Wandering around I found an office marked Radiology and there on the desk in the unattended room was my chest x-ray report. I read my death report: "Multiple secondary tumours throughout both lung fields."

It was sometime before the Colonel arrived and showed me my new film. In the middle was an awesome shadow. Summoning my courage I pointed at it and asked what it was. He looked at me in concern "That is your heart, doctor." The new film was completely normal.

That was the third time I was unwanted by God. I never knew what had happened, presumably someone behind me in the queue had his film muddled with mine. I do know that in the stunned minutes waiting for the Colonel's comment I had grown up a great deal.

Later, feeling at my fittest I attended a naval medical board. I knew there was likely to be a problem and it soon appeared in the form of the Ishihara test for colour blindness. I knew the right answers to this test and was able to hide most of my serious defect of colour vision. But the examiner was doubtful and stood me in front of a Martin lantern. This device shows a point of light whose colour can be changed rapidly by the operator. My task was to shout the colour each time it changed: " red, red, green, green, red"... and so on. After a moment the dead pan examiner asked: "You really want to go in the Navy?"

Thinking he meant rather than RAF or Army I nodded.
"There's a problem: I've only shown you a white light."

They needed doctors badly. At grade IV colour vision, unable to distinguish between a port and starboard light at a hundred yards I was in the Royal Navy.

Square bashing was awful but I remember spending a whole morning being taught how to salute on the march with a sword: a splendid accomplishment and one which I have never been called upon to use. I enjoyed the splendour of the uniform dignified by the thin red line of medicine between the lieutenant's twin stripes of gold braid but the formality of the RN Barracks Portsmouth was terrifying.

Then I was attached to the Royal Naval Hospital at Haslar presumably to be indoctrinated into behaviour appropriate to a young naval surgeon. It was terribly boring and I had little to do. Once, reading a Life of Nelson in the mess, I exclaimed aloud 'God, Nelson was a bastard!' A Surgeon-Captain crossed himself and others looked anxiously at the ceiling expecting it to fall in. My naval career was probably compromised from that moment but I have since changed my view of Nelson.

Mess nights were a riot. They began extremely formally with observance of tradition but after the port rapidly deteriorated into singing and games of Hicockleorum, a cross between a tug of war and a rugby scrum. Young officers had been know to suffer broken backs in this extraordinarily violent game. Sometimes Mess nights were open to wives when, if behaviour was more discreet, drinking was not. Once at a ladies night the port circulated generously and one Commander was seen walking with difficulty as he escorted his battle-axe of a wife to their car. As he left the barracks a senior policeman stopped him and asked where he was driving. With difficulty the Commander wound the window down and carefully enunciated "Bog-nor" and the termagant beside him froze.

"What a stroke of luck, sir, you see I have a young constable here who has just wrecked his motor bike, he lives in Bognor would you be so kind as to give him a lift?"

"Deligh-ted" said the Commander as the temperature in the car dropped several degrees.

Concentrating carefully the Commander drove miles out of his way. When the grateful constable was dropped on his doorstep the battle-axe demanded "Why the Hell did you say we lived in Bognor?"

"Shimply, me dear, becosh I didn't think I could say Shishester."

In April 1957 I travelled from Harpenden to Portsmouth, stayed the night in a seedy hotel and reported for duty early next morning in Loch Class frigate HMS Loch Fada as her medical officer. I knew that she was bound for the East Indies and would be based in the Persian Gulf for a year. This was almost exactly what I had hoped for. It is just about the hottest area I could be in and, though I had hoped for the Far Eastern Fleet in the China Sea, this was the next best thing.

I was warmly welcomed into her very friendly wardroom and soon realised I was in a community such as I had never experienced. I mentioned my previous night's accommodation adding that it was the first time I had stayed in a hotel in Britain. There was astonishment all round at my naïvety and I realised that I was among men used to a much more affluent lifestyle than I and that perhaps prudence should govern my tongue. In many ways I found the ratings more akin to my own background than the officers but I was separated from them as much by rank as I was by class from my fellows in the wardroom. I began to wonder how I should manage these social gulfs if I should have to cope with serious life-threatening disease or trauma. I suppose the ship's company was eyeing me in much the same way; we were to be away from home for a year and it must have occurred to them that at some time their lives might be in my hands.

The Captain, Commander David Loram, Royal Navy whom I liked immediately, had recently been Naval Equerry to the Queen. The first Lieutenant, a Scot called Archie Smith had a dry humour that I also came to appreciate. The Navigator, Michael Roope, was the son of a naval Captain who had been awarded a posthumous VC in the war. He had a strange habit of walking about with a handkerchief in his mouth but apart from that was fun and a great reader. Other officers included the engineer, 'the Gingerbeer' he called himself, Lieutenant-Commander Chris Wynne who was a delightful, quiet man, but expert at Mah Jong. 'El', Jack Ludbrook, the electrician, bubbled with good humour and 'Guns' Ernie Roshier, one of the sub-lieutenants, was a warrant officer promoted from chief petty officer [CPO] who was full of naval wisdom and protocol. I was to come to learn that good CPOs, or 'chiefs', were the salt of the earth, who combined humanity and discipline in a way that made them respected by the ship's company. Others in the wardroom included a marine officer, an underwater weapons expert and Sub-lieutenant Sidgwick the supply officer. The latter considered himself an expert at poker dice and we played frequently for after dinner liqueurs, which I usually won.

Accompanying me in the Medical Department was Sick Berth Attendant [SBA] Evans to whom I owed much as he guided me through the routine of shipboard life, language and tradition. Evans was the equivalent of a nursing sister and was both a technical assistant and professional confidant. At times of difficult diagnosis or worry he was a great support as I could think aloud to him. He bubbled with humour and loved, when I was syringing ears, to hold the receiver to the ear opposite the one I syringed! I soon learned our relative importance when a rating knocked on the sickbay door, saw me at my desk and smartly apologised saying he was looking for the 'Doctor' as SBA Evans was known among the ratings. Later I learned that on the lower deck the medical officer was called 'the prick farrier' conjuring up a mental picture of hammers and anvils! There was reason behind this nickname: life at sea seems to stimulate sex drive and after every port of call Evans would be busy preparing slides for the diagnosis of gonorrhoea. As a matter of prevention one of my tasks was to lecture the ship's company on sex. There are two ways of avoiding clap: abstinence and the use of a condom. It was quite apparent that a lecture on abstinence was a waste of time; the sailors were too keen for what they referred to as 'black ham'! I soon became a specialist in venereology so justifying the lower deck name for me. In the interest of prevention I put in enormous orders for condoms which waited for us in crates as we arrived in new ports of call. Loch Fada gained a reputation for its appetite for this particular item of Naval stores. However Ratings were strangely reticent about asking for them so I let it be known that the sick-bay was always open for them to help themselves. Evans saw to it that my policy was well known to the ship's company. When, late in the commission, we spent Christmas in Aden Evans designed a notice to be left with the condoms which he decorated with robins and holly with the legend "... And the Medical Officer says 'A Happy Christmas to you both!'"

Years later I was given a copy of the Royal Navy Officer's Pocket-book issued in 1944 which detailed the responsibilities of medical officers. Today it makes sobering reading and I doubt I had any concept of just what might have been expected of me. In fact I regarded the whole adventure as something of a joke. I was to grow up considerably in HMS Loch Fada in the company of her splendid complement of officers and ratings among whom I was to be confronted by life-threatening illness and death.

There is some mysterious chemistry, such as one sees in a year at university, a ward in hospital or even a general practice, which makes a corporate personality of a group and that renders the group happy or unhappy. It is hard to analyse but seems to depend on humour and a desire to succeed. This was at its most obvious in this floating iron box full of men at sea. Loch Fada proved to be a very happy ship and she, with 155 souls aboard was to be my home and very general practice for a year.

My cabin was a tiny box about five feet by five by eight tall with a recess for the foot of my bunk jutting into my neighbour's cabin. This small space accommodated a wardrobe, a huge chest of drawers with my bunk on top, a large writing desk and a chair. Going to bed involved climbing from my chair to my desk from which I vaulted into my bunk. When I first saw it my cabin was almost filled by my two trunks! The sick bay was large, though at present ill equipped since I had yet to pick up my stores. It was built as a miniature hospital with two cots for admissions. Evans asked my permission to sleep in one when it was not required by a patient. He was probably better housed than anyone in the ship including the captain but this was a privilege usually extended to the sick-berth staff. He moved out without a grumble whenever a patient moved in. I was very fortunate in my SBA

The Captain had invited Prince Michael of Kent, whom he had known at Buckingham Palace, to visit Loch Fada for a week. Prince Michael joined us a few days after I was officially installed and was accommodated in the Captain's day cabin behind the bridge. He was just like any other teenager of the time and, though neither would admit it, just as overawed as I was at the unfamiliar language and behaviour of the wardroom. We were busy 'working up' that is training for our task in the Gulf. This meant embarking every conceivable requirement from armaments to condoms and from malt whisky to chloroform and all the medical stores I might need to cope with any disease, or trauma that might come my way. I used to lie awake thinking of an emergency and mentally list everything I'd need to cope with it. An exciting if somewhat daunting challenge but one which I had reason to be thankful that I had rehearsed.

Most of the workup comprised putting the ship through every kind of drill: action against submarines, surface vessels and aircraft, controlling damage from enemy shellfire, putting out fires on board and so on. It was hard work but actually quite fun in a boy scoutish way. During the inspection which followed officers were suddenly challenged with ingenuity tests. The Inspecting Officer might suddenly say 'get me a fried egg' or 'a bloody Mary' and the officer so charged had to serve an egg or make a cocktail in the shortest possible time. Prince Michael and I were given the task of making a 'Jolly Roger'. The Yeoman of signals gave us a black pennant and we made quite an impressive skull and crossbones with sticking plaster from the sick bay. The flag was then flown from the masthead whilst we were attacked by six low flying aircraft. I was commended for the artistry of the skull but it was pointed out that, not knowing top from bottom of the pennant, I had made it upside down. The Yeoman, having respectfully shown me my incompetence said he would fly the pennant 'arsy-tarsy' so nobody knew!

Meanwhile I was attending to a dummy casualty on the bridge. Carrying a casualty about on a ship in a Neil Robertson stretcher is not easy and we got stuck in a narrow companionway when the unfortunate sub-lieutenant expired and returned to the bridge to carry on with his job.

Writing home I commented "Prince Michael is a pleasant boy– quiet and reserved but prepared to take an interest in everything. I have just been showing him the sick bay and teaching him how to use a stethoscope. By the way I can always say I have treated Royalty–he cut his finger and I had to put an elastoplast on it! Afterwards at tea in the wardroom I could see he wanted to ask something.

"What is it Sir?" I asked.
The prince went red in the face and said
"Please could I have another piece of cake?"

There could hardly have been a better demonstration of the normality of young Royals.

By early May we had completed working up and I had begun to find my way about. The ship's company had leave before sailing. I acquired my stores to prepare the sickbay for any eventuality during our commission. I had serious thoughts when opening my chest of surgical instruments: the first I found was a skull trephine;

it was a sharp reminder that I was responsible for treating anything that happened even if it required brain surgery.

We sailed two weeks later but developed engine trouble and had to return to harbour for two days while the problem was fixed. This always spells disaster for many a tottering marriage fell apart when a husband sailed. Once a ship made six attempts to leave Portsmouth but each time had to return. As a result there were 24 divorce cases! We only had one such case but I was not involved; the Naval Welfare Officers coped. An Able Seaman's wife tried to commit suicide after he sailed and I spent many hours trying to sort it out—finally arranging compassionate leave and for the rating to fly out to join us later. I had to travel 30 miles to see a petty officer who was supposed to be unfit to come with us—he had migraine and I managed to get him back to the ship where he is now better and quite happy. I was very glad to see the back of Portsmouth on Sunday evening. The coxswain's mate assured me that if we had not a) sailed on a Friday and b) had a priest on board to give communion on the day of sailing we would not have had to put back the first time.

I enjoyed the first leg of our passage out seeing all sorts of interesting beasts, many whales and sharks and lots of Portuguese-men-of-war, large jelly fish which have an air filled sail which they stick out of the water to catch the wind. The sharks were huge brutes 12-15 foot long. The Captain kept a rifle on the bridge to shoot at them*. Just as on my trip to Ecuador I was unable to identify the species that I was seeing and I was beginning to realise the immensity of my ignorance; it was like starting medical school again and every bit as fascinating.

Our first port of call was Freetown. There, before we had even tied up, transport was waiting to take me to the Military Hospital where I met an army captain from whom I got the odd medical stores that I needed. He showed me round his small hospital and then took me to the mess where I met his Colonel and was invited to lunch. I got back to the ship at about 2.30 and set to work setting up the

---

*One shark, shot by a junior officer on the quarterdeck after being hooked on a meat hook baited with beef provided supper for the ship's company.

evening's cocktail party. Such social occasions are a major part of showing the flag. Sometimes it seemed our most important task was fixing drinks! Often these were just informal gatherings in the wardroom as 'the sun was over the yardarm' when officers would invite friends for a drink. Once an officer entered the wardroom escorting so pretty a girl that all conversation stopped in admiration. Into the silence he asked her what she would like? She replied so all could hear 'I'd just love a nice cool John Thomas'*.

Our quarterdeck party at Freetown was a great success; the Governor Sir Maurice Dorland and Lady Dorland and everyone who mattered were there. As soon as the guests departed I dashed off and changed again and went ashore for dinner. No sooner had we arrived than the phone rang for me. A marine had gone berserk with a knife–so I had to go back to the ship. My host drove me back and sat in the wardroom drinking scotch while I sorted out the marine. Fortunately he had done no harm but it took me a long time to sedate him and get him turned in in the sickbay. I then went back with, by now, a rather drunken host to our very pleasant dinner.

We were due to sail the following day. In accordance with Queen's Regulations and Admiralty Instructions (QR&AI) I had put a request to Commander Loram for permission to grow my beard from that morning†. Sailing was delayed because of the obstreperous marine who, despite sedation was still violent. A deranged man is a potential danger in a warship and my Captain was acutely aware of this because before I joined a boy seaman had broken into a case of grenades and threatened suicide. He was disarmed by the gunnery officer but only after several grenades had exploded over the side. As we debated what to do the stubble grew on my face. Eventually it was decided to evacuate the marine; I had to arrange this with the senior medical officer in Freetown, a very disapproving RAMC Colonel who stared angrily at my quite correctly unshaved chin! But then the army never did understand the ways of the Senior Service! My brother Charles an RAMC

---

*A popular cocktail of the time was a Tom or John Collins.

†Permission was needed because a beard might make a man unrecogniseable; it was accepted that after a fortnight's growth either the man or his commanding officer could elect to discontinue growing.

Major during the war always grumbled at the sybaritic life of the Navy: "Why," he said, "you could even go into battle in comfort with your pink gin in your hand!"

It was very peaceful to be at sea again, even though I had a rating turned in with pneumonia and a large number of venereal cases to deal with. In the relative peace I wrote home describing the incredibly colourful town that was Freetown: "The vegetation is glorious. The bougainvillea is covered with red or purple flowers and makes a very vivid show. Another very fine sight is the flamboyant or flame-of-the-forest which is a large flat-topped tree with scarlet flowers which looks, as its name suggests, just like a forest fire from a distance..."

On 2nd June we crossed the equator which was an occasion of high jinks quite unlike my earlier experience in *Frubel Monica*.

Just after we left Freetown when it was quite dark, Neptune's Herald, accompanied by two bears, boarded the ship by the bows amid spraying water from hoses and fire and smoke from fireworks. He read a proclamation from his King announcing that Neptune would come aboard next day to meet the Captain and to initiate those among us who had not crossed the line. The Captain replied that he would see that the ship was suitably prepared to receive King Neptune and so, in a fanfare of trumpets the Herald returned to the sea.

Next day everybody off watch gathered on the quarterdeck. King Neptune came on board and made a present of a steel chain with seven keys on it to the Captain*. The court consisted of Queen Amphitrite, a number of bears, guards and attendants. Neptune, armed with his tripod was resplendent in a brass crown and a beard made from spun yarn. The Queen was radiantly dressed in mosquito netting and a very sexy pair of transparent black pants! Her flowing hair was again made of spun yarn and her figure adequately padded with sick bay cotton wool (underneath she was none other than the migraine-suffering Petty Officer I had rescued at the last moment from near Portsmouth). Neptune and

*The ship's crest is a horrible Sassenach pun; there are seven Lochs Fada in Scotland; hence seven keys for seven locks.

Amphitrite sat on their thrones, surrounded by their court, before a canvas swimming bath erected on the quarterdeck.

Those of the ship's company who had been charged were then brought up for trial. My own case was to have been first but I was at the time reloading my cine camera so the Royal Marine Officer went first and I followed. The clerk shouted my name and I was captured and forced before King Neptune where I knelt at his feet. My charge must have been longer than anyone's because two had been made out against me, one by the Electrical Officer and one by the ship's company. This indicates the rather special relationship there is between the doctor and the ship's company. By no means was I really a naval officer and was treated as a respected guest, and one whose services might be helpful, even life saving. I was naturally found guilty on all charges and King Neptune consulted his court as to what he should do about me. Amid a general shout of "throw him to the bears" I was placed on the chair with its back to the swimming pool. There it was decided that I needed various forms of treatment. I was given a pill, an injection and a dose of medicine by the 'Court Fishishian' and then the barber gave me a quick haircut and shave (the scissors were about two feet long and the shaving brush as large.) After the shave I was anointed with talcum (a large supply of which is obtained by sweeping the 'Charlie Noble'*!) and with a tip of the chair thrown to the bears who were eagerly awaiting their chance to duck me, throw me into the air and duck me again two or three times before I was considered free of my crimes and initiated. Then followed numerous other members of the ship's company who had not crossed the line before. The party eventually broke up with the King, Queen and all the court being suitably immersed in the bath themselves! A good time was had by all.

On 11th June we arrived at Simonstown which proved less busy than Freetown. It was mid-winter and we had changed back into blue uniform. As usual I was the first ashore to call on the local medical authorities to arrange for medical stores†, dental appointments and so on. The Cape was very beautiful with mountains rising steeply above the sea. Though they are only 3-4000' they were impressive

---

*The galley chimney.

†Most commonly condoms; the sailors seemed to get through masses of them but they saved a lot of infection.

and I wished I had had time to climb some of them. I was depressed by the political situation, dominated by the Apartheid laws. All transport had separate seats for blacks and whites, there are separate lavatories and even separate benches in the parks.

A few days later we were in the Mozambique Channel steaming up the east coast of Africa for Dar-Es-Salaam accompanied by a wandering albatross which followed the ship for several days This was the first albatross I had ever seen and I felt like the ancient mariner. I was beginning to look forward to getting ashore for a bit–two days in harbour was not enough and I spent most of the time working with not enough exploring! But again I was disappointed. We spent two days at Dar-Es-Salaam where I was invited to Government House but did not go because a marine corporal got fighting drunk. I had to stay on board to keep an eye on him. Soon we were at sea again off the Arabian Coast and due in the Gulf in a couple of days. We had run into the monsoon and had been battling gale force winds for three days. The sea had been quite remarkable–huge white crested waves the size of a house breaking over the ship. The wind was astern so the ship's movement was tolerable. I was not sick but with the rolling of the ship and the increasing temperature I felt pretty tired and looked forward to getting into the Gulf where it would be calmer. 'There are thousands of flying fish here reminding me of the Caribbean: the sailors collected bucketfuls of them from the deck, where the wind had blown them inboard. The quarterdeck, where most of them land has been out of bounds for the past three days because it has been awash in the rough sea.'

We arrived in the Gulf on 3rd July and spent the afternoon ashore swimming at a place called Khor Kuwai, a narrow strait of water between an island off the Musandam Peninsula and the mainland. 'The land is dry and barren but there are occasional wonderful sandy beaches between the cliffs. The sea is perfectly clear and very warm. I had bought a face mask and flippers so I was able to swim around watching the fish. I have heard how delightful this is but in reality it beats all descriptions. There are myriads of fish of every conceivable colour swimming over the coral and I spent hours just gazing at these colourful creatures.'

However there were other nasties: sea urchins have long spines which penetrate deep and painfully. Once I was called to the engine room to catch a live sea snake which had been caught in the weed trap of the salt water intake. The snake, which is extremely venomous, was about three feet long and one of the hazards of swimming here. Fortunately, like the big sharks, they keep out in the deep water away from the beaches. This one was injured and did not last long.

Medical work was never pressing but often quite worrying. Once I treated a rating's chest infection with sulphonamides and, despite my order to drink plenty, he developed anuria. The high humidity caused formation of crystals of sulphonamide in his kidneys. For some hours I was a very anxious man and grateful for the support of 'Doc' Evans. Fortunately in the cool of the sickbay with plenty to drink he soon recovered. On another occasion a senior Chief Petty Officer, old enough to be my father, sat down beside me in the sickbay and burst into tears: nobody had ever told me how to cope with that in medical school. In a few moments that man taught me things I did not know about doctoring. On another occasion a Somali lad, employed as a sweeper, was found hanging in his mess deck. He was cut down and brought to me with little more than a rope burn on his neck. The man did not speak English but, through an imperfect interpreter, I learnt that there was a criminal and very lucrative gold-smuggling trade between East Africa and Pakistan. The boy's extended family had sunk their entire wealth in buying gold which the boy had to deliver in Karachi. As an insurance policy tribal elders had placed him under a conditional curse; if he absconded then the evil eye would fall upon him. Somehow thieves got the gold and the youngster began to dwindle and became suicidal. I had the difficult task of persuading a senior RAF psychiatrist to admit a case of acute evil eye. I never knew what happened to him, I suspect he dwindled and died. Later this experience was to influence my understanding of both Australian Aboriginal health and of palliative care but at the time seemed a strange tribal curiosity.

In July I was busy, in temperatures up to 105° in the shade, for many sailors were down with Asian 'flu. At Bahrein I was also caring for the ratings at the shore base where they have no sick bay or medical officer. I now had an epidemic beginning on board. However I enjoyed Bahrein; after midday work was impossible because the heat was enervating. I spent the afternoons in the pool attached to the wardroom of HMS Jufair, the 'stone frigate' or shore base at Bahrein. The pool was also used by the Foreign Office girls who work at the Residency where the British Agent lives, so there has been some social life as well. Like everyone else I was already feeling the sex starvation consequent on the monastic milieu of the ship. I could sympathise with the queues of ratings consulting me after encounters in African bordellos. No wonder QR&AI laid such tiresome instructions to medical officers when dealing with 'unnatural offences'. I had one such case in the ship and was obliged to carry out an unpleasant examination of the man concerned. The fermentation of so much unrequited testosterone in a warship has made me wonder how the modern navy copes with women at sea. That is nothing new of course; women often went with their men in the old days. This has had its effect on present day custom. The morning cry of 'show a leg' dates from the time when a man and a woman might share a hammock; a feminine leg shown gained a few minutes longer to sleep while the men dressed. Another term 'son of a gun' came about because gunners often had more free time than other sailors. This meant that a gunner was more likely to be the father of a child conceived at sea. Another intriguing explanation relates that when labour was slow the poor woman was lashed to the breech of a cannon which was fired with a blank charge; the recoil pushed the foetal head well down into her pelvis.

Sailors collected their daily rum ration in a mug called a fanny. This was named after Fanny Adams, a prostitute who was murdered in a naval dockyard. Her body was dismembered and scattered round the dockyard. The crime attracted much publicity at a time when naval victuallers introduced canned mutton into the sailor's diet. Inevitably, given lower deck humour, this food became known as Fanny Adams and later the lady's name was prefixed with 'sweet'. The container, abbreviated as SFA, proved a useful receptacle for rum. Freud was well aware of the genital symbol of such a container; fanny took on a new meaning and FA was expanded as 'fuck all'. Language, even when obscene, often has intriguing history!

We sailed for Basra where we were due to stay a week and I looked forward to seeing it as it was reputed to be 'a good run ashore' in the Gulf. But Basra was extremely busy and disappointing (apart from the quantities of delicious shrimps taken from the murky waters of the Shatt-al-Arab doubtless fattened by waste effluent and the bodies of countless victims over the centuries). Apart from some of the sick whom I sent to hospital I was the only person allowed on shore because we were quarantined. I was ashore on medical business reporting to the Port Medical Authority on my epidemic, and I was entertained to a first rate lunch; there seemed to be no restriction on me but everybody else was confined to the ship under its yellow flag indicating fever on board. So much for a good run ashore for the ship's company.

After two days we were ordered to Bahrein to embark a large quantity of arms and ammunition for the Trucial Oman Scouts at Dubai because of a revolution in Oman whose Sultan had appealed to Britain for help. The trouble was in the mountains about 300 miles inland so we did not anticipate any excitement other than searching for gun-running dhows along the Batinah Coast of Oman. That meant steaming up and down the Omani shore looking for dhows. With air temperature at 110° and sea temperature 92° humidity is so high that sweat continually poured off me. We inspected several dhows but found nothing.

We had an afternoon in Muscat which was a strange place set in rugged mountains, which end in high cliffs at the sea. It was guarded by huge medieval Arab forts which looked like the forts in Foreign Legion films. I commented in a letter home 'Muscat is the hottest place I have ever been in, but I think one of the most attractive and genuinely Arabian cities I have yet visited. It is original, looks as if frozen in the fifteenth century and is not grossly and hideously modernised with oil wealth. With the Marine and Supply Officers I explored the city admiring stately mosques and the Sultan's palace on the waterfront. The people are very friendly though they are all armed. Their guns are quite extraordinary, many must be nearly 50 years old and often bound together with string.' Every man wore a great curved knife, called a khanjar, in his belt as a mark of status.

'The women, like all Muslim women, keep themselves veiled. However here in Muscat, instead of being completely shrouded in black veils as they are in Bahrein or Basra, they wear the brightest possible colours. I took some cine films of them but later heard that this was a punishable offence.'

The buildings were most attractive, especially the mosques with fine domes and minarets. The bazaar was a maze of alleyways between shops selling a peculiar mixture of oriental and occidental goods. The Sultan was reputed to be a character who disapproved of western new-fangled ideas such as spectacles so everybody was half blind. He also disliked the internal combustion engine and had forbidden cars in the Sultanate. He owned a Mercedes himself but had a trained team of donkeys to pull it! In my letter home I added: 'Muscat is a good place to visit once but I don't think would bear a second visit!' *

The best part was the harbour set in a rocky bay where, like others before us, we painted the ships name on the rocks. We spent hours swimming in the clear water of the bay hunting fish and capturing delicious crayfish. Less pleasant were sinister barracuda and huge Moray eels which lurked ominously in rock-clefts. I often felt I needed a rear view mirror when swimming in the Gulf.

After sailing from Muscat, our Leading Writer, one of the National Service supply ratings, reported sick with appendicitis. In view of the importance of the patrol we are engaged in I did not feel justified in asking the Captain to make for hospital several hundred miles away. I sent a signal to HMS Modeste, another frigate, about 100 miles distant and she came to meet us. Her doctor gave the anaesthetic and I operated. The patient had a very nasty appendix so

*How wrong this was; Oman was later to become one of our favourite countries *vide infra*.

I was fully justified in my decision to operate and he did very well. The operation itself was rather protracted. The chap helping me had trouble with the anaesthetic, because in the high temperature the volatile ether evaporated before being inhaled by the patient; it took two hours to get my patient flat enough for me to go ahead. I took about an hour doing it but I have only done them before in proper theatres and at sea I had to be my own theatre sister, sorting out my own instruments and threading my own needles instead of just asking for them as one does in the luxury of a proper theatre. In fact we inadvertently put the ship in danger; the anaesthetist used so much ether that it was smelt in the boiler room and ether vapour is highly explosive.

Later the Captain and I went ashore to call on the local Wahli who is like a mayor. The visit was partly medical and partly social as we had had a signal requesting medical assistance at another place where we were to call the following day and so, just in case there are any sick today I was to go along too. The trouble tomorrow may be anything from a full scale epidemic of plague to an in-growing toenail!*

'That trip ashore was fun. The motor cutter couldn't beach as it was too shallow so we had to wade ashore. Everyone ashore was delighted to see us but the local boss-man was away. We wandered round for a bit asking where we could find his deputy. Eventually the deputy turned up and we all shook hands and told each other what good fellows we were. Then I set up surgery sitting cross legged on the beach. I only had half a dozen patients of whom most had nothing much the matter. Most had been treating themselves by heating charcoal red hot and putting it on the place that hurt and so had burns. One man had an injured wrist which I strapped. The last patient had an advanced cancer of the stomach so I advised him rest, his tumour was far too advanced to do anything. We then left after exchanges of goodwill. I doubt if I have done any good at all from a medical point of view for I was little better than an 'elastoplast doctor' but socially the visit was a great success.'

---

*In fact it was a false alarm.

Next day we had another visit at a place called Dibah on the Batinah Coast. Just before going ashore I held my usual morning surgery and another man reported sick with probable appendicitis. I turned him in to await developments while I went ashore. Again everyone was delighted to see us. We called on the local Big Man who took us to a rough building with the most splendid rugs and cushions where we sat for two hours carrying on a desultory conversation through an interpreter. Although we had been warned that medical assistance was needed nobody had asked for a doctor. However patients soon turned up and told me their troubles. Again there was very little I could do. Many of them had backache and seemed to enjoy having liniment rubbed on! Their eyes were in a terrible state. Trachoma is very common and most have diseased eyes either with it or resulting from it. Trachoma is a very infectious virus condition which could be treated if only they had some medical organisation. Out here, however, where there is oil there is everything, where there is no oil there is nothing. After a long wait a meal was provided for us consisting of mangoes, dates and chapatti washed down with fresh lime juice and followed by coffee. We left presents of flour, sugar and tea and went back to the ship.

That afternoon I decided to operate on the second appendix so we made for Khor Kuwai, which is more or less our base during this Omani trouble. There we met HMS Modeste and her doctor again gave the anaesthetic. By now we had little ether left so my guest anaesthetist used pentothal, I infiltrated the abdominal wall with local anaesthetic and with the ether we had I removed the worst appendix I have ever operated on. The appendix perforated as I removed it and the rating developed localised peritonitis but his temperature is normal and he is feeling well. Perhaps I should have operated sooner but in retrospect his illness had not appeared as severe as the earlier case. It is amazing that we should have three appendicitis cases (the first I sent ashore) and I think we have now had our ration. We now have two appendices as trophies pickled in wardroom gin which we show off at cocktail parties! There was no doubt my stock was high on board!

The tedium of patrolling was broken by a kusi with the Sheikh of Um-al-Kuwain, one of the Trucial States. I went with the Captain and three other officers, dressed in my best white uniform and wearing a sword. After formal greetings at the Sheikh's fort we were shown to his dining hall. At one end was a large mat about 12 feet in diameter with carpets distributed round its perimeter. The mat was laden with food. As usual the main food was whole sheep*. In the centre was an enormous dish about a yard across laden with mutton and rice cooked with saffron. Arranged round this were ashets piled with beautifully cooked rice and beside each plate of rice another bowl of mutton. The last circle of dishes on the mat contained tinned fruit, dates and mangoes. We each squatted, sitting on the right foot with the right leg tucked underneath and the left knee bent with the left foot firmly placed on the ground–most uncomfortable but it is very disrespectful to show your host the soles of your feet. Then we dug in using the right hand only. The food was very good but rather messy to eat, especially since by now I was heavily bearded. The Sheikh was a delightful old boy who did not seem to be worried by the lack of conversation. Silence apparently is not an indication that Arabs are not enjoying themselves–rather the reverse. After an hour we were all so cramped we needed help to get up!

Occasionally a passing ship would signal asking if we had a doctor on board. This produced medical challenges. One such case was extremely ill. A Russian seaman had injured himself by diving into the Suez Canal while his ship was anchored there. He had become unconscious a week later when the tanker was in the Gulf. The man was barely rouseable with a three inch healing laceration on his forehead. I examined him carefully with especial attention to his nervous system. My only finding was a very slight right facial nerve weakness. I suspected a subdural haemorrhage and, after discussion with the tanker's captain, arranged air evacuation.

On another occasion a signal from a tanker had me hurrying in the motor cutter to a severe head injury in a rating who had fallen onto the deck from rigging. I feared that I might after all have to use the trephine from my surgical kit but the man was dead when I reached

---

*Mercifully it had filtered through to our host that British officers did not care for the delicacy of a sheep's eye.

him. I reported this to the tanker's captain who was furious that I had been called as he had had to slow down to pick me up. Even a few minutes loss of time in a full oil tanker costs a great deal of money. I was relieved to be spared an attempt at brain surgery but distressed by the tanker captain's attitude.

We resumed patrol looking for the leaders of the revolt who were supposed to be making their escape to sea so we, with two other frigates, searched every dhow we met. Nobody really expected to find them for this coastline is full of little rocky bays and inlets where anyone could hide–but we had to keep looking. By now I was officially in the dhow boarding party*. Though I boarded several I found nothing except a beautiful tame gazelle which one was carrying."

After two months in the Gulf I suddenly became ill. I turned in one evening with pain in my back. During the night I woke with rigors and soon found my temperature was 106°F. Then I had so profuse a sweat that my sheets were soaked. By morning help came when SBA Evans came to check on me. As the only other member of the medical department Evans immediately took charge. He admitted me to the sick bay and reported my illness to the Captain. Later I was to hear he thought I had poliomyelitis. I felt so ill I wanted to be left alone. As a seaman-like precaution a canvas bag was prepared in case of need for a funeral at sea. Evans looked after me devotedly as my fever waxed and waned. The Captain made for Bahrein where I was admitted to Bahrein Government Hospital at Manama. Shortly after I was admitted I developed jaundice due to infectious hepatitis and remained in hospital for a month while Loch Fada sailed away without me. While Fada was at Bahrein I did very well for visitors since all the officers came to see me several times and the Captain came three times. I felt absolutely bereft when the ship, which had become my home, left.

As soon as I was able to take notice of my surroundings I saw a familiar scarred face in the next bed. It was my Russian seaman patient. He had been lucky to survive tetanus from his wound. What I had taken for a right facial weakness was the beginning of

*Armed, in contravention of the Geneva convention, with a revolver.

the classical *risus sardonicus*–the sardonic grin of tetanus, which had increased muscle tone on the left. This was the only case of tetanus I was to see in my professional life. It crept in to much of my writing*.

In early October I was discharged from hospital after arrangements had been made for me to spend sick-leave in Cyprus and I was flown to Nicosia by the RAF. From Kyrenia I wrote that Cyprus was beautifully cool after Bahrein. By now I was pretty fit but tired easily. On the flight to Cyprus I had met a Major Dickerson, who lived in Cyprus. He had visited Bahrein in connection with a court martial and had returned home on leave himself. I think he was glad of someone to play with and he was very kind. He took me to Episkopi in the South near Limassol from where I travelled into the mountains at about 4500' where it was beautiful and delightfully cool.

After two months away from the ship I rejoined her at Bahrein in early November where we immediately sailed for the Batinah coast again. I was really glad to be back on board with my friends in the wardroom.

Our visit to Karachi was dominated by taking part in a large multinational naval exercise. Karachi was fascinating and the engineer officer and I explored the markets. The carpets here were magnificent, I had never seen such wonderful colours in carpets before, but they were prohibitively expensive. I could not find one that flew but for the price of them they might have been expected to do so.

I visited an elderly Begum who was a friend of neighbours in Harpenden with Chris Wynn the engineer officer. The Begum was of an old aristocratic family in Kashmir which was still in dispute after the partition of India by Cyril Radcliffe†. She invited us to join her at a later date for dinner and we were looking forward to that and to learning at first hand of the troubles of Kashmir.

---

*Infective Disease in Primary Care. Chapman and Hall. London 1987.

†Viscount Radcliffe of Hampton Lucy [1899-1978] who became a
neighbour and patient of mine.

Karachi exhibited the usual squalor one found throughout the Middle East but that somehow was part of the picture and horrible though some of the beggars were they belonged as much as red busses did in London. Everyone chewed betel nut in the street and there was the ubiquitous aromatic scent of spices in the air.

One day I went to a shoot about 50 miles north of Karachi in the Sind Desert. Our host was planning to take us to a lake where he had shot duck seven years ago. Unfortunately we got lost but, by great good fortune we got back to the car and went off to another place where we had about two hours of magnificent sport with partridge and pigeon (later identified as see-see partridge and eastern stock pigeon). I got a brace of partridge and four brace of pigeon and was able to feed the wardroom on pigeon pie that night. I had never had a day like it and it was the best day I had had since I left home. Spending a whole day in the country itself like that was great fun–I learnt far more about what it was like than just seeing the coastal area. The birds were wonderful. There were hundreds of parrots and parakeets, many different kinds of hawks and at least three species of beautifully coloured kingfishers. How I would like to learn more about the natural history of this amazing sub-continent.

The exercise with Pakistan Navy kept us very busy culminating in a review by the King of Afghanistan*. Next day we were unexpectedly ordered to sea to resume patrol. This meant that we missed our dinner with the Begum and had no means of communicating with her; I still feel guilty about this apparent lapse of manners.

In this part of the world there is always something happening and so our movements are totally unpredictable but we were promised Christmas at Aden. This, as I anticipated, was hectic and alcoholic. I met up with an old friend, Barry Lovell, with whom I went to Paris, when we were housemen. He was an RAF doctor there. We explored Aden together and climbed Shamsan, the highest point in the crater of the extinct volcano.

*King Zahir Shah was king of Afghanistan from 1933, after the assassination of his father, until 1973 when Zahir was overthrown by military coup because of severe famine in Afghanistan while he was receiving medical care in Italy.

Christmas aboard proved too much for many officers. For me it started with a sick bay parade in the normal way and then I went to prepare the wardroom for the party we were giving to the Chiefs and Petty Officers. I made up a large quantity of rum punch. They arrived at 11 o'clock and the wardroom was packed–and they consumed all the punch. We then moved on to the messes. It is a Christmas tradition that officers visit the messes and drink rum with the ratings. It is also tradition that you may not refuse a drink. Before very long the officers were being helped to bed one after another! I put the navigating officer to bed three times as he fell from his bunk four feet onto the deck; his Boxing Day bruises were spectacular! With a monumental hangover I played my last game of rugby on Boxing Day on a pitch that felt like concrete; I vowed never to play again!

Early in the New Year we visited Djibouti in French Somaliland. Djibouti was very French and hardly anybody spoke English. We went to the Governor's Palace to meet H.E. and were entertained to champagne for half an hour whilst we struggled to communicate with each other. Few of them spoke any English at all but I found one or two with whom I could converse in German.

One evening five from Fada's wardroom joined some French officers for a picnic on the beach. Imagine a party with a lot of excitable Frenchmen on the beach under palm trees and a tropical moon–unfortunately there were only four girls who were all very much attached or it would have been very romantic. Mike Roope had the misfortune to get stabbed in the bottom with a palm frond, the ends of which are very hard and sharp. I ministered antiseptic from a bottle of whisky and the following morning I had to cut it out of him with the result that he could only sit on his port side!

From Djibouti we went on a Cook's tour of the Gulf of Aden. We were diverted to Berbera in British Somaliland. There was a strike on there and it was feared that there might be rioting but in fact all was quiet when we got there. Berbera was an attractive place and I made friends with a very pleasant doctor and his wife who arranged an evening's shooting for us. The Captain, Mike Roope and 'Guns' and I, armed with a mixture of weaponry went off into the desert where we saw plenty of gazelle but were unable to bag any.

We had great plans for our stay in Berbera: I was going to help at the hospital, where the doctor was very busy, and we hoped to fix up more shooting. Unfortunately as the supposed strike had settled down without civil unrest, we had orders to sail again the following morning.

From Berbera we anchored off Socotra where there was no harbour. Though its beaches have heavy surf we managed to embark two heifers into our whaler which was then towed out to the ship by motor boat. The poor cows were then hoisted by derrick with huge canvas slings under their bellies. They took the whole operation stoically and are now happily chewing the cud in specially constructed stalls on deck. They seem to have taken very well to the idea of naval life. We then returned to very familiar waters on our way to Bahrein to gladden the heart of the Socotran bull who lives alone there. We were to be in Bahrein for 24 hours before sailing to Karachi again for our refit giving us ten days in harbour. I hope to get up country again for more shooting. I very much enjoyed these trips inland. I remember how delighted we used to be when going on holiday when we first saw the sea from the train: I get the same sort of feeling now when it goes out of sight!

In Bahrein I found an excellent jeweller and bought a couple of very nice pearls for my sister together with a sapphire which will be her combined Christmas and birthday present. It was great fun buying them as I had hundreds of pearls and stones to choose from which an old man emptied out of tissue paper packages all over the top of his desk. There were pearls half an inch in diameter and sapphires, rubies, emeralds, opals and aquamarines by the score. It was quite fascinating; I bought an emerald because I thought it was beautiful. It cost me £20* but as it has a fault in it I believe it is genuine. I am not sure what I shall do with it.

Gradually the commission drew to an end and it was time to go home. In March we celebrated leaving Khor Kuwai for the last time with a party. We built an enormous fire and cooked sausages,

*£333 in 2006 prices

steak and bacon and washed this down with litres of wine before basking in the sun in a temperature of 140°F. After we had recovered we wandered round the island after partridge and I saw my first hoopoe. But trouble was not over for, within hours of departure from Muscat, I was shaken in the night to see 'Guns' who had been taken ill with a perforated gastric ulcer. I reported to the Captain asking him to return to Muscat. I had a trying time looking after the officer until we got him ashore where I assisted a local surgeon* to operate on him in the Mission Hospital at Muscat. I was glad to hear after we sailed again that he was doing well despite the inevitable delay before surgery It is a difficult looking after one's friends when they are seriously ill.

My last incident in the Middle East was in Aden in April 1958, where there has been trouble with the Yemen. We were ordered to stand by but had not had to do anything. There was one spot of unpleasantness when a fanatic threw a home-made bomb into a cafe. Two of our ratings† were injured and are in hospital. After visiting them in hospital in plain clothes at 2 am I decided to walk back to Loch Fada unaware there was a curfew. I was arrested by a terrified RAF other rank who mistook his tanned bearded prisoner for a Yemeni terrorist. I was duly identified and driven back to my ship.

* * * * *

My final adventure occurred the day I left Loch Fada and was to affect the rest of my life. When an officer, particularly a popular one, leaves his ship it is traditional to throw a party. I left Loch Fada very drunk and travelled to and across London with difficulty. I was just sobering up when I reached the station at Harpenden, my home town. I was encumbered with two trunks which I had to collect from the guard's van. It took a few moments to sort out my baggage and I noticed a girl also walking to the guard's van. With horror I recognised that my mother knew her mother and I greeted her in what she afterwards described as 'a gale of brandy'.

---

*Dr Donald Bosch.

†One was badly injured with bomb splinters in his bladder.

For a moment the girl froze, then reading my name on a trunk, she realised that her mother knew my mother and that we lived close by each other. There was only one taxi and it took two minutes to arrive. In that time I learned that she had just left Bristol University and decided that I was going to marry her.

I had six weeks leave in which to woo her and convince her that this was a good idea. I had the lovely half carat emerald that I had purchased in Bahrein as my only armament. I bought a clapped out old Morris Post Office van and with Gillian as my driving instructress learned to drive it. Her mother, a painter, asked me to sit for her. Little did I know that this was an investigation into my suitability. I passed the mother-in-law test but convincing the daughter was less easy. But by dint of proposing at least three times a day adamantine refusal was overcome and with a bare three days of leave left we were engaged and a date was set for our wedding in St Albans Abbey four months ahead.

Gillian was 22 and had read French at University and was from a very musical family. Through her architect father she was a keen hill walker and has always known far more than I about wild flowers. We had so much in common of which most important was a huge desire to travel. The future looked incredibly exciting.

But the navy, as always, had no regard for lovers and, my leave over, I was ordered to the Royal Naval Hospital Chatham. If the service up to now had been challenging and great fun the full tedium of being a general duties medical officer now hit me. I was attached to the surgical division of the vast empty hospital where my professional day started at 0830 hours. Officially, apart from when I was duty medical officer, it ended at noon but in effect there was little to do by nine o'clock. After the frenetic life of the NHS when a junior doctor's day seemed never-ending and one had to run to keep up with the demands of the job, this was boring in extreme.

My old friend Peter Barnard was at RNH Chatham and commented that he had devised all sorts of routines to stop himself going mad from sheer boredom. Despite this he spent time researching the

Navy List and found that there were more Surgeon-Rear Admirals than permanent Surgeon Lieutenants. He commented: "If you could bear it signing on gives almost certain odds of reaching the top."*

I was intensely irritated by service life ashore in which everything was dictated by rank. The correctness of diagnosis was more dependent on the gold on one's sleeve than on intellect. Some senior officers were splendid doctors and charming gentlemen but there were others for whom the necessary respect for rank was hard to simulate.

Despite this there was fun among the junior officers which largely depended on rivalry on the croquet lawn. The huge perfect grounds of the hospital were ideal for this peculiarly devious game which we took extremely seriously. I loved it and it passed the time until my longed-for marriage.

I managed to get to Harpenden to see Gillian every weekend that I was not on duty and wedding plans developed apace. We toured the Hertfordshire lanes in the battered van teaching each other a great

Naval Wedding, St Alban's Abbey, 4th October 1958.

*He did sign on and after a brillaint career in underwater physiology became Surgeon Rear Admiral.

deal of natural history, some of which had to do with wildflowers, others with birds and bees. Perhaps it was these idyllic weekends that made the Navy seem so boring.

At last the great day came when Gillian and I were married in St Albans Abbey where the Dean, himself ex-naval, was delighted to have uniformed officers in the Abbey. I wore a sword that day but was not required to 'salute with it on the march'! Gillian and I were mystified by a private joke shared by our parents. At last it emerged that when my parents considered marriage it was Gillian's grandfather who had so strongly cautioned against it. All agreed that as a result of his strong sense of humour he must now be chuckling in heaven.

We honeymooned in Burgundy pub-crawling among the famous wine chateaux before returning to a lovely home called Cobb Cottage, idyllically situated in the village of Shorne near Rochester, which belonged to a Commander presently at sea. Here we were taken under the wing of a delightful elderly couple called Russell who introduced us to the village, had us for dinner and invited me shooting. We sang together in the Rochester choral society until I was completely thrown by The Dream of Gerontius and 'retired hurt'. I did better when playing the lead in Noel Coward's *Nude with Violin* in Shorne's dramatic society production. Gillian was working on a tapestry but doing so very slowly. I chided her that any fool could sew like that and, hardly surprisingly, she challenged me to prove myself a fool.

High above the Kentish shore of the Thames Estuary we gardened and explored the woods. Gillian's botanical knowledge was far greater than mine but I was better at birds. We had much to teach each other. The woods were full of woodcock. One spring I noticed a shiny berry in the undergrowth. I was mystified that there should be fruit among the primroses. As I looked in puzzlement at the berry a shape began to form around it and I realised I was looking at the eye of a sitting woodcock not five feet from me. The camouflage was so perfect it would have deceived all but a colour-blind eye.

I suppose it must happen in doctors' families quite often because I knew Gillian was pregnant before she did. I told her that she was due in the middle of February the following year adding "but next year's a leap year. I bet you go a fortnight overdue and have the baby on the 29th."

Then, into this state of connubial bliss, Their Lordships of the Admiralty struck a bitter blow. I had been dreading it for weeks because there was trouble in Iceland. I received orders to repair at once to Rosyth to join HMS Trafalgar as surgeon in the emergency of the 'cod war'. Armed with a new tapestry canvas I set out for Scotland. In a crowded train the unusual sight of a young man plying a needle stopped people in the corridor to watch the madman. Soon I had the compartment to myself. If for no other reason tapestry has its rewards.

On June 13th I wrote to Gillian from HMS Trafalgar at Rosyth that I was not alone as several of the officers did needlework and the Captain was also a tapestrist. Trafalgar was much bigger than Loch Fada but I found myself quite at home. The wardroom was a big one and they seem a very pleasant crowd. I met the doctors from the other two Battle Class destroyers, Dunkirk and Jutland, before I left Rosyth. Together we have a practice of about 1500, 200 in each destroyer and about 900 in the trawler fleet and scattered over thousands of square miles of Arctic Ocean: quite a daunting prospect.

The next day we sailed north in a hurry into the teeth of a full gale. It was hell; a destroyer at speed in rough weather jumps around all over the place. I lay in my bunk, vomiting and praying for death.

A few days later, in the Arctic Ocean, life became more bearable and I wrote to Gillian explaining what was happening. Iceland had extended her fishing rights from 3 miles to 12 from the coast. The British Trawling Association recognised the increase only as far as 4 miles and continued to fish outside that limit but inside 12 miles. According to the Icelanders this was illegal and they tried to arrest any trawler within the area. In addition to this the trawlers now lacked the shelter of Icelandic harbours in case of illness, mechanical breakdown or storm. We were there to provide medical and engineering assistance and to prevent Icelandic gunboats arresting British trawlers. Trafalgar patrolled the northerly fishing area of Iceland inside the Arctic Circle; HMS Jutland was west of Reykjavik; and HMS Dunkirk on Iceland's east coast.

My first case in the trawlers was a man with a broken arm; I brought him back to Trafalgar, infiltrated local anaesthetic into the fracture site, reduced and immobilised the fracture. The second, was a crushed hand, which I treated in the trawler. The means of transfer to the trawler in choppy sea was dramatic. I embarked in a rubber dinghy and was dropped over the side of Trafalgar and hauled over by line to the trawler. When I had seen my patient I re-embarked in the dinghy and was cast loose to drift and wait for the destroyer to pick me up. The first time I lost my breakfast–but I soon got used to that. When it was calm it was very pleasant with the midnight sun shining and I enjoyed the trip. It is something to have been in a raft in the Arctic Ocean!

We had a press representative on board who was the only person in Trafalgar whose sea-sickness was worse than mine. He had been too ill to witness my home visiting jaunts and wrote a story for the press based on what he thought might have happened. I was to learn later that Gillian, teaching at a secondary modern in Gravesend, received a visit from The Daily Telegraph who announced that her husband had "performed a deed of heroism in the Arctic". She replied that that did not sound like her husband and the Telegraph was the only paper not to publish the story under such lurid headlines as **MERCY MISSION BY MAN IN RUBBER RAFT.** It took a long time to live the episode down when I returned to RNH Chatham when I was chided with 'When are you going to the palace for your medal!' Most of my time in Trafalgar I had nothing to do and was thankful for my tapestry.

After another trip in my rubber raft I picked up an old trawlerman whom I thought had cancer of the lung. I did this transfer in dense fog and Trafalgar's captain was concerned that I might get lost–the thought did not amuse me very much either! They got us back eventually but we sat in the dinghy for quite a long time and could not see Trafalgar. I made my patient comfortable in the sick bay but heaven alone knows why so ill a man had gone off fishing.

My next letter discussed naming the baby before becoming passionate; the trip was getting to me as indeed it was to the entire ship's company. Increasingly ratings' letters home were marked KORW* for, after a week at sea, the ship was bulging with testosterone. However sex starvation was relieved by sickbay tasks: I put a skin graft on the butcher's finger, filled aching teeth, opened abscesses and gave 120 TAB inoculations. The rest of my time I spent wandering round the ship, sewing my tapestry or playing bridge and drinking the large stock of Chianti the ship had embarked on a recent visit to the Mediterranean.

Unfortunately we were not patrolling the best area for good fish. HMS Dunkirk, patrolling off the SE coast, was feeding on scampi which the skippers throw back when they take it in the trawl. However they did give us a single halibut of 365lbs enough to feed the entire ship's company. By now I had a tremendous admiration for these fishermen: they have a hell of a life, they get about one weekend ashore between trips which last 3-4 weeks. Storms up here, even in mid-summer, are no joke; in winter they must be appalling. The liaison skipper we have on board tells me he paid £3000 income tax last year! But even with such financial inducement I don't think I should enjoy such fishing.

Shortly after that the lovers were reunited and my prediction turned out to be right: Fiona, a maid of Kent, was also a Leap Year child born on 29th February 1960. I still have a notice from the RNH wardroom notice board inviting officers to an RPC† to wet the baby's head.

Looking back on my brief naval career it was probably one of the most educational experiences of my life: I was tested with responsibility and respected for rising to it; I travelled extensively but, probably more important than anything else, I mixed with people such as I had never met before, broadened horizons in

---

*Knickers off, ready and waiting.

†RPC: Request the Pleasure of your Company is the standard naval signal meaning 'drinks on me.'

many ways and even learnt a few social graces. Speaking from my own experience it is a great pity that obligatory national service was abolished.

Chapter 5 Leamington & Aberfeldy

I was due to leave the service just before the baby was due. I applied to the Admiralty for a three month extension to avoid moving around the time of Gillian's confinement. Such an application had to pass through the Surgeon Rear Admiral commanding RNH Chatham. I did not get on with the SRA whom I regarded as a pompous twit. I and another Surgeon Lieutenant had founded what we called 'the Purple Admiral's Club' for that was the effect we seemed to have on him. When the SRA saw my request he sent for me and was in a towering rage.

"You seem to think, Hull, that the Navy is here to suit your convenience!"

But he was obliged to send my formal request to the Admiralty who not only agreed immediately but pointed out that this would increase my terminal gratuity. Chatham had not been a success but my report from Loch Fada was so good my empurpling of the Admiral at Chatham was overlooked. I got my revenge after I played the lead in the local naval drama competition's production of JB Priestley's *An Inspector Calls*. The adjudicator singled my performance out for praise.

The SRA said rather coldly "Hull, you should change your profession."

"I am, sir, I am leaving the navy." He went purple again.

At Cobb Cottage we pored over the back pages of the British Medical Journal where all the jobs were advertised. After so long with only a wholly masculine practice I felt it essential to get experience in obstetrics and gynaecology. At that time there were many applicants for every GP practice and an essential qualification was the diploma of the Royal College of Obstetricians & Gynaecologists. The knock-on effect meant that obstetric jobs were hard to get. I applied for several, often did not even get an interview or, when I did, was turned down.

One evening lying before the lovely log fire with a bulky wife and Penny, our first Labrador, an advertisement for an obstetric house job caught my eye.

"Where's Leamington Spa?" I asked.

Gillian did not know either so we got out the road atlas and started dreaming.

"Look," I said, "it's in Warwickshire. Perhaps if we got that job it might be a good place to hunt for a practice." My finger moved southwest on the map. "The Cotswolds are not far away. I bet that's a lovely rural area. I want to live in the country again..."

"And I love the Cotswolds," added Gillian.

The dog, hearing the excitement in our voices, thumped her tail in agreement and I wrote a letter of application immediately. Shortly after that Fiona was born: I was a father at 29.

I went to Leamington for interview and met the consultant, Mr Christopher Swan, and immediately liked him. He was an ex RAF officer who seemed pleased to have a serving naval officer applying for his job. He appointed me on sight.

In April, when Leamington was a mass of cherry blossom, I was once again employed by the NHS. My first night at the Warneford Hospital, as was my wont in the Navy, I put my shoes outside my cabin door to be cleaned by my servant. Someone peed in them, bringing me sharply down from being an officer and a gentleman to the earthy NHS.

Naval habits died hard and I used the terminology I had become so used to in the service. Mr Swan supervised my first forceps delivery. It is a rule that the left blade of the forceps is applied first. I examined the patient with the boss standing behind me watching.

"Where's the suture line?" he demanded.

I felt the baby's fontanelle and checked the lie of the skull sutures.

"Fore 'n' aft, Sir," I replied, like a well trained sailor.

There was a chuckle behind me, "Good; put the port blade on."

That delivery was easy but somehow forged a link between the older surgeon and me which was to have a lasting effect on my family.

We were very hard up for junior hospital posts were poorly paid. My naval gratuity was earmarked for the car I must have to work in general practice. Gillian and Fiona went back to live with her parents in Harpenden, Penny stayed with my parents and I resumed a reluctant bachelor existence in the Hospital. I was off duty alternate weekends when I hitch-hiked seventy miles home to be with my wife and daughter. People giving me lifts were surprised to be picking up a hitching doctor five years after his qualification; but few people knew the pittance junior hospital doctors were paid.

In some ways it was like being at sea again; the same note of passionate longing entered my letters, but they included the excitement of returning to a busy job without naval red tape and the incompetence of some of my seniors. Soon I was reporting that I was enjoying the job immensely. 'Swan, the boss, is a splendid fellow and a very good teacher. He has a great sense of humour and tolerance of his houseman's ignorance. It really is a pleasure to work for him- and, mind you, there is plenty of work. You have no idea how good it feels to be doing something myself after all these years and I am very pleased to find that I still enjoy medicine— a fact I was beginning to have grave doubts about—I am feeling pleased with myself: I have just done my first forceps delivery and a manual removal of placenta. I miss you terribly when work is slack: The boss pulls my leg about being so keen; he doesn't realise that I have little to do if I am not working. Tonight all is quiet and I find myself missing you terribly... still it's only six months and it could have been much worse if I were at sea.'

Obstetrics is a very human branch of medicine which made me ponder my own marriage in a letter to Gillian. "Love is an extraordinary emotion: it seems to be endless and it continues to grow the longer we are together. Fiona has made you all the more precious; I often think of you when I am delivering someone. Despite the pain, the blood, mess and ugly looking newcomer it is a moment of tremendous triumph and I find it amazingly satisfying even though I have really had extremely little to do with it. But each time I am glad you've been through it and that I did have something to do with that... "

Two months into my six month appointment hints about our future kept recurring in letters home. "I shall be glad to settle down somewhere together... I have several irons in the fire with regard to the next job but doubt if any of them will come to much–though at a party one of the registrars passed on Swan's observations on me which were flattering so I hope he will give me a good recommendation at Stratford*."

Chris and Marion Swan, as I later came to know them were extremely good to us. He was amused at my hitch-hiking home and made good-humoured references to sex-drive. He was probably the best consultant I ever worked for. He always came in very early and liked to read night sister's report of the happenings of the night which usually reported on my doings. Sometimes, when it was obvious that I had hardly been to bed at all, he would say "It's all right Hull, I can do the round alone, you go and get your head down." I had never experienced such consideration from my consultant.

Gillian planned to spend a weekend with me when I told her: "Mr Swan was surprised at us planning to sleep in my single bed! He has invited us to stay with him on what he calls a bed & breakfast basis- so that we can come and go as we like without feeling we have to be sociable! This is extremely kind of him and I have accepted but I may have to be on call so I suggest you spend

*Two practices in Stratford were advertising for assistantships with view to partnership. There were some thirty applications for each. I was bidden to the interviews for both.

Friday with me at the hospital and we will move to the Swans for Saturday, Sunday & Monday."*

Two jobs came up in Stratford and went to other would-be GPs, Hamish Nicol and John Lewis. Perhaps it was just as well for it left me free for a third job which my boss thought would be much more suitable. "Third time lucky", said Chris Swan when he heard that a special friend of his, Lawrence Mackie, in the village of Wellesbourne, near Stratford-upon-Avon, was looking for someone to replace Dr. Christopher Hill who was, like so many others at that time, fed up with poverty and was emigrating to Australia. I met Dr. Mackie, an austere reserved man, whom it would take years for me to address by first name, at his branch surgery. But we were both ex-naval officers, both were rock-climbers, and most importantly, had similar philosophy and humour. We were also heavy cigarette smokers then. I was engaged on the spot and soon began 18 years of close work with one of the finest doctors I have ever known.

There was a gap between jobs which I filled with locums. I wrote in answer to an advertisement for a GP locum in rural Perthshire in November. Though not the best month to visit Scotland I thought if I could get work there a Scottish locum might be fun. Three weeks' work should be worth £50, which would buy our new bed!

When the Leamington job finished and I was the proud owner of a shining new Triumph Herald I started a locum at Wellesbourne while my predecessor and his wife spent two weeks saying goodbyes before emigrating to Australia. This was my first experience of general practice anywhere but, except for the many house calls, in many respects it resembled my sick parades at sea. Soon I was writing to Gillian " I am completely bewildered at present but very much enjoying myself. Mackie is a very nice chap–very helpful and understanding about my complete ignorance of practice. This locum is going to be very useful for my real start in December. I am sure you will like him and his wife is delightful. He is extremely reasonable about terms of agreement which we are going to discuss with the accountant. I have seen the practice accounts and to my

*The room he gave us had two single beds so we ended up in one after all!

119

untutored eye they look very healthy. We are to rent the Hill's house in Chestnut Square in the centre of Wellesbourne. Work at present tends to be rather slow and laboured because everything is so new. The patients are delightful though they all tell me how sorry they are to see Dr. Hill go. I got caught in the bar last night by some of the locals who, when they discovered who I was, tried to fill me with beer! Mackie tells me when he joined his first practice the same thing happened to him!"

I was worried at following such a popular doctor as Chris Hill. Gillian's mother suggested that I told them the only difference between Hill and Hull was a change of 'I' for 'you!' As soon as the Wellesbourne locum finished I drove to Harpenden and next day set off for Perthshire with Gillian and Fiona. From Harpenden we took the Great North Road to Scotch Corner, crossed to the west and started up the A74 into Scotland staying the night across the border at Crawford. Next day we started early, by-passed Glasgow and went through Stirling to reach the Highlands at Crieff. We were enchanted by Perthshire as we traversed the spectacular Sma Glen. Then we entered the moors and for the first time saw white hares bounding through the heather. Further on we came to a small loch* beside the road where quantities of red grouse sat on roadside walls shouting "go-go-go back, go-back" at us. A moment later we descended the long winding hill to the Tay valley with a magnificent view into the lush green strath with the peaks of Schiehallion, Carn Mairg and Meall Buide further west. Then as we neared Aberfeldy the Ben Lawers massive filled the western view.

Gillian was ecstatic and said "We've got to get up that."

I reported to the practice and was told I was not needed until the next day. I said to Gillian that I had heard there was a spectacular place called Glen Lyon. And so, on that brilliant last day of October, with Perthshire at its full autumnal magnificence, we explored what we still believe to be the finest glen in Scotland. We were in love and had fallen in love again with Perthshire.

---

*Later we came to know this as Loch na Creige where in winter we sometimes see black-throated divers.

That locum was to influence the rest of our lives, but how much we could not then begin to conceive. Much of my work was spent visiting in the long narrow practice in the Tay valley, nearly 50 miles in length but never more than five in width. The population was scattered, immensely hardy but welcoming to an obvious Sassenach barely improved by having a Scottish mother. Many of the hardy folk I met later crept into my writing as characters in novels or as case histories in medical journals.

Dr. Watty Yellowlees was away on an obstetric course but we got to know his wife Sonia well and met him briefly on his return. Dr Swanson, the senior partner, was an old school general practitioner such as Cronin might have described. He was a medical politician and a workaholic fuelled by draughts of whisky. He would do a full day's work in the practice, catch the London sleeper, spend the day sorting medical politics at BMA House. Then he caught the next sleeper back and arrived in time to do morning surgery. He was gruff, intolerant of fools and was worshipped by his patients (then and now, nearly half a century later and long after his death). However he never wrote any notes; everything was committed to his elephantine memory. He asked me what I liked doing and when I said, shooting, fishing, climbing and natural history he waved a hand saying: "Then ye're in luck. It's all round ye here."

In autumn the haughs* in the valley bottom were densely populated by the first greylag geese I had ever seen, recently arrived from their summer quarters in Iceland. Swanson got me permission to shoot at them. I and a friend from the guest house where we were staying got up early every morning and crawled through hoar frost to try and get a shot. Probably Old Swanson knew the geese were far too fly for us to bag one. However our shots fired as the skeins took noisily to the air served to warn them off the farmer's fields. I learned a lot about greylag geese and came to respect them as magnificent social animals.

Visiting was fun though an inefficient way of delivering care. I once visited a nonagenarian living alone in the remotest dwelling. I drove a long way to see him, left my car to walk across several

---

*Haughs are flat grasslands flanking the river and in England might be called water meadows.

fields, opening and shutting gates behind me. Then I rowed across the River Lyon and walked up the path to my patient's home. Thirty yards away was another obviously occupied house. There was not much amiss with my patient but I remarked that this was a very isolated place for a gentleman of his years to live alone... "but," I added "you do have neighbours across the way."

The old Scot looked at me in astonishment and expostulated "I hanna spoken to they for thirty years." Such indomitability was characteristic of many of the patients. One old lady living alone in Aberfeldy I described later in *The Healing Island*:-

"Hearing the noise of sticks being cut I walked round behind the house. Maggie was outside splitting kindling for her fire. I hesitated, watching this bent old woman whom I knew to be both blind and totally deaf, wielding an axe. I could see, as the wood split before it, that the blade was razor sharp. How could I let her know I was there? A false move and she might injure herself, or me. She was remarkably accurate, cutting the wood with precision based only on touch. She was thin and obviously very strong for her eighty odd years. Suddenly she put down the axe, scrabbled the kindling together with her foot and turned to me. I saw, above a nutcracker jaw, the opaque eyes turned on me and noticed the deep wrinkles of her face engraved with the soot of her peat fire.".

Another tough old character was Hughie. He was the McPhee of McPhee, the clan chief, panjandrum himself. Not that the McPhees were the greatest of Scottish nobility; they were the tinkers, travelling people living in humpies, tunnelled tents of tarpaulin stretched over hoops of hazel branches. One very dark night I had a call to one of these humpies. I was told the camp was behind the Mains farm where I splashed my way through torrential rain. In the gloom I noticed a bit of high ground; knowing it would be dry I stepped heavily onto it and my leg sank above the knee in a fresh midden. Eventually, smelling strongly of cow dung, I found the humpie. Inside a fire blazed in an oil-drum and in the sweltering heat, by candlelight I was shown a teenager with a high fever. Diagnosis was impossible and

I withdrew before my trousers scorched on the fire. I reassured the mother, suggested heat was quite unnecessary and promised to see the lad next day.

In the morning I retraced my steps even noting the dunghill I had blundered into but of the humpie and my undiagnosed patient there was no sign. After hunting about I left to get on with my round. There was a new call, again to the tinkers. In the light I found this camp quite easily. There I was confronted by an adolescent with a fever. "Odd!" I said, "I saw someone just like you about two o'clock this morning but that was miles from here."

"That's right the farmer moved us on in the night" The boy had infective hepatitis the same ailment that had laid me low in the navy.

I met Hughie long after it had happened, but even then it had its drama. Years before I had even heard of Aberfeldy Hughie had had a little trouble. In the hardy fashion of a clan whose lifestyle would have made the Spartans seem sybaritic he 'tholed' it without complaint. But it got too much even for Hughie and he summoned up the necessary pennies for a phone call to the surgery.

"If the doctor was down his way on the morrow would he be kind enough to call?" he asked in a voice that gave no hint of discomfort. He did not wish to enlarge to the lady taking the message which was accepted at face value. But the following morning Hughie phoned again to cancel the visit since "it had burrrrst". This time the receptionist was alarmed and got the doctor to talk to Hughie on the phone and in a few moments he was on his way to the disused railway hut that was the McPhee palace.

Hughie had gone into acute retention some weeks before and had ruptured his bladder. Urine had tracked through fascial levels into his scrotum, which then distended to his knees until, with a malodorous gush, it indeed 'burrrrst' and the greater part of his pain was dissipated. After months in hospital the McPhee plumbing was reorganised leaving his grossly infected pelvis draining through colostomy and ureterostomy and Hughie returned to his shack.

I was asked to see him in a week of intense frost. The stench in the hut was mephitic. Fighting nausea I asked Hughie if he could be undressed when I called first thing next day. On my return Hughie was at the door smoking his pipe and contemplating the patterns of hoar frost drawn into horizontal icicles on every grass stem by the wind. He was stark naked. I admitted him to the cottage hospital; fortunately it was the last day of my locum for Hughie was never a popular patient and fumigation was needed after his departure.

Later Watty Yellowlees told me that Hughie used to save up his butter ration to give to the doctors. Even after years of rationing Watty said that when Hughie removed his gift from caked trousers they had sorrowfully to consign rare butter to the incinerator.

I loved my round of visits being greeted as a guest in the houses of my patients where kettles permanently simmered in case of chance visitors needing tea with scones or Dundee cake. But the real joy was the unspoiled countryside, stark glaciated scenery where hobgoblins and gremlins might lurk in what I later described as 'Tolkienesque' territory. There were monoliths in the fields as evidence of people who shifted massive rocks with primitive ropes and rollers. There were mysterious cups carved into rocks with circles round them; there were elfshots* which the fairies used to curse cattle; this was an enchanted land where lions and witches inhabited wardrobes and where Hobbits and Ents might dwell. Both Gillian and I were enthralled.

But above all this was a land rich in wild creatures; eagles floated on thermals, peregrines haunted cliffs where ptarmigan flaunted their winter whiteness. In the great wide strath, gouged by the ice ten thousand years before, there were drumlins and huge accidental boulders like illustrations in an open text-book of geology. Here, where the geese fed all winter, foxes picked off the weaklings exhausted by their long flight from Iceland. Momentarily, with all these wonders about me I regretted taking my practice in Warwickshire. The Scotland of my mother's birth and schooldays in Arran called me back. Then, I reflected, with all this beauty, this wildness, these rivers to fish and mountains to climb how would there ever be time for medicine?

---

*These were Neolithic arrowheads which are sometimes turned up by a plough.

124

One adventure involved all three of us. When I reported for work one afternoon Dr. Swanson beamed at me. "I've just one visit for you, Dr. Hull, it's at Pubil, I'll show you on the map."

Pubil was the village created for the dam-builders thirty miles away, right at the head of Glen Lyon. I was delighted and rang Gillian "Bring Fiona, we've got a splendid afternoon trip."

We started after lunch but nobody had told me how many gates there were to open and close before we reached the tiny hamlet by the dam. The patient expected us, tea was laid with fresh scones and honeycomb and before any medical business was transacted our hostess had to admire the baby and discover our entire life histories. Eventually she told me she wanted a repeat of the thyroid tablets she took for her long-standing deficiency. It was 5 o'clock before we started home after what seemed a needless visit. As we negotiated our way through the gates towards the village of Bridge o' Balgie we pondered on the task of a doctor in remote places where the commonest dis-ease was often loneliness.

But we had been noticed. Even after two weeks my emerald green Triumph Herald was known throughout the practice. Outside every croft there was someone with a hand up; "we wouldn't trouble you normally, doctor, but since you're in the glen..."

There were boils and blisters, piles and pimples, lacerations and lumbago galore. In Bridge o' Balgie a concerned party greeted us 'Mrs McTavish's hadna been seen, a neighbour had investigated and she couldna rise.' She had a fractured femur and had been lying in front of a burnt out grate for hours. Admission was arranged and we waited for the ambulance to take her to hospital. By now Fiona was hungry, wet and protesting. The Post office reopened for us and emergency baby food and nappies supplied; the doctor helped the community who, in turn helped him. In this remote Scottish village I learned a fundamental principle of general practice, mutual inter-dependability. It was after eleven o'clock when we got back from the visit to Pubil.

On the last Sunday I believed I was off duty. Sonia Yellowlees said she'd look after Fiona so Gillian and I could climb Ben Lawers. We were both very fit and experienced hill walkers so we decided not to follow the standard route but to attack the mountain from the north from Glen Lyon itself. It was a very long walk through snow but we made the summit and enjoyed the magnificence of nearly 4000 feet. But it took a long time and Sonia was glad to see us back. She mentioned that Dr Swanson had asked after me.

The following day he looked at me sternly.

"Where were you at the practice meeting yesterday?"

I said I believed I was off duty so I climbed Ben Lawers.

"A doctor is never off-duty!" Swanson boomed at me.

How different things are nearly 50 years later.

Chapter 6 Practice in Wellesbourne

The practice, I told my friends, was set in Arden. Where? they asked, but I was unable to answer with accuracy. Certainly Shakespeare lived in Arden; that was his Mother's maiden name and he wrote about it frequently. Rosalind and Orlando, and the Melancholy Jacques loved and philosophised in its Forest but, like much of Shakespeare's geography it is hard to put on the map. But such an area, part real, part fantasy, roughly in the heart of England is a good place in which to work; its combination of reality and dream suggests the greenness of rural England.

The Forest must have covered a huge area in Shakespeare's day with many clearings where the fertile land was farmed in strips still visible as a corduroy pattern of ridge and furrow in many fields. How big the Forest was is unknown but it must have extended widely as hunting ground for the nobility and grazing for animals and their attendant shepherds and swineherds so well portrayed in Winter's Tale and As You like It. Shakespeare, in his pastoral scenes, leaves an Arcadian touch but life must have been short and brutish for the majority. In the poverty and the poor hygiene of the time the ravages of infections such as measles and scarlet fever culled the children while smallpox and syphilis took their toll of those spared by the violence recaptured in Shakespeare's histories.

Now things are different. It is actually difficult to know where the forest was, though it is hinted at in place names such as Henley-in-Arden. Some old, proud oaks still stand that might, as saplings, have helped to populate the forest but most have gone to yield timber for ships, or even the great beams of the three hundred year old house I came to live in. Man has swept aside the great forests throughout the world as his need for fuel, building material or space, expanded.

Walking my Labradors high above Shakespeare's Avon, looking down on a landscape beribboned by modern housing development where dense woodland has given way to huge, hedgeless tracts of arable and scars where mechanical mastodons extract gravel for the new motorways one wonders at change. Perhaps Shakespeare walked here himself with his dogs (I cannot believe he did not have them) pondering the lines of the plays he set in just this sort of country. If he came back he would be surprised at the ecological change, surprised too at the huge population of the former forest and at the numbers of old people. He would see that in Arden now few people die of infection or of violence but live longer to end with heart disease or cancer. He would see greater health in this geriatric population but what would he say of the foetuses 'untimely ripped' from wombs at the demand of the unwillingly pregnant?

For the first time since I left my childhood home of Harpenden I was living in the country. It was a breath of fresh air and at last I lived among woods and fields that teemed with wildlife and plants. An early experience of driving down the Fosse Way amidst the splendour of autumn accentuated this sensation. The leaves had fallen and the woods resounded with the noise of guns for the pheasant season was at its height. The practice area, some fifty square miles of rural South Warwickshire teemed with game especially grey partridge and multitudes of hares. Wildfowl congregated on the lakes and rivers which held many species of coarse fish, chub and barbel, and an occasional trout. The principal river was Shakespeare's Avon, home in season to water voles, kingfishers, common sandpipers and elusive water rails. The hedgerows of my daily round were alive with finches, yellowhammers and the winter fieldfares and redwings.

Warwickshire was a horsey place with an important hunt. Centuries of hunting had determined the shape of the land. Broad gallops ended in low hedges as jumps and small frequent copses provided cover for foxes. Perhaps because of the hunt there were plenty of foxes. Mostly they preyed on rabbits though the myxomatosis plague had reduced their numbers drastically and Reynard was becoming more urban. Another mammal we often saw plodding along the roadsides of late night visits was the badger. They lived in huge, centuries-old setts which must have been there since Shakespeare's time. Lawrence Mackie hit a pregnant sow driving home from an obstetric case and for a moment considered a post-mortem caesarean section but the thought of looking after premature badgers daunted him and the chance was missed.

The main surgery was in Dr Mackie's home. Lawrence was never punctual; his bathwater was often heard gurgling away long after the patients had arrived for morning surgery and the receptionist had to be inventive in providing excuses for his 'absence'. During my first experimental locum I lived with the Mackies and as I appeared one morning quite early I met Elizabeth Mackie leaving the house on some good work. "Breakfast's in the Aga," she shouted as she left. I had become used to rather short commons during my stay and was pleased to find a reasonably substantial fry-up which I ate with gratitude. Inadvertently I ate my new boss's bacon and egg as well, though, typically he did not mention the matter until years later when we were having one of our rare disagreements!

The practice was dispensing and we had a tiny office-dispensary filled with pills, potions and galenicals. Worryingly there were huge quantities of potassium cyanide stored amongst the medicines. In those days country people bought cyanide to destroy wasp's nests; they always had too much and brought it to the doctor for safe keeping. It used to terrify the receptionists who mixed up medicines! This was to lead to one of my great embarrassments. When the Mackies were away one of the dispensers and I decided we could not stand keeping enough poison to wipe out the entire practice. I rang the fire brigade who suggested talking to the police so I rang a rather disinterested village constable, who was well known to us as a patient. He did not know either but said he would make enquiries. The next day I had a formal visit from a sergeant who inspected the cyanide and wanted to know its provenance, its method of storage and what I intended to do with it. I told him what I knew and he departed. Next day I had a visit from a police superintendent whose questioning left me feeling distinctly criminal. It then went ominously quiet until our village bobby rang up.

"Doctor," he said, "you haven't half set up a hornet's nest. My top brass are in a dither and don't know what to do about you and your cyanide. Frankly they wish they had never heard of the stuff. Take my advice, its unofficial you understand, and sling it down the loo."

With some misgiving we did just that. I was worried that there would be a disaster in the local waterways. To my immense and amazed relief nothing appeared to happen at all, though I expect a few sewer rats succumbed. I cannot imagine what would happen if several pounds of such highly toxic chemical were to find its way into a sewer today.

Adjacent to the dispensary there was a tiny waiting room (even as early as 1960 we ran an appointment system so there were never too many waiting at once) and our very few private patients were always seated in the drawing room in the house. The consulting room was exceedingly cluttered with a desk, a huge chest of drawers where notes were stored (but rarely used) and there was an examination couch where, when feeling brave, we undertook messy minor surgery and suturing. Occasionally in the summer the Mackie's cat would leap through the open window and land on a naked and often pregnant abdomen on the couch. Sometimes it was easier to send the patient home and visit them where we could examine them in bed. We used to carry our syringes and needles in small stainless steel boxes which periodically we sterilised in the surgery boiler. Looking back, it is incredible how little damage we inflicted with our methods of sterility which would be quite unacceptable today.

Conditions at the branch surgery were even worse. Two rooms of an old cottage were used as waiting room and consulting room; the rest of the cottage was unaltered with a rusting bath and a bedroom complete with original wallpaper and detritus from previous occupants. There was no heat and in cold winters I rarely took off my overcoat while doing surgery. In one hard winter the 'indigestion mixture', a white alkaline brew, froze solid in its half-gallon storage bottle cracking it open to reveal a gigantic antacid ice lolly.

Old people always say how much more difficult things were in their day but there can be no doubt that Warwickshire general practice in the early 1960s was tough going and very poorly paid. Dr Mackie was adamant that the telephone must always be manned; either by the duty doctor or his spouse*. The relentless, alternate nights of duty through epidemics in a practice with 100 deliveries a year, mostly at home, was exhausting. In the spring after I joined there was a major measles epidemic such as we never see today. Then I had never seen measles (except when I had it myself at Christ's Hospital) - it was not a disease that was taught in medical school. The epidemic was incredible, the disease spreading like wildfire through the schools hitting each non-immune child. Measles is misery but rarely very serious though it has many complications especially affecting the ears and eyes. Some cases developed a worrying secondary pneumonia and there was always the remote possibility of brain involvement leading to death or permanent disability. We were frantically busy, every case had to be seen, diagnosed and notified, most needed two visits some four or more where there were complications. A family of eleven boys were smitten together and I was long remembered for a certificate that 'All the Cotons' were unfit for school. Poor Mrs Coton (who, incidentally recommended a novel use for the Daily Mail to me *vide infra*) must have had a busy few days. In one day I calculated that I saw 99 patients, mostly in their homes which involved driving scores of miles. At bedtime I remember praying for just one more call so I could boast of a 'ton' of consultations.

In the middle of the epidemic Lawrence asked me how I liked practice. I said I'd rather be back on the house in hospital it was less exhausting! In that epidemic we lost one patient, an 88 year old man who caught the disease from a grandchild. As I signed his death certificate I thought it rather humiliating to live to such an age and then die of measles

But, though exhausting it was immensely rewarding and very good fun. After my first year in the practice I became junior partner sharing half the work of the practice with a third of the profits. On

---

*My non-medical Gillian somtimes found this difficult. Once lying in my morning bath I heard her answer the phone, but she did not summons me. I dressed in a leisurely fashion and at breakfast she asked casually: "Darling, what does 'coma' mean?" Fortunately at that moment the phone rang again and the caller said "not to worry the doctor, they got some sugar into the patient and he was concious again!"

assuming partnership I asked Dr Mackie to estimate my income. He said he could only guess but that it should be not less than £2000 a year [equivalent to about £30,000 in 2006]* peanuts for extremely hard work.

In 1961 a young woman came to Dr Mackie's house for an interview. That was Gillian Byrne [Jill], appointed that day as receptionist. She, later dignified with the title of Practice Manager, supervised the growth of the practice in Wellesbourne until long after I had left. During the formative years of the sixties and seventies it was she, Lawrence and I who started the conversion of that little country practice into an extremely efficient and internationally known medical partnership.

In 1962, after we had moved to our own house, our new surgery was adapted from the house in Chestnut Square where Gillian and I had first lived when we joined the practice. The Victorian house was converted to hold two consulting suites, each with a separate examination room and a small operating theatre for minor surgery. Later we took on extra staff, secretaries and nurses under Jill's supervision and soon we were to become a teaching practice with our own trainee general practitioners. The first was an unofficial trainee. Out of the blue we had letter from an Aberdeen hospital in which a young woman doctor announced that her name was Ann Welbourn and that she was writing to us on impulse in reply for a request for a locum because her name was so similar to that of our village Wellesbourne. She said she wanted experience of rural practice. Perhaps her decision to write to us was tinged by her parents being dons at Cambridge, though she did not tell us that at the time. We so liked her that Ann came to work for us, and everyone adored her. Years later Lawrence Mackie was to write of her 'What a splendid butterfly hatched out of that unlikely chrysalis!' Indeed Ann, when she came to us, was a rather subdued person, so depressed by her experience of hospital medicine that she was considering abandoning medicine altogether. Lawrence responded immediately and so encouraged her that he changed her mind. Ann was with us for nearly a year before resuming what

*Calculated from Purchasing Power of British pounds from 1264 to 2006
- internet.

turned out to be a very distinguished medical career working with an underprovided Mohawk community and culminating in a chair at McGill university and the Order of Canada. While with us Ann achieved notoriety by wiping out a police car in the snow with her mini; she also became a life-long friend and later Godmother to our third daughter Emma.

After Ann we found that trainees were enormously stimulating as well as being very helpful in the practice. Ann was succeeded in turn by Robert Hodkinson, David Hewat-Jaboor, Ben Richardson, David Gordon and Susan Warren, all of whom spent a year with us. Robert Hodkinson was our first formal trainee who came to us as a newly-wed with his charming wife Kate who for a time I was able to employ as a part time research assistant. They eventually settled in practice in Longridge where we frequently visited them *en route* for Scotland; they, too were life long friends until Robert's life was cut short by cancer.

After several years in the surgery in Chestnut Square we found that, spacious as it had seemed when we adapted it from the simple house it had been it was very cramped for a rapidly growing teaching practice. We took our first new partner Dr Graham Parfitt who, like me, had been Chris Swan's houseman in Leamington. He was with us for two years before moving to a single-handed practice in Coventry. By now we were definitely growing out of Chestnut Square and were planning to build what seemed then to be an enormous new surgery which Lawrence and I called 'The Palace'. Indeed it was palatial and the finances were daunting. When building started we needed a new partner, since Graham Parfitt's departure for Coventry, and soon appointed Dr Henry Meadows who bravely took on what was to become known as Hastings House when it was at foundation level. At that time this endeavour was literally frightening and it was entirely due to Lawrence's vision that the project was carried through. The palace was designed with four consulting suites each with a purpose built examination room. There was a small minor operating theatre, nurses room where a succession of nurses coped with a great deal of work leaving the doctors free for more specialised care.

In addition there was a common room cum library for the Doctors and extensive office space let to the local health authority.

But all that was in the future.

One day a notice in the British Medical Journal caught my eye. It was for a weekend course in hypnosis; unfortunately it was for a time when I was on duty. When I asked Lawrence if he would swap he studied the notice and said: "No, I'm off and I shall go."

The following Saturday evening he rang me fizzing with enthusiasm and invited me for a drink to hear all about it. By midnight we had had each other into so many hypnotic trances we hardly knew where we were. That ushered in what Jill Byrne always called the 'hypnotic phase' of the practice. We tried it for everything: asthma, smoking, stuttering and especially in obstetrics. We found hypnosis a great and fascinating addition to our practice. I taught an antenatal patient autohypnosis so that, when in labour, she would go into a trance at the onset of a contraction. She called me to the caravan where she lived with her husband one evening, thinking she might be starting. When I arrived her husband was going out, shotgun under arm, to bag something for the pot. The next morning she was in the obstetric unit in established labour and apparently sleeping through each contraction. Standing beside her in the labour ward I enquired if her husband had shot anything the night before.

"Yes," she said brightly, "two pigeons and a rab....."

Interrupted by an intense uterine contraction she was silent for a minute or two before concluding:

"...bit."

Later I delivered her by forceps with minimal local anaesthesia. She said the whole experience was terrific.

At the time I was playing with the Loft Amateur Dramatic Society in Leamington in Christopher Fry's *The Lady's Not for Burning*. As the curtain went up Tony Matthews, one of the leads, developed asthma and could hardly breathe. In the interval he demanded that I do something. In costume with nothing with me the only thing I could try was hypnosis. We had to be quick for he was due on as soon as the next act started. He seemed responsive and went quickly into a trance. I left him with the post-hypnotic suggestion that his asthma would stop and that he would perform better than ever before. When the curtain came down the producer met us all on stage.

"What happened to you Tony?" she asked. "At the beginning of Act I you were awful, then you suddenly changed and acted everyone off the stage."

"I dunno," he replied, "I was a bit wheezy to start with, then suddenly I felt fine."

That sounded as though he could not remember our brief consultation. So it transpired that my best hypnotic subject was not even a patient of mine. He was capable of such hypno-suggestibility that I could stick needles through his arm and I used him in several demonstrations of hypnosis at GP courses. In one course I induced total deafness in Tony. One has to be careful doing this because the subject can no longer hear verbal instructions so it is essential to leave him aware that a touch on his shoulder will restore his hearing. With my victim totally deaf I was able to fire a starting pistol in his ear without waking him though it certainly made the audience jump. Perhaps it was this incident that first suggested to me that drama could be very effective in teaching

However, because there was comparatively little positive return from what amounted to a great deal of work the 'hypnotic phase' gradually passed but not without raising a considerable interest in other aspects of para-psychology, such as dowsing and extra-sensory perception which later stimulated my writing of fiction.

In 1962 we bought our first house. It was a new, detached three bedroom house standing in half an acre of unmade garden. It cost £6300 [nearly £100,000 today] and took every penny we could raise. My paternal grandparents had almost the same Christian names as Gillian and me. They called their house in Mobberley, Cheshire 'Oakhurst' and it seemed traditional to follow their example. Fiona, a heavily pregnant Gillian and I moved into Oakhurst in October and Lawrence delivered our second daughter, Janet, on Armistice Day 1962. Saddled with a mortgage we were desperately hard up, had no holidays away from home for four years and I frequently came home to tears over grocery bills.

There was much rejoicing at Janet's birth, but the wise women of the practice were concerned that we had no son. One* even went so far as to take me aside and tell me to incorporate a newspaper in my bed. "Do it on the Daily Mail, Doctor, that'll get you a boy."

My first few years in practice were making me realize more than ever the inadequacy of my medical education. Lawrence Mackie, my senior partner, taught me a great deal and stood behind me at every point where learning by trial and error inevitably led to mistakes. An example of how he dealt with complaints about 'the new doctor' occurred during a smallpox scare in 1961. A suspected case of the disease in an officer recently returned from the Far East to a nearby RAF station caused panic throughout Warwickshire. Hundreds of people lined up for vaccination. At that time certification of vaccination attracted a fee. It was some satisfaction to know that lots of half guineas were coming in as a result of the hours of extra work I was doing. We put on special vaccination clinics and asked people with other problems to come to normal surgeries. In the middle of the vaccination queue was a man with a sore shoulder. I put my needle down on my desk. As he slipped his jacket off he accidentally stabbed his thumb on it. The following week he presented to Lawrence extremely angry about a beautiful cowpock on his thumb. He was breathing fire and ready to sue. Lawrence, who was six foot two, stood over him, and examined the thumb, 'That will be ten and sixpence,' he said and we never heard another word.

---

*Mrs Coton vide supra.

Lawrence, like Dr. Swanson in Aberfeldy, was of the old school of doctors, an excellent clinician, indefatigable in his care of the very sick but, having little time for trivia, he did not suffer fools. Communication was not a strong point in this big but surprisingly shy man. Often his consultations were conducted in a series of grunts. Once a woman came to him complaining of a sore throat. Seizing a torch and spatula Lawrence commanded 'Open wide'. He looked and grunted. The patient, feeling she had not had her money's worth, said: 'And I've got bad piles too.' The doctor gestured to the examination couch and requested a display, again he grunted and muttering, 'give you something,' pottered off into the dispensary. In those days we used penicillin lozenges (now quite outmoded) and he counted out twenty and wrote on the package: 'One to be held in the cheek until dissolved'. The patient returned a week later with a stupendous rash covering her buttocks and the complaint that she 'had to stand still for bloody hours to get those things to dissolve'.

Dear Lawrence, he inadvertently taught me the need for communication skills.

By the early 1960s I was beginning to feel more confident and was getting skilled at applying forceps in the home. Domiciliary obstetrics was forced upon us. My old chief Chris Swan simply did not have room to take the many patients of those baby-booming years.

'Damn it, Hull,' he would say, 'I trained you to be a safe obstetrician, get ahead and do it.'

Primiparity then was no indication for hospital confinement and I spent many hours with our two splendid midwives, Miss Schofield and Miss Fyfe, earning premature white hair and the respect of patients. I learnt that the most important ways in which a young doctor builds the trust of his practice lay in obstetrics and in the care of the dying. The doctor who was there when Little Johnny came, and when Granny went, was remembered, trusted and sometimes revered. They never taught that in medical school.

I learned never to underestimate the power of the women of the practice especially when organised into committees. Take the Women's Institute, that butt of rural humour, purveyors of Jam and Jerusalem, of monthly meetings and interminable gossip and there you have a major source of health education. So I used to tour the W.I. meetings giving talks about anything that took my, or the ladies', fancy. Natural or, especially, local history or more professionally something about the practice. Whatever the subject I would always end with a few minute's commercial. This was the time to plug the need for keeping the children's tetanus immunisation up to date (the area was full of horses and the soil rich in *Clostridiium tetani*) or the need for cervical smears. Husbands too could be reached via the opinions of their wives for blood pressure screening, advice on smoking or, if I wanted to make the ladies chuckle, testicular examination. The subjects the ladies of the Women's Institute most wanted to hear about were the female cancers of breast and cervix. Breast cancer, the commonest site of malignant disease in women was also the commonest cause of death of women in their early forties. Its prognosis was poor and detection of the disease early offered a better prognosis. So talking to the ladies of self-examination may help. Even more important was the ventilation of the dread word cancer. Though it is true that terminal breast cancer may be painful it is not always so and pain may be relieved. But the pain of terminal cancer is not solely physical, it is also psychological even spiritual. Physical pain is relievable by opiates but other types of pain, exacerbated by anger, fear, depression and the boredom caused by the inactivity of debilitating disease respond less to drugs than to understanding. So in the Institutes we talk of early self-diagnosis but then went on to ask about the effect of the disease, not just on the breast, but on the woman. How does she feel, think or agonise about cancer? Can she say the word 'cancer', which in the 1960s was more forbidden than other more vulgar words? Does she want her doctor to be frank in his discussion? Or does she want him paternalistically to say "Don't worry your pretty little head. Its only a tiny lump, we'll take it away, shine rays on it and give you medicines that will make your hair fall out..... but don't, whatever you do, concern yourself in the least"

So in the last few minutes of a talk on collecting china or growing roses we ponder life and death questions in the Women's Institute. A show of hands indicate that ninety-five percent of the ladies want their doctor to talk openly about their breast cancer, taking them into partnership in the business of managing their disease. Above all they want a doctor they can trust, who will deal with their real and imagined fears; trust is not fostered by lying or evasion. The ladies of the institutes are wives and mothers anxious for their families. It is with them that health care starts. They have power to influence behaviour–we harnessed that power.

We had many a laugh at our patients especially at their requests for 'sistificates' One youngster denied a certificate to excuse him from school avenged himself by scrawling 'nity ol kwak' on the message pad in the surgery porch much to the delight of Lawrence Mackie at whom it was directed. Many of our patients were poorly educated or, as one of them averred, 'higorant as pigs'. One hypochondriac father developed acute interest in his genitalia and discovered his cremaster muscle which controls movement of the scrotum. One day, in great anxiety, he held his scrotum up for my inspection saying in a terrified voice "look at 'em , doctor they're wrigglin'."

Most of all we enjoyed letters from patients, some of which came from a delightful rural character called, we thought appropriately, Mrs Belcher. Married to a Neanderthal looking agricultural worker Violet Belcher had a family of sons who resembled their father and one astonishingly beautiful daughter also named Violet but known as Wig. On Friday nights Mrs Belcher would relieve all her men folk of their pay packets and then, having locked them in their cottage, she took a taxi to the pub. That was the sort of character she was and having no telephone she wrote splendid letters which often took some interpreting, for example:-

my dear doctor

could you plese come up to seea my son Frank because I am not Saturfided with him but he hurt his back on lifting heave hirions Pypings and he walks

like a old man, is worrying me but I am keeping on
Purpis to seea him on a surprise I dont want him to
know I sent for you doctor come quitley helse he
may dart away if he seeas you

come Sir come

before dinner please Sir

my Dear Sir

could you give luke a Bottle of mesnen or sopme
Pilly I think I got the Flue because when I pass my
watert it seems to Scalls me and I got a heavy head
Sir but dont come up I shall be oright not without
you think you Better but you can Please your self Sir
but send word with Luke dont worry

V Belcher

Mrs Belcher was a delight and adored us all. At Christmas she
would make 'a pointment' and deliver garish parcels with a cry of
"There's yer bloody Christmas present then." When her beautiful
daughter Wig came to see me because 'she hadn't seen' she was
four months pregnant and when I asked if she had told her mother
she replied "I dursn't."

"Would you like me to tell her?" I asked.

Wig was much relieved and undertook to get her mother to make
'a pointment'.

Mrs Belcher in her best finery including a fur wrap appeared in the
surgery a day or two later when I explained Wig's predicament.
The old Lady looked astonished:-

" 'E musta bin 'aving connections wiv 'er."

I agreed that seemed probable.

"Well, fancy 'im doin' that behind my back!"

I couldn't resist it: "He was hardly likely to do it front of you!"

Mrs Belcher roared with laughter and Wig was forgiven... though in her mother's eyes there was little to forgive. Wig had her baby at the Warneford Hospital and a triumphant note arrived from her mother:-

> My Daughter Got a Baby Son
>
> She had it on Monday knight Dear I am pleased with you to Doctors What you have done for my daughter
>
> x x x Happy Christmas to all

A year after my arrival when I became a partner I took on a post of clinical assistant at our local mental hospital. This was partly to gain psychiatric experience and partly to boost the practice income. Lawrence did not like psychiatry and thereafter called me the 'practice shrink' and referred all the confused, anxious, and frankly mad patients to me. This led to considerable psychiatric responsibility for much of South Warwickshire for I became recognised under the Mental Health Act as being sufficiently experienced to sign commission orders admitting patients to the mental hospital. In those days Mental Hospitals were huge institutions where people were constrained often for little more reason than being a 'bit odd'. For some institutional life was a comfortable refuge from the 'slings and arrows of outrageous fortune.' Once, signing the death certificate of an elderly inmate I looked through his notes and discovered he had been in hospital for over fifty years. Modern drugs had relieved many of the horrors of earlier mental care. One severely deranged lady had been controlled on a drug called chlorpromazine. She was a nice, placid septuagenarian who daily thanked her doctors for the new wonder drugs which made her well enough to work embroidering an enormous cushion. One day, walking across the ward with her cushion in her arms she collapsed with a fatal coronary. The cushion burst open and tens of thousands of chlorpromazine tablets scattered across the floor.

A most bizarre case concerned a husband who suffered morbid jealousy, a condition sometimes called the 'Othello syndrome'. This is extremely difficult and my patient kept coming to me with circumstantial tales of his wife's infidelity with tradesmen and postmen visiting the house. The lady in question was appalled at her husband's accusations and, indeed, seemed the most unlikely person to have so sensational a sex life. A case of 'Othello syndrome' may come to violent end* involving homicide, suicide or both. Eventually after much heart-searching and consultation with a psychiatrist, the man was committed to hospital under section.

Threatened suicide was a common problem often arising from domestic problems fuelled by alcohol. Most led to overdosage with drugs, usually responding to gastric lavage in hospital followed by tender loving care. Others were more violent involving cut throats, hanging, drowning or shotguns. Whenever called to a suicide I felt guilty that I had not recognised severe distress before the irreversible act. Often there was nothing that would lead one to predict self destruction but in other cases I felt that, had I been sufficiently observant, I might have prevented death. One such case in a young woman in my early years in practice scarred me and led to the production of a teaching video-tape on the topic.†

There was one schizophrenic lady who so adored Lawrence that she would not leave him. Every time she called to see him she brought a gift, always a variation on a theme. Sometimes a parsnip and two small potatoes, or a cucumber with two tomatoes or a large carrot with two small beetroot.

"Do you think," he asked me, "she is trying to say something?"

---

*As in my novel *Silver Sea*.

† 'Suicide' made at Birmingham University Television and Film Unit with Tim Betts and Paul Morby.

Neither Lawrence or I were happy about the introduction of 'the pill' in the early sixties feeling that disturbing a young woman's menstrual cycle in order to prevent conception was laying up trouble for the future. Even my old boss, the gynaecologist Chris Swan, felt some apprehension. In some respects before the oestrogenic component of the contraceptive pill was reduced we were justified however time has shown that our suspicions were largely unfounded. Our reluctance to prescribe the pill meant there had to be an alternative. On a course I learned about the intra-uterine contraceptive device (IUCD) popularly known as 'the coil'. Soon I was spending an afternoon a week fitting coils to women from all over Warwickshire and even from as far away as Brighton because so few doctors offered the service at the time. Once sitting in the village pub having a pint by myself I burst out laughing. There were seven men in the bar who demanded to know the joke. I could not possibly tell them that I had fitted each one of their wives with a coil! Such is general practice, it provides a ring-side seat at patients' most private lives and is a wonderful place to study the natural history of one's own species.

Thanks to the Doctors' Charter of 1965 renaissance had begun. As I later wrote 'Life changed dramatically after the Charter, suddenly there was more money to develop practices by increasing staff and by acquiring new equipment and skills. Even the domestic budgets of young doctors showed signs of easing.'*

By 1969 I was able to publish a report on experience of 100 cases of women using the IUCD. In that paper I commented ruefully that when there was a method failure producing a son the boy was usually named Robin because it was all my fault!

Case histories were as often tragic as funny and many of these found their way with altered names into my later writing. For example Captain Nicholson RN was a most charming septuagenarian. I always enjoyed my visits to the house which usually culminated in a pink gin for old times sake. The captain suffered badly from arthritis and his increasing disability from his hips had led to my making an appointment for him with our

*See "Just a GP, a biography of Professor Sir Michael Drury." Radcliffe Medical Press. Oxford. 1994.

143

mutual friend Robert Duke, the orthopaedic surgeon. A few days before the appointment Mrs Nicholson rang me to ask if I would call as the captain's pain was so much worse. I found him lying in bed sweating with anxiety and pain. The arthritic right hip was held in spasm and I could elicit no movement whatsoever. Though there was no history of a fall he really gave the appearance of a fracture. I gave him a small shot of morphine and rang my friend Robert and arranged an urgent domiciliary visit. The morphine settled the patient and I left him to get on with the rest of my visits.

An hour later consultant and GP converged on the captain's house. We were met by his wife coming down the stairs to let us in. "I am so glad you're here he thinks he's dying.... he's just said goodbye to me". We hurried upstairs and as we entered the room the captain glanced at us in greeting.... and was dead.

We tried to resuscitate him to no avail and then went down to break the news to his wife. Both of us had to confess total amazement at the turn of events. Driving home thoughtfully I suddenly realised what had happened. As I entered my home the phone was ringing. It was Robert and we said simultaneously; "ruptured aortic aneurysm". Sometimes such a rupture is preceded by a leak which may produce severe pain referred to the hip. The pre-existence of arthritis had been a red herring which prevented earlier diagnosis.

Aortic aneurysm is not rare but this was an uncommon presentation. Sadly exactly the same thing happened much later to my revered colleague Lawrence Mackie who presented with severe backache as a manifestation of an undiagnosed leaking aneurysm and subsequently died on the operating table. Such cases can be very difficult to diagnose: as with many difficult diagnoses being aware of the possibility is vital to success.

My interest in natural history often helped with diagnosis. My father had taught me to observe and to question which helped with my friend Luigi. He was a Sicilian cowman who was neither very bright nor intelligible. He had never really mastered English despite having been a prisoner here for many years during the war. But he was ever cheerful and always had a wave for the 'Dottore'. Luigi was a neighbour in charge of the cows at the farm near my home. Gillian reported having heard that Maria, Luigi's wife, was worried in case he lost his job, there had been some problems with calving and the farmer was cutting his splendid Friesian dairy herd. Indeed I noticed that I had to wait a shorter time for the lowing herd to cross the road in front of my impatient bonnet when I tried to pass the farm. Then I saw that some of the best pasture was put under plough and there seemed to be something less cheery about Luigi's wave as I passed him in the lane. That was odd and I remembered my father teaching me that if things looked odd they needed investigating for that was when something really interesting cropped up. But general practice was far too busy to spend time worrying about a cowman's employment prospects.

Then Luigi asked for a call one hot August day. I found him lying in the bed where I had delivered his two sons. He was drenched in sweat and he greeted me with "I gotta da flu". Suddenly the whole story jumped into focus. There was no influenza at this time of year, the calves, the dwindling herd, the ploughed pasture all now made sense.

"No, Luigi, you have not got 'flu, you've got acute brucellosis".

Such spot diagnosis is of course highly suspect but in this case it was confirmed by blood tests and the patient soon became quite well. Poor Luigi he did not last long for a few weeks later he was killed in a motor cycle accident.

Another case concerned an irritating man called Somerville Farquharson. He upset people from the moment he arrived in the village. The vicar was first to call and was embarrassed when a voice responded to his knock with a shouted "Bugger off". To make it worse the vicar's arch enemy the grocer in the next door shop overheard and went off visibly chuckling. The grocer, who was also churchwarden, knew that the newcomer kept an African grey parrot whose vocabulary revealed his education in a sleazy Kampala suburb.

Farquharson annoyed me too. He sent his card in with the receptionist, perhaps expecting that the CBE which it advertised would get him in ahead of those who had appointments. It didn't. When he did come into the consulting room he was clearly put out at having waited for half an hour. What's more he made it plain he had expected to see a more senior doctor. Dutifully I enquired about the CBE. "Oh, water engineering in East Africa", he replied with an assumed casualness before requesting referral to a specialist. I enquired if he had medicine or surgery in mind and his pomposity eased a little. "I just don't feel well and I seem to run a fever at night, at least I have profuse sweats." There was little else: despite several years service in Uganda he had never been ill there and had been scrupulous in taking antimalarials. Indignantly he denied overuse of alcohol and he had never had any external blood loss. Examination was normal apart from a large and tender liver. Fortunately I had seen just such a case before. "Yes" I said "I will refer you. I have a colleague who is particularly good on amoebic hepatitis."

It was a gamble, of course, but my hunch proved right. The consultant rubbed salt into the patient's wounded self-esteem by congratulating him on his GP's diagnosis. After that Farquharson became a model patient; the African grey succumbed to Warwickshire winter and the vicar got a new churchwarden.

Another case widened my knowledge of natural history to a study of molluscs. Martin Gray was a quiet unassuming, but obsessional man, who kept the sports-ground of the local secondary school in immaculate order. He never came to the surgery but I knew of him because his vegetables won so many prizes at the village show. Late one summer day he appeared in evening surgery clearly ill, with beaded sweat across his forehead on a cool evening. He said he had been feeling ill for some time with what he took to be 'flu but this evening he had started getting quite severe upper abdominal pain and a feeling of nausea. His abdomen was slightly distended with marked tenderness over his liver and I was perplexed. The appearance was one of an acute abdomen but with no localising signs.

Wondering about inflammation of the gall bladder I phoned the surgical registrar at Warwick who took him in immediately leaving me to get on with running a delayed surgery.

Later the registrar phoned me back "That chap Gray you sent in... he's interesting; we were just taking him to theatre when we got his blood count back. He's got a high white blood count with 40% of eosinophils*. I've asked the physicians to see him but we don't have a diagnosis yet. Can you help?"

Beyond saying such a blood picture indicated a parasitic infestation I could not. Discovering that his wife had gone home to await the outcome of his expected surgery I went round to see her. Together we explored all she knew about his work and anything unusual that might have brought him into contact with a parasite. We drew a complete blank but she was glad of my visit and, in the way of country people wanted to give me something as I left. "Do you like watercress?" she asked. "Martin has found some marvellous cress at work and we've been having quite a lot of it, he likes it in his sandwiches." I accepted a large dripping bundle and looked forward to the morrow's salad.

It was only on the way home that the penny dropped, but they were ahead of me at the hospital where a clever physician had already diagnosed liver fluke disease. Three days later Mrs Gray was also in hospital as a result of my discovery that she too had eosinophilia. The consultant and I, armed with shrimping nets, visited the stream separating a sheep pasture from the school playing fields where we caught specimens of snails of the genus *Lymnaea*, the intermediate host of the flatworm *Fasciola hepatica*. Both the Grays did very well after the parasites stopped munching their way through their livers.

For four years after we bought Oakhurst we were stony broke, having a large mortgage and a small income. During that time we did not have a holiday away. Then Malcolm MacGregor, the paediatrician, offered his cottage, Cwmllan, in the Gwaun Valley near Fishguard. The rent was nominal, the valley gorgeous and

*Eosinophils are a particular form of white cells which increase in cases of parasitic diseases.

Fiona and little Janet adored it. Nearby there was a secluded beach with a good pub where I, who detest lying on a beach, could suppress my allergy to sand. Better than anything was the river which meandered its way to Fishguard harbour. It was alive with small brown trout which could be caught with a worm cast upstream under overhanging branches. In spate there were sea trout, or sewin, as they were called in Pembrokeshire. I took over responsibility for cooking the evening meal so long as I could fish afterwards as well as early before breakfast. I loved that little river and soon knew every inch of it.

One night our neighbouring farmer came knocking at the door after dark:

"Come fishing with me boyo?" he asked, "it's all right so long as you pay half the fine!"

Armed with a huge trident he led me to the stream where his mate had a twelve volt battery strapped to his waist. In his hand was a powerful lamp. They explained that when poaching salmon the fish would rise to the light and could be taken with a gaff. Sewin on the other hand lay on the bottom and had to be speared with a trident. In the dark the lamp was turned on the stream. It was fascinating and I could see the little brown trout just where I had predicted them lying behind rocks or in the slack beside the main current. Then suddenly there was a commotion in a pool nearly five feet deep. It was a huge sewin. Soon it settled lying at the bottom of the gin clear water apparently mesmerised by the bright light. Seizing the trident the farmer slipped in to the pool in his chest waders. He inched his way towards the fish while his mate kept it still with his beam. The farmer's toes were right up to the fish when he slammed the trident down and hurled the 8lb sewin onto the bank. It was fun and ever since I have dreamt of catching such a fish legitimately*.

But it was not just the fishing (though once for a heart stopping second a salmon took my worm and I saw it as it broke the flimsy

*Years later, in Scotland I did so with a 7lb 8oz rainbow trout taken on a small black fly.

tackle I was using for six ounce trout) there were signs of otter but I never saw the animal. There were buzzards and peregrines on the cliffs as well as terns and gulls. Sometimes from the cliff tops we watched gannets diving on a shoal of fish. That is a magnificent sight as the great birds fold their wings and plummet vertically to explode into the sea in a plume of spray. The cliff walks of the Pembrokeshire coast were superb and a wonderland of wildflowers. Then the moors above the Gwaun valley teemed with other species we did not see in Warwickshire such as wheatear, stonechat and whinchat. Once on the way to Fishguard I nearly crashed the car when I saw the rarest British raptor, a red kite. During those holidays in the Gwaun I started listing the birds I saw. That was to become life-long hobby and was to lead later to a huge archive of bird observations and much ornithological writing.

For Gillian the Gwaun was respite from the chores of a doctor's wife. In the practice she was tied to the phone when I was on duty and was responsible for taking messages and finding me in the depths of Warwickshire when things got urgent. In addition to looking after our daughters she was expected to do good works such as meals-on-wheels ('wheels-wheels-wheels' the children called it) and entertaining the local old folks at a weekly tea-party. In the Gwaun it was just us; we had no money but my fishing rod fed us and our bird and wildflower hunting cost nothing. There were no mountains in Pembrokeshire but the cliff paths and moors beckoned. Sometimes we went to the Preseli hills where there was a splendid Neolithic burial chamber at Pen-tre-van. In many ways Pembrokeshire was a prelude, much later, to the wildness of Perthshire.

In 1967 we were again at Cwmllan for a less active holiday as photographs show that Gillian was again pregnant. However even the Daily Mail did not alter our run of girls and Emma was born on 25th November and the ciné films of our next holiday in the spring show her competing with her sisters in doing headstands at the age of four months. She was aided and abetted by our friend and the children's honorary uncle John Parr [always known as UJP] who often visited us. But the family was growing up and by 1970 we felt rich enough to travel further afield.

Gillian's younger sister Alison, after reading botany at Bristol University, married Peter Clark, a doctor who was working as a trainee assistant in Lewis in the Outer Isles. They had often holidayed with us at Cwmllan and invited us to Stornoway. This was my first visit to the Outer Hebrides and I revelled in seeing unfamiliar birds such as great skuas, harriers, corncrakes and black guillemots. But the real joy was the fishing, for by now I had learned to cast a fly. Peter and I would bring home large catches of beautiful brown trout and even a couple of salmon.

In the practice my habit of recording things was growing and I amassed data on various aspects of my daily work. As well as my paper on the use of the IUCD I was fascinated by the methods of diagnosis used in general practice which were quite different from those we were taught as students. I published several papers on the subject as well as a collection of cases of brucellosis inspired by the cowman Luigi. Collecting and analysing all this data demanded a system of coding disease; so I invented one without realising that with the coming of computers this was an important field. My paper on Disease Coding in the Journal of Royal College of General Practitioners attracted world-wide interest*.

Despite less poverty and better holidays the early seventies were black. After long discussions between us Gillian elected to prevent further pregnancy by using an IUCD. At first this suited very well until she woke one morning with severe abdominal pain. I was frightened and telephoned Lawrence saying as calmly as I could:

"I think Gillian has a ruptured ectopic pregnancy."

My partner wasted no time and soon she was making an agonising trip to Hospital in Leamington Spa by ambulance. Mercifully my diagnosis was wrong the cause of her pain was an acute pelvic inflammation a known complication of 'the coil'. It was ironic that this should happen to the wife of such an exponent of this method of contraception. With antibiotics she made a swift recovery without surgery.

---

*Disease Coding - Journal of the Royal College of General Practitioners 1971.

Late in 1970 I too developed lower abdominal pain which defied diagnosis by Lawrence's friend and neighbour surgeon Christopher Savage. This culminated in an exploratory laparotomy to exclude cancer. Mercifully nothing abnormal was discovered and my appendix was removed. We convalesced by visiting Amsterdam for a few days in which time Gillian and I fell in love with that attractive city.

Meanwhile I had decided to attempt a thesis for the London MD based on the research I had done in the practice. That took many months of work mostly late at night sifting data, reading, writing and rewriting. As the thesis progressed I needed more and more time so I got up earlier and earlier. Eventually I could not sleep after about 3 am and was getting exhausted. The matter came to a crisis; one afternoon I went to Lawrence and burst into tears. To anyone but me the fact that I was seriously depressed was quite obvious. Depression, with its horrible conviction of worthlessness, is something I would not wish on an enemy. Time, the loving support of my wife, Lawrence's understanding and anti-depressants got me through. The illness left me with a far greater understanding of the anguish many of my patients endured and a heightened awareness of their often unspoken suffering. The MD was failed but with the recommendation that I rewrite and re-submit it.

While recovering I scribbled my first attempt at a novel which Mary Ariss, one of our receptionists, typed for me. It was soon to be awarded multiple rejections from many publishing houses. The world apparently did not like my non-medical writing. So, still taking antidepressants, I took the family with Alison and Peter on a fishing holiday to Connemara. We had an unheard of drought and the rivers were so low it was virtually fishless but very beautiful. Soon after we returned our beloved Penny, the first of our long string of Labradors, died of old age. The whole family was distraught but it was not long before we heard of a litter of labs born in the practice just at the time of the decimalisation of British Currency. We soon had a beautiful black puppy. She, as our New Penny, was christened Cent and was the first of a long line of Labradors all with monetary names.

By now finances had eased a little and despite the mortgage there was a little surplus cash. We used this to buy a small inflatable dinghy which soon paid for itself with fish caught and ice-cream not bought. With that and our new puppy, in the spring of 1972 we had the first of many holidays in Arran in a rented cottage in Whiting Bay. The children loved it and, after initial caution, loved the boat too. Emma, always, adaptable, felt no fear and simply fell asleep in it and once nearly slipped overboard in her sleep. We were so delighted we managed to book a tiny cottage called 'the wee hoose' for a summer holiday from a wonderful bow-legged Arran character Walter Marshall. We spent alternate days climbing the mountains and fishing in Lamlash Bay in the boat. We lived off mackerel and delicious flatfish from the bay. That holiday marked the beginning of my recovery from darkness though the black cloud of depression still lingered for, exciting though much of general practice is, it has its routine which may sometimes be soul-sappingly boring to a doctor trained in science and experienced in the major diseases of hospital. As I began to feel that general practice no longer frightened me as it had at first so I began to feel dissatisfaction with myself. I remembered that friends and teachers at medical school had predicted a career in hospital and I wondered if I had made the right decision. I also remembered the words of Lord Moran, a former dean of St Mary's Medical School and later Churchill's doctor, who described the medical school as a ladder up which students climbed to become specialists; those who fell off the ladder became general practitioners.

While pondering my career I read a paper by someone called Crombie who was writing arrant nonsense about the diagnostic methods of general practitioners. I was so incensed at the arrogance of this paper that I felt it essential to prove the man wrong. He gave a good description of his research method so I repeated what he had done. That taught me a lot for my results were almost identical with his. I learned from that that good research should be repeatable. Even more importantly, I realized the truth of Mark Twain's dictum 'it ain't what I don't know as makes me a fool as what I do know that ain't so'!

It was through this that I met two men who were to influence my life enormously. The author of the paper I had so despised, Donald Crombie, became a life-long friend as did that most remarkable of Midlands doctors, Robin Pinsent. Years later another friend, Michael Drury, was to write in Robin Pinsent's obituary, after his death on Christmas day 1987 at the age of 71: 'Robin's genius was for inspiring others... he was a master at encouraging others to take those first few uncertain steps into research.' He certainly inspired me.

Robin Pinsent was heaped with honours but remained a modest man devoted to gardening and fly fishing. He had a total laryngectomy for throat cancer but the only thing this prevented him doing was fishing, having promised his family not to because they feared he might drown. Unaware of this, I invited him for a day's fishing as a way of thanking him for the enormous help and support he had given me. He was torn between his promise and not wishing to refuse me. He came fishing, caught trout and demonstrated that fishing was not incompatible with a tracheostomy. After that he fished for the rest of his life, several times with me. I am not sure how popular I was with his family but I am glad I was able to reintroduce him to one of his abiding passions. Just before he died he sent me a fly* he had tied that I still use to tempt trout.

Between them Donald and Robin taught me the essentials of general practice research, opening up a new area of interest and challenge that, for a time at least, softened the fall from Lord Moran's ladder. Robin and Donald were always ready to see me at the College's Birmingham Research Unit and ever encouraging. Once when I was considering abandoning the project Robin looked me in the eye and croaked, in his oesophageal voice: 'Problems are made to be overcome!' There was no answer to that.

Part of the cause of the depression was the huge burden of debt we had saddled ourselves with in building the palace. At that time, though we were helped by considerable loans from a government sponsored organisation, the risk seemed colossal to a young father still coping with a large personal mortgage. However the palace

---

*A Montana nymph with which I took my only specimen of
Salvellinus fontinalis.

was quite a showpiece for general practice. We had many visitors and the practice of Mackie, Hull and Meadows was beginning to be recognised and talked about. Before long we added Dr. Susan Warren, a former trainee, to the team. She was later replaced by Dr David Rivers and, later still. Dr Steven Desborough.

Strangely I never kept a diary before 1972 and after that it was almost entirely for ornithological observations (such as the date of the first swallow or chiff-chaff) for fishing or social dates but increasingly there are notes of speaking engagements in and around Warwickshire. In early 1973 I attended my first lesson in doing vasectomies adding another skill against world population to the practice armament.

Some months after recovering from depression, but still in doubt about my future, on a Friday in March 1973,1 was doing evening surgery when a patient failed to keep an appointment. The *British Medical Journal* had arrived that day and it fell open at an advertisement which asked: 'Would you like to go to North Carolina?' For years following the example of Dr. Ian MacWhinney, a neighbouring practitioner in Stratford who, like Dr. Michael Drury of Bromsgrove, had won a Nuffield Travelling Scholarship, I had wanted to visit the States. I had applied twice for a Nuffield and had been short listed not long before my depressive illness. I picked up my pen and wrote on a piece of practice notepaper 'Yes please, what sort of guy do you want?' I tucked in a copy of my *curriculum vitae* and put the envelope in the post. All in the ten minutes of a failed appointment. The rest of surgery was so busy that I forgot the incident and did not even mention it to Gillian.

Two weeks later I received a letter asking me if my application were serious and if so would I mind sending in a proper one. This time I did discuss it with Gillian and with a growing sense of wonder I replied to the letter. By return I had a letter bidding me attend for interview. I replied with apologies as I was to be holidaying in Scotland.

'Very well,' came the telegraphed answer 'we will interview you *in absentia*.' I asked if they would pay my air flight from Edinburgh to London to attend the interview and this was granted.

On 31st of March we drove to a holiday cottage at Ardtrasgairt near Aberfeldy where my diary contains records for April: 1st: Siskin, 2nd: Capercaillie, fished Tay, 3rd: to London. These entries were laconic in the extreme both the siskin and the capercaillie were my first sightings of these species; when fishing the Tay I was casting into a snow storm and as for the London trip....

The interview was extraordinary, I remember Pat Byrne, Professor of General Practice at Manchester, and Dr. Ekke Kuenssberg and Dr. James Cameron from the British Medical Association were on the panel. These were then the great and the good of general practice. My recollection is of telling Pat Byrne how to be a Professor before excusing myself because I had to catch a plane back to resume my holiday in Scotland. I must have been the most tiresome interviewee in history but as there was no chance of my being selected I set out to enjoy myself. As I got up to leave a doubtless exasperated Professor Byrne said: 'Sit down, Hull... you've got the job.'

I do not believe I will ever be so astonished. It transpired that my facetious letter, written in two minutes of evening surgery, had crossed the Atlantic to land on the desk of a Dr. Robert Sullivan. Bob, later to become a great friend, chuckled and then wondered why my name was familiar. Then he saw that on his desk was a copy of the paper I had written on disease coding which he had read the day before. He wrote 'get this chap' on my letter and sent it back to the selection committee in London.

Lawrence, phoned from Heathrow, was as amazed as I was. Slowly the implications of a six month visiting professorship in America began to dawn on us. He said; 'I need to think, phone me tomorrow morning.'

"It is quite impossible," Lawrence said after a night's sleep, "you are due to go in eight weeks... how can we arrange cover for the practice? But... there is something even more impossible and that is that you should lose this opportunity. I don't know how we'll manage, but we will fix something."

That is the sort of man to have as a partner.

Two months later I found myself teaching family practice residents and students in Professor Robert Smith's department at the University of North Carolina (UNC) at Chapel Hill. The six months visiting professorship was financed jointly by King's Fund and UNC.

Just before we left we held a farewell party. Among our guests were Michael and Joan Drury who announced they would be in Washington during our time at Chapel Hill. Little thinking of consequence we invited them for a weekend.

Part III Academia

Chapter 7 American Adventure*

My introduction to Academia began with a jolt at UNC before becoming a more gradual easing until a complete transfer to that direction in 1985.

At 10 pm on 29th June 1973 exhausted and disorientated Gillian, Fiona, Janet, Emma and I arrived at Raleigh-Durham Airport where the heat and humidity of a Southern summer night, noisy with cicadas, hit us forcefully. Around us we heard the slow, deep, drawl that passes for speech in the South and noticed that every other face was black. We had arrived in an alien world to be met by the friendly English face of Dr. Peter Curtis.

Driving in the dark to Chapel Hill Peter told us what a beautiful place we had come to with its glorious campus combining English parkland with fine Georgian architecture. The whole area, he told us, is a forest where birds are magnificent, though difficult to spot among the vegetation. Alarmingly he spoke of snakes including cottonmouths, coral snakes, copperheads and rattlers all of which can be lethal and there are also black widow spiders. Through my jet-lag I heard him tell how to identify the deadly coral snake from its harmless imitator:

Red on yella, killa fella,
Red on black–good for Jack.

Early next morning I explored the house set in a wooded back street called Burlage Circle and let to us by a professor away on foreign leave. It was delightful and filled with books. Suddenly an excited voice summoned, "Daddy, come quick there's a bright red bird in the garden." So Fiona and I saw our first cardinal, the glorious scarlet State bird of North Carolina.

Arrival in America has a peculiar effect on visitors from England. The plane loses five hours as it whisks across the Atlantic. Jetlag combined

*Much of this chapter was written in 1974, just after our return from USA, comments and descriptions made then may not be valid today.

with the strangeness of the place, disorientates one completely. To this must be added all the little differences: phones make a different sound, light switches are off when down, money and banking are confusingly different, taps turn and loos (called 'comfort stations') flush in unfamiliar fashion, car mechanisms are transposed, and of course they will drive on the wrong side of the road.

The emptiness of Appalachia is stunning. Most people live in cities, leaving great tracts of land sparsely populated. Parallel to the East Coast run the Appalachian mountains, clad to the summit in dense forests of hickory and oak. These formed a barrier to the westward spread of early settlers, so early colonies were littoral.

Historically the south, with its semi-tropical climate, developed into an easygoing, sophisticated land-owning culture. The north, colder and more puritanical, with huge natural resources for its industry, produced the brisk, go-getting Yankee. The south, needing agricultural labour, turned to black Africa, while the north, looking for workers for its factories, turned to its own children and immigrants from Europe. So developed the dichotomy which led to Civil War, in an attempt to preserve different cultures. The defeated south was plunged into poverty from which it has taken more than a century to recover.

Violence has long been part of American life. Settling white men had to defend themselves against bear and cougar, rattlesnake and Indian and needed firearms for protection. This established the cherished American right to bear arms which, enshrined in the constitution and exaggerated by civil war, has led to the present proliferation of firearms. Though personal experience of violence during our six months' stay was fortunately very slight, violence was ever-present among patients and gunshot wounds were a frequent cause of attendance at the emergency room. Homicide ranks second and third respectively as the cause of death for females and males aged 5 to 45. Even my 22-year old secretary told me she slept with a revolver under her pillow!

The Sunday Preacher on the radio exhorted: "Jus' remember, you sinnin' heathen, there's a great big lake of sulphur waitin' jus' to sizzle y'all up", reminding us forcibly that we are in the Bible Belt. The poor are everywhere. Most are negro, but include what the middle-class blacks call 'white trash'. The towns have their shanty sections where the poor live in squalid hopelessness, their only relief found in drugs or alcohol. Much of the South is dry, which means it is impossible to buy liquor by the glass, and in some areas alcohol is legally unobtainable. Where spirits can be bought they are obtained at the Alcoholic Beverage Control (ABC) and there is an ABC store in most towns—customers being rationed to a gallon of spirit a day! All alcohol must be wrapped and it is not unusual to see men walking down the street drinking out of gurgling paper bags. Despite being cheap, the poor cannot afford enough to produce the anaesthesia they seek and cheap substitutes with names like 'moonshine', 'stumphole' and 'white lightnin' are commonly and illicitly distilled, sometimes even in a car radiator.

American women are fascinating. They are often very attractive, of warm personality and show a paradoxical mixture of the modesty, expected in the 'Bible Belt', and sexual provocation. The lovely girl seen scantily clad at the swimming pool is the same modest creature who either refuses to undress or, having done so, wraps herself in paper to baffle the examining physician. (When first confronted by a woman with chest pain cocooned in paper I tore the wrapper from her in order to examine her, whereupon she remarked to the nurse: 'He don't look much but he's all man'.) Sexual permissiveness and variety is such as to make Britain seem a nunnery. The bookshops offer large quantities of lavishly illustrated books on sex with many variations on a theme. This led to such confusion about sex that one young woman came to me because she had been told she needed abdominal surgery. She was 18 and complained of severe tummy pain. While I took a history her pain became increasingly vague and eventually she said that she was always tired. She was weary because she and her boyfriend had sex on going to bed and then sat up for the rest of the night debating whether they had succeeded. Hence her tiredness, hence her pain. Our ensuing conversation went like this:

'Can you swim?'

She looked puzzled. 'Sure I can swim.'

'Before you could swim what did you do when you went to the pool?'

She clearly thought me mad, 'I sat in the shallow water and splashed like the other kids.'

'Now, I want you to do something for me. Go away and sit in the shallow water and splash and in one month's time come and tell me how you're getting on.'

She backed out of the office and I thought I'd seen the last of her. But she did come back, pain gone and all smiles. 'I just want to tell you', she said, 'sittin' in the shallow water 'n' splashin's a load 'o fun.'

Peter and Carolyn Curtis took us to a barbecue at the Faculty Club swimming pool which was at a place called Old Mason Farm. The 'farm' belonged to the University who preserved it as a nature reserve. I explored somewhat nervously, astonished at the magnificent butterflies and, puzzled by a new avifauna, added Carolina Wren, Towhee, Blue Bird, two woodpeckers and the beautiful Blue Jay to my new North American list. When Gillian joined my cautious exploration a sudden movement in a bush had us almost leaping into each others' arms in terror as a covey of Bobwhite Quail erupted at our feet.

The first days were spent on formalities in the University and being shown round the superb campus shaded by stately oaks. The oldest building dated from 1797, most were early 19th century. Just after we arrived July 4th was celebrated by a carnival in the football stadium with lots of fireworks. No work was done that day. My chief memory of that Independence day was someone in the crowd singling us out because of our 'East Sussex accents!' Though I insisted it was not us who had the accents we were bombarded with requests to say anything, "'cos they jus' love list'nin' to the way we spoke". I suspect any early lecturing success depended more on the way I spoke than any wisdom I imparted. Once when we called at The Playmaker's theatre, the delightful campus theatre, the unseen producer of a Sherlock Holmes play shouted from within "Get that posh Limey accent I want him to play Dr Watson!" I was sorely tempted but really had enough on my plate without added thespianism.

So I found myself at Chapel Hill as Visiting Assistant Professor of Family Medicine in the department of Family Medicine. My task was to see patients in the Family Practice Unit (FPU), to help to build up the practice, to engage in research and to teach family medicine to undergraduates and newly qualified doctors working in the Family Practice Residency. Before I could contribute I had so much to learn.

The Department of Family Medicine was under the Chairmanship of Professor Robert Smith, an Irishman, who was in overall charge of the FPU. Peter Curtis, a general practitioner from rural Hampshire, and also a visiting professor of Family Medicine, was director of the FPU. Dr. Curtis had been in NC since January 1973 and had achieved the remarkable feat of establishing the practice so that it was able to start its official existence on July 1st.

Much of my work involved seeing patients in the FPU. Sometimes cultural differences caused incidents. An attractive patient I asked about her contraception replied, "Don't need it. Ma hubby 'n' I prefer it orally." As soon as she left I found Peter and recounted this. The attending Psychiatrist overheard and looked at me sharply.

"Did you tell her, Robin?"

Feeling nettled at what I mistook for criticism of an omission I asked, "What should I have told her?"

"Shoulda told her it was fattenin'."

On another occasion I took Gillian round the FPU and I showed her how women were placed in stirrups for gynaecological examinations. 'Barbaric' was her comment. I managed to find an old examination couch such as I used at home. With that I could examine the ladies and do their 'pap' smears in a much less undignified position. To my horror I heard that the message was going round the hospital 'Go down to Family Medicine and you can have it The English Way'.

Patients attending the practice consisted of the families of students, nurses and junior faculty who had joined because of the offer of comprehensive round-the-clock care at reasonable cost. The second group of patients were the rejects of other departments or were brought to us by residents from the ward because they urgently needed care and had no place to get it. These patients, predominantly black, were the flotsam and jetsam of the North Carolina poor. They suffered from severe chronic, disabling social, mental and physical disease and for some their problems seemed insurmountable. The commonest physical diseases were high blood pressure, diabetes and obesity. The major social disease was poverty which bred depressed hopelessness leading to high and frequently illegitimate birth-rate, alcoholism, drug addiction and violence. Alcohol related death was high in the list with cirrhosis and acute pancreatitis as its henchman.

American medicine had changed from a poorly trained and organised profession in the early 1900s. In recent years there had been increased scientific orientation away from the person to the disease. In a country which loved gadgetry, medicine must have all possible technology, and access to this had led to a centripetal drift of doctors to centres of excellence, leaving a dearth at the rural periphery. In addition to this spatial maldistribution there had been no control of entry into the specialties, with the result that a town might have six times as many neuro-surgeons as primary physicians. There was really no shortage of doctors; they were just the wrong sort in the wrong place.

It had become very difficult to find a personal doctor and, when found, the bill for the tests he felt he must do could be astronomical.

Doctors got busier and drew patients from a wider area; home visits became impracticable and the relationship between the patient and his physician grew strained. With the burgeoning of science in the last two decades this vicious circle had strangled the old bonds of empathy. In the UK we are well aware that family doctoring is not so much about illness as about people who have dis-ease. Doctors in the States still command respect, but it is a respect tinged with fear more than love. A recent American survey had shown that public confidence in doctors was only a whisker ahead of their confidence in garbage collectors.

North Carolina is the size of England and its population is just over half that of London. The logistics of supplying medical care are insuperable. The United States as a whole had 134 counties without physicians, 55 million, over a quarter of the total population lived in rural communities where health care is either inadequate or essentially nonexistent.

With doctors poorly deployed, and engaged in examining the healthy and treating the wealthy, the American people explore other sources of care. So the universities, saddled with the task of providing primary care, have started departments of family medicine.

Legal repercussions hang over the doctor like the sword of Damocles. A patient was sent to see a neurosurgeon because she had a ten-year history of monthly pre-menstrual headache preceded by flashing lights in the periphery of her visual field. She often vomited and had to lie in a darkened room; the following day she was better. On reading the doctor's letter the neurosurgeon ordered a work-up which consisted of routine blood chemistry, chest and skull X-rays, brain scan, electroencephalogram, lumbar puncture, air encephalogram and, finally, carotid artery angiogram. These done, patient and surgeon met for the first time, when he said, 'My dear, I'm happy to tell you all your tests are normal; I think you have migraine!' The bill was considerable. In defending himself the neurosurgeon would explain that he had to exclude the remotest possibility or fail in his job. Examination, he would claim, told him little that the tests did not; if he failed to carry out the tests and missed, say, a symptomless meningioma he would be liable for an action for malpractice.

Difficulties in teaching were many: subjectively I had doubts as to my ability particularly arriving in a highly scientific medical school so long after leaving my own school. My lack of academic and of recent hospital experience made me feel inadequate and this was not eased by the aggressiveness of the American student. In addition there were the very considerable objective difficulties inherent in a different culture and language whose nuances of meaning are so important in teaching. In the face of these difficulties I discovered that I had much to teach and I became so angry at what I saw that it would have been difficult to stop me, but my hosts were too charming to do that.

After two weeks I was a mass of conflicting emotions; depression at my inadequacy, home-sickness (such that, if I could have returned to Warwickshire without loss of honour, I would have done so) and most of all anger. In a teaching session I lost my British cool, thumped the table and said "For God's sake Don't you know you're doing it all wrong?'

There was an embarrassed silence then a senior resident started clapping as he drawled "Ya'll jus' be awright from now on."

He was correct; from then on I adored everything that NC had in store for me especially when teaching. It was then that I realised it was my very difference that was the basis of my teaching especially in my approach to collecting data on which to make a diagnosis.

There was a free and easy relationship between teacher and pupil which from an early age encouraged argument and disputation. By the time a youngster had passed through school and undergraduate college into medical school he was ready to cross swords with anyone. This produced a medical student quite unlike his British counterpart: his attitude to his professors was usually one of polite tolerance. He seemed to look at a teacher and, not liking what he saw, determined to find anything he could within his mentor which might forward his education, even if this meant tearing the professor apart. They did not know what to make of the strange 'Limey': the best ones were brought up short and were stimulated to think; the others just ignored me.

Formal teaching was quite informal; smoking, reading, talking and eating, were accepted lecture theatre occupations and, of course, mass walk-out in the face of a tedious address was not unknown. In my first formal lecture to over 100 students as well as a number of academics who wanted to see what their visitor was like, I was very nervous but by now had decided that what little strength I had lay in my difference. I waited until there was silence and calling up all my theatrical experience I began: "Listen. I am going to tell you a story"; and I recited the nursery rhyme 'Ring a-ring o' roses'. I then made them imagine themselves in a village in the south of England in the 14th century. I described a stranger approaching the village. He looked ill and was staggering. On entering the village he fell dead. Some of the more curious villagers came to look; they were some of the first to die….

Their attention was caught by my choice of bubonic plague to introduce a lecture on infective disease to students just about to start anatomy and physiology. It worked; for some time the proverbial pin could have been heard. Later I spoiled it a bit: I needed a volunteer. A girl clad in brief shorts and a halter top came up. Trying hard not to stare at her cleavage I asked her name:

"Gee I'm Randy ," she replied.

"So am I," I said " but this is hardly the place."

That lecture probably did much to determine attitudes towards me! To my surprise the academic organising this course to introduce new entry students to the complexity of clinical medicine wrote to me saying my lecture was 'beautiful'. That unexpected, totally un-British epithet alone said so much about the difference between American and British teaching. Though often plunged into highly technical medicine I stuck to first principles, to the work I knew dealing with sick people at their first contact with health care. It seemed to work for, though I often felt the ice beneath my skates was paper-thin, it was apparently successful.

Sometimes in lectures we were harnessed with highly sensitive microphones. I took part in a quartet of 'experts' on alcoholism before a very large audience of students and faculty. My remit was to talk about the difficulty of diagnosis of dependence on alcohol in practice, I was followed by a physician and then a pathologist who gave their views. The last speaker was an internationally expert psychiatrist. He was also very boring and droned on and on. When he was explaining dream analysis in alcoholics he said dreaming of drinking was a favourable prognostic sign. Forgetting the microphone round my neck I nudged the pathologist next to me and asked "is that what they mean by a wet dream?" Two hundred students went mad with glee and the famous psychiatrist never spoke to me again.

American universities have enormous teaching faculties. At UNC Medical School there were four hundred each of students, beds and professors. This high ratio of staff meant that teaching was less pedagogic than in England, making more use of small-group and tutorial teaching than of formal didactic lectures. But there was a dearth of clinical experience. In consequence students had a wealth of theoretical knowledge and this imbalance was largely responsible for the greater importance laid upon laboratory rather than clinical findings which, in part, contributed to the depersonalisation of medicine.

Some of the faculty were outstanding teachers. Head and shoulders above them all was Dr. Jim Bryan. Every year the students voted for the best teacher and Jim won that accolade with monotonous regularity. He was an inspiring teacher and I learned from him that, though teaching fact was difficult, instilling wisdom was much more so. Once Jim was delayed on the ward and I started chatting to his group of students about a recent television programme on Sherlock Holmes. When Jim arrived he listened for a moment and then spent the session talking about the famous detective. He knew the work of Conan Doyle in detail and was enthralling. I recognised what he was doing but the students thought they were getting an easy session. Jim concluded an hour's impromptu talk by saying. "Y'all just learned more about making a diagnosis than you've heard since you came to medical school" and, with his inimitable laugh he rushed back to the wards. His teaching by parable was hardly new but was certainly inspirational.

Another interesting innovation, introduced by Peter and me, was home visiting which was virtually unknown and initially considered by the residents to be the anachronistic obsession of the two Brits, and of questionable value. It was with some pride that we noticed that residents were setting aside some of their hard-pressed time to see patients in their homes. I was sure we did too much home visiting in Britain but was equally sure that general practice would suffer enormously if doctors stopped visiting altogether. The residents were quick to appreciate how much can be learnt from a brief visit to a patient's home and how the patient's illness became more understandable in the context of his environment. American patients showed their appreciation of visiting and the whole doctor-patient relationship became incomparably warmer.

Once, visiting a middle-aged black lady who had a thrombosed leg vein, I was balancing on the side of her trough-like double bed bandaging the leg when her telephone rang. She answered, listened and said "Can't talk now honey I got Doc' Hull right in the middle o' ma bed."

One afternoon I saw a black man in the emergency room with a severe burn as a result of sleeping off his 'moonshine' with his foot against a hot pipe. The foot was a mess but his reason for attending was a broken nose after being hit by a drinking companion. I dressed his foot and sent him off with instructions to see me again. He failed to keep his appointment because he was subsequently imprisoned for shooting his boozing chum dead. I had the interesting experience of doing several 'house calls' in the jail to dress his foot. I liked both the murderer and the sheriff who guarded him and this most unusual 'home visit' put a new light on the term 'carer': 'I was in prison and thou visited me.'

The most exciting teaching was at a clinic improvised by the students themselves. Chapel Hill was well integrated but had not always been so. In the late 1960's the Civil Rights movement was strong and produced much change for the better in black-white relations. Because of lack of integration, cost and social problems the blacks had inadequate medical care. At the same time students felt they were not getting enough hands-on experience with patients. A number of highly motivated students led by Toby Atkins (who later became one of Family Medicine's second year residents during my stay in North Carolina) approached the Medical School with a proposition: ' We need patients,' he said, 'and the blacks need medical care. Why not put us together?' This raised many problems in a community only just emerging from segregation but they were eventually overcome due to the persistence of the students and also the leaders of the black community and the Student Health Action Committee (SHAC) was born!. SHAC found a disused school and opened a weekly clinic which was run by students and provided free care for the indigent. For legal reasons it was required that a member of faculty be present at the clinic to countersign each patient's chart and to approve prescribing. The clinic started at 7 pm and went on until there were no more patients, perhaps 4 to 5 hours which, in the non-air-conditioned clinic in a Carolinean summer night was a marathon. It was a very exciting to see the drive with which the students worked. It was rather like a hopelessly disorganised but very enthusiastic general practice. The patients presented mostly for routine physical examinations required by law prior to work or marriage but sometimes there were very considerable medical or social problems. The opportunities for teaching were first class. The first patient I was asked to see was a case of sarcoma of the femur in a boy of 18 and later I taught on the first case of tuberculous epididymitis I had seen since

---

*Toby Atkins came from a wealthy northern family. Rumour had it that when the dean opposed his proposal Atkins replied "See here, Mr Dean, if you don't agree I'll buy your medical school." Though apocryphal the story could have had some truth in it!

I was a student. Writing to Lawrence Mackie I commented 'how immensely refreshing it is to be back in an academic atmosphere where there is time to discuss, to argue and to think.'

However SHAC also revealed the inequality of care. The boy with the sarcoma was seen by an orthopaedic surgeon, the diagnosis was confirmed and he was discharged the same day because he could not pay for surgery. The boy with tuberculosis of the testicle also was found to have open pulmonary disease and so posed a public health risk. He too was discharged without follow up because he was moving out of state. To my way of thinking both cases constituted malpractice.

Most weekends the family spent exploring Chapel Hill, the nearby University Lake and the farm. The kids were having a whale of a time, mostly in the water, and were brown as berries. Once I saw an enormous black snake only a hundred yards from the swimming pool. At the time I believed these to be benign but it served as a warning that even this Eden had its serpents.

In a letter to Lawrence I wrote: "I saw Gaitha, a delightful black lady three weeks ago with acute depression who was taking a host of expensive medicaments from the six doctors she had seen in the same week she saw me! I spent a lot of time talking to her without examining her or taking blood all of which had been done repeatedly by my colleagues. Gaitha, worked at SHAC, was a pillar of her church and a prominent civil rights worker. She found her alcoholic husband was hard to live with. After I had done with explaining her depression she made a pretty speech about 'Limey Doctors' and then flabbergasted me by saying she was off to see another doctor from whom she could get the antidepressants I prescribed more cheaply than from the hospital! Happily she responded to stopping all other therapy.

"This place is so beautiful particularly in regard to its natural history. The birds here come in vivid primary reds, blues, yellows and greens and are superb. At present the flowers are exciting us and we are collecting and pressing. It is fun to see cultivated flowers–rudbeckia, golden rod, coreopsis and ageratum blooming wild. I often think of my father's patient raising of *Lobelia Cardinalis* and his triumph over it when I see superb specimens blooming in the fields! The kids all started school today and first impressions sound favourable. They have made so many friends at the swimming pool* I doubt they will have many problems. All three adore America especially the swimming, the clothes and the ice cream. Actually we all enjoy the food and all have weight problems but are munching our way through sweet potatoes, okra, acorn squash, hush puppies and dills, some with approval some with distaste."

I had applied for a course in Maine on Lawrence Weed's Problem Oriented Medical Record which was sending me out of my mind at the FPU. The University gave me time off and funded my journey which included a visit to Montreal so the family came too. At Montreal we were met by Ann Macaulay (nee Welbourn) who had worked in our practice in Warwickshire. Ann has made tremendous strides, as well as having a couple of babies. She is now general practitioner in charge at an Indian Reservation near Montreal. It is clear that she is loved by the tribe who have given her son honorary tribal status with a quite unpronounceable Indian name. It was obvious as I talked to her patients that Ann had not only helped them medically but had given them encouragement to help themselves into improving their incredibly decrepit hospital and regaining some of their national pride. Through her example they have so impressed the legislators that it is highly probable that they will have considerable state aid towards a new hospital.

After a weekend at Ann's idyllic lakeside cottage we drove through Vermont and New Hampshire to Maine. I had always heard of the beauty of New England and it surpassed expectation. Before going to my course we visited the Acadia National Park on Mount Desert Island, a small glaciated island of deep valleys, pine covered mountains, murrain ended lakes with a ten mile fjord. We climbed Mount Cadillac, the high point at 1500 feet. The rock is a pale pink

---

*Most afternoons Gillian and the children had the pool to themselves; Watergate was at its height and everyone rushed home for the latest episode of what seemed to be the soap opera of the day.

making a splendid contrast with the vivid green of the trees and deep blue of the water. It was a pleasure to walk without fear; in Chapel Hill we are always conscious of the copperhead and anxious for the children. In Maine there was nothing venomous though a skunk could be an embarrassment. We all fell for the raccoons with their pert, masked, gangster faces and a look suggesting shrewd intelligence and had the pleasure of observing them closely. I did not enjoy the course but it did help to pay for a wonderful trip.

In October the owner of the rented house at Burlage Circle was returning so we had to move. This caused problems to the University who, as part of my contract had to house my family and suitable accommodation was hard to find in Chapel Hill. I was asked if I would mind living in the University Chancellor's official residence.

"Mind?" I asked "Anybody would give his teeth for the chance."

So we spent the last third of the job living in an exquisitely beautiful modern reproduction of an ante-bellum southern mansion. I forget whether we had six or seven bathrooms reached by a superb staircase such as Scarlet O'Hara might have used. The furniture was magnificent for the forests of NC provide wonderful timber for tables and chairs. We even had a grand piano for Gillian to practice on. This splendid house made a good place for tutorials for groups of students. From the Chancellor's house it was a short but enjoyable walk through the campus to work. This allowed a few minutes to look at wildlife. I became well acquainted with a family of chipmunks who scurried along in front of me as well as many species of woodpecker among the trees.

I had an interesting letter from Michael Drury saying he had just been appointed as Tutor in General Practice at Birmingham University. He added mysteriously that he had a proposition to put to me. As arranged before we left Warwickshire Michael and Joan stayed with us at the Chancellor's House and over a gin and tonic in the magnificent garden he invited me to join him at Birmingham. This was a Godsend for, after tasting academic life, I was not sure if I could function without it. Gillian was immensely relieved, for

171

she feared a backlash after the stimulus of America.

By November I was extremely busy in the FPU and Thanksgiving brought welcome relief and gave us three days in which to visit The Outer Banks taking a ferry to Ocracoake and Hatteras lighthouse. We drove to visit the Wright Brothers Memorial at Kill Devils Hills and watched fishermen hauling nets leaving behind menacing looking Thresher Sharks. The natural history was superb on the major migration route from the north with many new birds and thousands of Snow Geese. One bird was so exciting I ran the car off the road and had to be helped out of the sand. But one does not see an American Bittern every day!

At Christmas Ann and her family flew from Montreal and we had a fine traditional Christmas following which we threw a memorable leaving party celebrating a dream-like six months with gallons of Bacardi punch and eightsome reels. Leave-taking was sad but we had the long journey south through Charleston, Savannah and the great swamp nature reserve of Okeefenokee. After exploring new country in Georgia and Florida, we flew home from Miami to an England plunged in gloom with the fuel crisis of January 1974.

Though my diary entry for 8th January, our first day home, reads ' An unspeakable day!' the whole American venture was a turning point in our lives. I had discovered I liked academia and surprisingly it seemed to like me. As a family all our horizons had suddenly been broadened, our philosophies altered and our prejudices challenged. After the blackness of depression, life took on a new and rosier look.

Gillian had once again been transported back to university, attending Italian classes and mixing with academics. Though there were features of American life, particularly its violence, inequality and gun culture, which she disliked there was a wonderful peace in the great campus with its quadrangles filled with stately oaks and Georgian architecture. Once a senior academic wife asked her what she did in England and on hearing that, like a good country doctor's wife Gillian did good works she said: "Never mind, my dear, you will grow out of it." That prophecy, given the stimulus of Chapel Hill, was soon to come to pass.

For me the change was even more profound. I had gone to NC full of self doubt, wondering, not for the first time, whether I had been wise in choosing general practice, or even medicine, as a career. I had returned with new ambition to restore that humanity to medicine which I had sensed that Britain was losing and whose loss was so obvious in the over-specialised and highly technical profession in the States. But I was also excited by the enthusiasm and hope that I found in the students, though immensely saddened by the degradation of those virtues by a form of medical education that seemed to depend on rote learning, heavily didactic teaching and multiple choice examination. I had also discovered, or perhaps rediscovered, a love of teaching instilled into me by my own teachers at St Mary's.

At the interview for the North Carolina post Professor Byrne had asked me what I would do in America. Rather pompously I told him that I would spread the philosophy of British General Practice. Perhaps America gave me a chance to formulate that philosophy; now I wanted to promulgate it more than ever. The future looked incredibly challenging but how was I to find a way to meet the challenge?

Chapter 8 Early Academic years 1973-85

Return to Wellesbourne brought reunion with Lawrence Mackie, the practice and my patients. All were looking at me seeking change but they must have been disappointed for return resembled coming back from a holiday. Then routine work slipped, like a well known jacket, back onto my shoulders. The endless demand and routine of daily surgeries and visits, performed against the clock, engulfed me, making my more contemplative, even leisurely, visit to academic medicine seem light years away.

But there were things inside bursting to get out. I wrote to Abraham Marcus, editor of the popular postgraduate GP journal *Update*, asking if he would be interested in my adventures in America. He was, and a series on American Medicine in Update was the real beginning of my writing career. Then Robin Pinsent approached me. He was also writing for *Update* and had started a monthly column called *Practice Revealed*. The journal appeared fortnightly and Robin asked if I would consider writing a similar piece to alternate with, and complement, his. So we sang a duet with *City* and *Country Practice Revealed* which was to continue for years and went on long after Robin retired with David Brooks writing from Manchester instead of Robin from Handsworth. This was just what I wanted; a regular slot where I could philosophise about the work of a country family doctor, and the habitat in which he practised.

Robin Pinsent and Donald Crombie introduced me to another organisation which was destined to have profound effect on my life. They and Dr Ekke Kuenssberg, an Edinburgh GP, and later President of the Royal College of General Practitioners* were trying to expand general practice research into Europe. Ekke had been on my interview board for the Carolina job so we already knew each other.

Britain had a head start in practice research for every GP had a formal list of patients, a known denominator of people against whom to relate the incidence of disease and which could be used as a baseline for epidemiological studies. This was one reason that the College

*The RCGP or, more often just 'the College.'

was able to lead Europe in general practice research. I attended the second meeting of a group of highly motivated European doctors who, over the years, were to become lifelong friends. Particularly I remember Poul Pedersen and Poul Krogh-Jensen from Denmark, Dag Bruusgaard from Norway, Echardt Sturm from Germany, Oleg Gorbatov from Finland, Gilbert Temmerman from Belgium and Chris Bruins and Govaert Dorrenboom from Holland among many others. We met twice a year in a different country to discuss and compare problems of national and international research. It was enormous fun and highly stimulating. Asked what the European General Practice Research Workshop (EGPRW) actually did I used to reply flippantly that we learned to say 'have another one old boy' in every European language. Certainly it had its social side but it also led to the publication of a huge range of papers comparing and contrasting different health care systems and their effect on the delivery of care. I became fascinated by the way doctors in different countries divided their time between various aspects of practice such as consulting, home visiting, hospital visiting, continuing education and so on. I was awarded a prize* financing the research and delivery of a paper on the 'General Practitioner's use of time' at a conference at Colle-Colle in Denmark in 1982. Another important spin off from EGPRW was that it enabled me to write some thirty articles for *Update* under the title *A Day with the Doctor*. To do this I spent a day with a family doctor in different countries so providing a subjective impression of international variation between doctors in the same way as Practice Revealed highlighted differences between two doctors in the same country.

Another spin off from America was that many of my former UNC students jumped at the chance of visiting Britain when they stayed with my family and followed my day's routine. In time the practice in Wellesbourne became an extension of the medical schools of at least three continents. I do not know if I taught them much but I know how much they taught me. Of course there were a few linguistic errors. One elegant southern gentleman with exquisite manners was due to do something with me early one morning. As he went to bed Gillian asked "What time shall I knock you up in the morning?"

---

*The SIMG-Janssen Prize (SIMG = *Societas Internationalis Medicenae Generalis*).

Our guest was astonished for her request had only one meaning for him. For a moment he stared in bewilderment before bowing to her with "Why Ma'am, that sure is hospitality!"

This international student exchange was another form of education for our three daughters who grew up with a cosmopolitan breakfast table. One Chapel Hill student so loved his attachment he subsequently revisited us with his wife on their honeymoon. Important in these student exchanges was King's Fund who had partly financed my trip to NC and through them we had many visitors so that over the next two decades we averaged 94 man/nights of guests a year from 28 countries and six continents. One year the beds hardly cooled down with 186 man/nights!

Gillian, by then, had 'grown out' of good works in the practice and when not being a hostess was working hard as a Blue Badge, French-speaking, Guide in the Heart of England. Her tourist work led her to study the history of the area and especially of early local doctors and soon she was publishing papers on historical medical men including Dr John Hall of Stratford (Shakespeare's son-in-law) and Dr John Wall who began the manufacture of Worcester porcelain. She also followed up Lawrence Mackie's preliminary work on the history of medical practice in Wellesbourne. This resulted in a slim volume entitled *Three centuries of medicine in a Warwickshire Village*.

In the practice it was business as usual. Other practitioners who took time out to do other things were often penalised by their partnership agreements and were obliged to draw a smaller income from the practice. I could not afford to do that so I bargained that every penny I earned as a writer or as a teacher should go into practice accounts from which I should draw my share as a partner. I brought more in than I took out and so I bought peace from those who grumbled that I was never there*. The practice was burgeoning with new housing estates and soon Lawrence Mackie, Henry Meadows and I had to take on an additional partner; we were joined by Dr David Rivers.

---

*With Michael Drury under the *nom-de-plume* of 'Gemini' I worte a semi-humorous piece in the *British Medical Journal* in a series called *The Pathology of Partnership* entitled "*You're never here - I'm never there.* [1982].

Lawrence was devoted to all his trainees and followed their subsequent careers for the rest of his life: a quiet, almost taciturn man, he watched over the men and women who worked with him almost as though they were offspring. On a day to day basis this was hardly noticeable and his regular lack of punctuality often jarred to the extent that his concern for the well being of his colleagues became obscured. For me, following my bout of acute depression, he was particularly watchful. When my schizophrenic life between Birmingham Medical School and the practice became overly hectic he would gently remind me of my history and urge a slower pace. But at the same time he was ambitious for me, writing letters encouraging me in the political maze of advancement within academia. We had frequent debates as to whether I should give up either my teaching at the university or my caring role as a country doctor. Often I wanted to choose between them but knew in my heart that the thing that made me a credible teacher was that I was working in the field, doing night visits, coping with emergencies and the routine decision-making of practice.

In November 1974 we bought a lovely old house called Jasmine Cottage in the then unspoiled village of Hampton Lucy, finalising the completion over the phone from a call box in Sannox in Arran. Jasmine Cottage was a dream where we lived for 23 years seeing our children grow up in lovely, if draughty, space. With six bedrooms there was room for us all, a study and ample guest room for all those visiting students. It also had the advantage of being four miles nearer to the medical school. In time, from Jasmine Cottage, Fiona went to Edinburgh University to read ecology, Jan to Sheffield reading geography and Emma to Cardiff following me into medicine. Two of them, Fiona and Emma, married in Hampton Lucy, walking across the village street from Jasmine Cottage to St Peter ad Vincula church.

In those middle seventies my workload seemed to grow by the day. I had two full days at Birmingham, was in wide demand as a postgraduate teacher all over the Midlands and sometimes as far away as Devon or the Lake District. Often I had as many as 20-30 articles and papers a year to prepare and I took my share of night duty and routine consulting and visiting. In 1974 just before we moved to Hampton Lucy I was elected a Fellow of the RCGP. Much to my disappointment the MD which had been referred for further work was failed. That disappointment could not last long for I was far too busy: certainly there was no hint of the depression it had occasioned two years before. It had to be accepted, *c'est la vie*.

At Birmingham it was all go. I was officially appointed as Clarkson Tutor in General Practice in 1975. Michael Drury had started work while I was in Carolina but at first things were very slow. The early GP foetus was wombed in a little wooden hut next to the 'Gents'. We had two desks and a telephone. Half a mile away in the teaching hospital we had a part-time secretary, the incomparable Sue Magwin, in the office of the Department of Medicine under whose protective wing we nestled. The head of the Department was the delightful South African Professor Bill Hoffenberg; he was always supportive and encouraging. Professors of medicine used

Emma, Florin, Janet, Guilder & Fiona at Jasmine Cottage, Spring 1980.

179

to frighten me a bit in those days and often I had to share teaching sessions with Bill. If he felt, as I did, that the gulf between us was vast he never showed it but rather stressed to students a general practitioner's good fortune in seeing a case from its outset and for detailed knowledge of the patient, his background and family.

Much of the time, in those early days was spent together with Michael Drury in the hut planning the future. Once I remember Michael looking at the phone on his desk with the words "wouldn't it be nice if it rang!"

From the start we planned an ambitious teaching programme trying to find a toehold in any part of the curriculum. One of the earliest programmes we called 'Before and After' and it was with these that I often taught with Bill Hoffenberg and with other consultant physicians across the complex chain of Birmingham hospitals which comprised the teaching resource. The idea was that a student should present a case as he had seen it in the ward. Where possible we would try to persuade the patient's GP to explain the circumstances leading up to admission to hospital and then we would all debate what might happen when the patient returned home The students loved it for it was so different from anything they had done before and made them think; but it was sometimes difficult to get GPs to join the discussion. They claimed shortage of time but I suspect they felt the same vulnerability that I had felt with the professor of medicine. Once we had a case of an elderly diabetic whose disease was out of control. The patient's doctor when invited to attend declined: "They'll get onto complicated biochemistry and I've forgotten all that." But we did persuade him. For a little while he listened as the student talked of keto-acidosis and elevated blood sugar till finally he could stand it no longer. He interrupted the student and said: "let me tell you about this man whom I've known for nearly forty years. He's lived alone with his old Labrador since his wife died. It was the dog that stopped him going to pieces then, he was devoted to it. Every day he and his black lab walked a mile across the park to a supermarket where he bought himself and the dog a nice bit of steak. Then the dog was run over; the patient was suddenly doubly bereaved of wife and dog. There was no reason to walk across the park; he went to the baker's shop next door for his supper. His exercise was reduced and his diet changed from largely protein to carbohydrate. You don't need your expensive technology. What you need is another dog!"

Those students never forgot that brilliant and simple teaching of which Hippocrates himself would have been proud.

Another very supportive senior member of staff was Owen Wade, Professor of Clinical Pharmacology and, later, Dean of the Medical School. Owen had come to Birmingham from Belfast where general practice teaching had been established with a chair held by Professor George Irwin. Owen Wade had used the Ulster GPs in his research and had become impressed with their potential. In consequence he was one of our greatest allies. Owen was an extremely forceful, sometimes controversial, character who had developed a novel way of teaching his subject which, despite its importance, was one that did not lend itself to student popularity. Each week he ran what he called a 'roadshow' spiced with his own variety of humour sometimes near the knuckle, much to undergraduate delight. The roadshows involved a case history and a rotating panel of students who had to prepare an argument, based on pharmacological principles, for treating the patient or patients involved. In addition he required two experts, one a hospital clinician and the other a GP, either Michael Drury or me. This was fun, the students loved it and attendance verged on 100%. despite being scheduled for late on Friday afternoon. It had two great virtues: students, all of whom had to take part in the panels, were seen themselves to be teachers, also it brought Michael and me to their attention.

Another innovation was Family Attachment. This programme put all first year students into contact with a family in the city. Families were selected by their GPs, because they were interesting or had difficult chronic diseases such as diabetes or epilepsy. Probably the largest group comprised families with a new baby. At first the students, boys and girls straight from school, were nonplussed;

they knew nothing and found it difficult to relate to their families. Each group of students had a tutor, often a GP, with whom they discussed their families. I found my tutorial group nervous and rather frightened. In many cases this was the first time they had been thrust into an unknown family often socially disparate from any they had experienced. To say they were thrown would be an understatement, some even pleaded to be excused. I hit on the idea of saying to them 'pretend you are writing a novel about your family. Describe them, tell me how you relate to them, how do you think you would react in their circumstances? Don't tell me you don't know enough about their problems; there's a bloody great library at the end of this corridor go and find out'.

The relationships thawed, students and families often became so close that students continued to visit their families in later years long after the official part of the attachment was over. Patients felt a particular interest in their 'young doctor', and were proud to have been part of his or her education. In all the years we only found a replacement family once. A good looking young man came with a problem. His family with a new baby was socially lamed by the husband being in Winston Green Prison. The lad was concerned, the young wife was showing signs of being attracted by him and he had learned that the husband was in jail for beating up a man he suspected of having an affair with his wife. Student safety took priority over educational rigour and he was reallocated.

Another first year activity was a practice visit. Parties of students were taken by coach to selected practices who entered into the spirit by showing them behind the scenes in a busy practice and then appealing to the youngsters with tea and buns. Our idea was to catch them young, before they were at an age to be let loose on anything but a very dead patient in the dissecting room. I had taken part in a similar course in NC and realised the importance of exposing the first year to at least a flavour of things to come and to the doctoring they had chosen as a vocation.

Soon after we were established at the Medical School Michael and I sometimes looked into the Staff bar for a pint to lay the dust of teaching or lecturing. There we were to meet two other people who had enormous influence on the way in which the renamed General Practice Teaching & Research Unit (GPTRU) developed. The first of these was a young psychiatrist, Senior Lecturer Tim Betts. Tim was forward looking in his teaching and among other novel methods was using television to demonstrate aspects of his subject. He introduced us to Paul Morby, often to be found, wineglass in hand in the bar in the early evening. Paul was an interesting man, effervescent, mercurial and very talented as a television director. Unlike most of us who used the staff house bar Paul was not an academic and liked to draw distinction between himself and the rarefied and, he said, aloof professors and lecturers. He was director of the University Television and Film Unit. As soon as he met us he invited us to produce programmes with him. This seemed a Godsend for, twenty-five miles from my clinical base in Wellesbourne, I was deprived of my best teaching material, my own patients. At first our programmes were simple interviews with patients starting with a young soldier made paraplegic by a bullet in Cyprus some twenty years before. This patient, Bruce Dutton-Cox, a close friend of mine, was himself a teacher and very willing to be interviewed on camera. The resulting videotape provided an excellent way of exploring the physical, psychological and social aspects of disability which was made all the more powerful because a popular member of the department of Social Medicine, Tim Marshall, was also paraplegic. After the success of this tape it was followed up by case presentations of Down's Syndrome, Haemophilia and a sick patient abandoned by her husband. The student's response to these tapes was interesting, used to television in their own homes these cases on the screen combined reality with a separation which allowed students to react to the portrayed people with a freedom they could not have if the patients were present in the flesh. I had to admit that spending a day in the studio with Paul and his crew of technicians appealed to my love of amateur dramatics but the results proved their success as teaching aids and soon justified a day off from 'real work' playing at television.

We then became more ambitious. I had always been fascinated by the pathway of diagnosis in practice and how it differed from that taught in medical school. In practice the doctor was faced with a torrent of symptoms. The trouble is the first symptoms of serious illness are often identical with those of trivial, self-limiting dis-ease. The trick is to spot the difference. Easily said but fraught with difficulty because so many barriers prevented such diagnosis. Some barriers are in the patient, some in the doctor and some are circumstantial.

I had recently had a contretemps with an American visitor who understandably had little idea of how the NHS worked. She rubbed me up the wrong way by turning up at my home one day before breakfast for advice about her cold. She then presented in the surgery with such bizarre neurological symptoms that she convinced me she was neurotic. Then, as she put it, 'I seemed to be having difficulty in reaching diagnosis perhaps I could help with a simpler matter, her contraception.' By this time I was getting fed up but, as she described her need to remain attractive to her husband she hesitated and became tearful. Clearly she was depressed and this was because she knew she had multiple sclerosis and was so disturbed and unable to come to terms with it that she tried to hide it from herself and even from me, her doctor. Once the story unravelled, though I could not cure her, I could at least help her to come to terms with her disease, her sexuality and her husband.

I discussed the case with Tim Betts and Paul Morby. I then wrote it up in detail and with a superb amateur actress we went into the studio and filmed "Neurosis or Neuropathy" which I used all over the world with generations of students for fifteen years. With it we were able to explore many aspects of what was later to become known as 'behavioural medicine' and to explore communication blocks between doctor and patient. This was the first of many major video-taped productions I made with Paul which were to go to medical schools world-wide and win us international prizes. There is no doubt that the sometimes strained relationship with Paul Morby paid off. I can remember violent exchanges between us which included what the BBC calls 'strong language'. I was probably as much at fault as Paul and his histrionic outbursts were undoubtedly part of his genius as a director.

Most of the first two years of the student's course consisted of preclinical studies of anatomy, physiology and biochemistry. This is an intensely academic phase of medicine at distance from the real live human beings that most longed to get to grips with. Therein, of course, lay our success in teaching in the early years. Once the major hurdle of satisfying preclinical examiners was cleared there was an intensive introduction to clinical medicine course. For some reason this course was unpopular with clinicians. Michael and I made it our business to volunteer for jobs others did not like and soon the Clinical Introductory Course (CIC) became wholly reorganised and largely taught by us. We could never understand reluctance to run this course for it came at a time when students were at their keenest and hungry for the hands-on medicine their vocation demanded. That course was a major part of our contribution to teaching. It was an enormous amount of hard work designing its content and structure and organising the best teachers from other disciplines of medicine but linking them to the patient. And who was the best person to portray the individual patient but his personal doctor?

In the CIC we used a lot of Paul Morby's video material. Drawing on Owen Wade's involvement of students in his roadshows I used the tapes to trigger student reaction. Stopping the tape at a critical juncture I would pick on a student at random and ask him or her to comment. Because I made it a rule to treat even the most inept contribution with humour and respect I won their confidence and some made extremely penetrating observations. With a whole year of 160 or more students this often meant literally running round the lecture theatre in order that no seat was exempt from my questioning finger; everyone had to respond. Though some students said they dreaded this inquisition the class was always full. Two comments from academics give some measure of these teaching sessions; 'Robin is the only person who can teach a whole year as if it were a small group ' and 'everyone knows when you are teaching the laughter is audible all over the medical school'. (The latter came from a senior Professor to whom I had relayed the common student comment that he was intensely boring. I parried his remark by saying that laughter was surely preferable to the snores of tedium).

In 1979 Michael and I tried to encapsulate what we were teaching in a little textbook called *An Introduction to General Practice* published by Balliere Tindall. Inevitably the book was Spoonerised as 'Dreary and Dull' by the students but it was noticeable that the several library copies were so well thumbed they fell to pieces.

Another task that fell to us was advising on student electives. I took particular pleasure in this since Lawrence Mackie, in a generous gesture of support to what we were trying to do at Birmingham, endowed a bursary to provide funds to help a student with travel on an elective project. All students, except the few who needed remedial teaching because of disagreements with examiners*, had an opportunity in the final year to spend six weeks on a self chosen elective course. They could do anything provided it was approved by a member of academic staff. Some studied music, drama or art but many elected to travel and look at some aspect of medicine abroad. One enterprising lad even managed to gain permission for a study of Midlands breweries. I subsequently read his report and was most impressed by his scientific approach to what was obviously a serious hobby! Because of my many contacts in Europe, America and later in Australasia I helped students find experience abroad. They had to write up their electives but in addition I always asked students whom I helped to report back to me verbally. One stunning girl I sent to a GP in South Australia came back with a vivid experience.

"One Saturday," she told me, "My doctor told me he was going to show me the Outback. We drove for miles on dirt roads through the most unbelievably empty wilderness. Suddenly, rounding a bend, we came on a car lying on its side. There was body lying in the road. My doctor didn't speak. He got out of the car and turned the body over with his foot. Then he bent down and shone a light in the man's eyes. He came back to the car and, opening the boot, took out a tool kit. Then with an ordinary brace and bit he knelt on the man's head to steady it and drilled a hole in his skull. Then he spoke for the first time: 'C'mon Sheila, help me get him in the car'. By the time we got him to hospital he was

*Birmingham had a system of continuous assessment but even so a few had such difficulties.

186

speaking; he got meningitis of course from the dirty burr hole, but his sub-dural haematoma was decompressed and he lived!" the student sat back eyes sparkling and added "By God! if that's general practice I want to do it."

Finally we gave students their major experience of general practice by attaching groups of them to practices for a fortnight. During this time each student lived with the GP's family in order to get a flavour of his lifestyle, workload and position in the community. These attachments began with a briefing session often at some postgraduate centre anywhere in the region and they finished with a day-long debriefing session at the medical school when we reviewed the experience of the group. Sometimes Michael and I shared a session, more often, especially when a lot of travelling was involved one of us would do it alone This teaching was arduous but immensely worthwhile. The attachment provided all students with first hand experience of practice, for some this helped them choose their careers but even more importantly it provided the only real insight into the problems of the general practitioner for future specialists.

In the summer of 1977 my father, whose health had been bad for some time, died of leukaemia. My mother had also died just after my family returned from America and Pater had remarried and had moved to Letchworth where we visited him on several occasions. The second marriage was strange and my new stepmother found such difficulty relating to us that she was never present at our visits. This strained my relationship with Pater though he remained the same patient unambitious man that he had always been with an expressed interest in my career and development of his three granddaughters. In his last illness I travelled as often as I could to his bedside at Addenbrookes Hospital in Cambridge. When I last saw him he was heavily sedated and I doubt he knew me. A few days later a dawn telephone call announced his death. His widow did not attend the funeral and I scattered his ashes on Harpenden Common near where he and I had camped to try out the new tent he bought in 1945.

All through those years with Gillian and our daughters and dogs we took time off in summer to visit Scotland in Arran, Mull, Skye and Torridon. These holidays were spent on daily alternation between the mountains and fishing in our inflatable dinghy. All the girls became active hill walkers and the Labradors adored it. Those were supremely happy days. The children, metamorphosing into young women, had surprisingly few teenage problems. Fiona, the eldest, was conscientious almost to a fault and her success at A level in 1987 was not surprising. In her first long vacation from studying ecology at Edinburgh University she went off to East Africa working on a research project involving antelope.

Janet was different and once said apropos her sister's A level results 'If you think I'm going to work like that you're mistaken!' But her friends at school were a high-flying lot and she did not want to let them down; at the last gasp she started work, got a commendable A level and started at Sheffield University to read geography.

I tried my best to dissuade all three from medicine, feeling that though women were good for medicine, medicine was not always good to women. With the youngest daughter Emma, I failed. Like Fiona she did well at school and later entered medical school at Cardiff.

Earlier in that summer of Pater's death, at a party in a friend's house a young solicitor I occasionally fished with arrived late. Glancing round the noisy room he caught my eye and mouthed 'I want to talk to you.' He fought his way to me and shouted "Come to the Himalaya with us." I shrugged and in turn got through the masses to Gillian and asked 'Can I go to India?' 'Of course,' she replied; so I told the solicitor I'd go.

So the single, most exciting episode of my life, which at times seemed it might be the last, started almost by chance. A group of climbers, having trekked to Annapurna base camp, decided they wanted to visit the Nanda Devi sanctuary in the Garwhal Himalaya in northern India. They had been warned that this was an exacting trek and decided that they needed to include a doctor in their party. John Penn, my solicitor fishing acquaintance, who knew of my interest in mountaineering, was given the task of sounding me out.

There is a major difference between professional mountaineers and trekkers. Experienced climbers set aside enough time to acclimatise to altitude. Trekkers condense as much as possible into the time available for their annual holidays. I was appointed as medical officer after plans to trek in the Himalaya had been finalised. The group consisted of ten men of varying age and mountaineering experience who were going into the Nanda Devi sanctuary, one of the holiest places of Hinduism. This involved crossing a ridge at nearly 14,000' on the third day of climbing on a route that Chris Bonnington had described 'as the worst walk in' that he knew. Reaching that elevation before acclimatization inevitably meant altitude sickness.

From Naini Tal in Uttar Pradesh we travelled to the holy town of Josimath, where everybody was tense and short of breath on exertion after three days' bus journey across the Gangetic plain from Delhi. Josimath was only at 7,000'; how would we be at nearly 16,000'? The bus took us a little further to the road end at the village of Lata. The guide told us that 'the short walk', to first camp was quick and easy. The heavy toll of 4½ hours of lung-bursting exertion took it out of all of us. Several climbers attended evening surgery with trivial problems indicating inner concern that this trek was much more strenuous than they had anticipated.

Next day was beautiful but even more exacting; the botany was superb; the turf, grazed short, by transhumed herds of goats, was full of gentians and redolent of herbs. Reaching camp at 12,100' I felt acute air hunger but before evening surgery I walked in the incredible beauty of these highest mountains reddening in the sunset. I began to feel an intense, emotion-charged exhilaration, which brought me near to tears. Indeed everyone was showing emotional lability and squabbles were already apparent among the team because of inadequate tents.

The third climb was to the testing camp at 14,000'. In brilliant sunshine we struggled slowly with magnificent views of the double peak of Dunagiri, 23,190', towering above us. The guide and I were last when at about 13,500' we overtook a labouring climber.

As I spoke to him I saw him go blue and realised his life was in danger. Descending a precipitous rock face to a campsite 1500 feet below the casualty improved with every foot we dropped. The porters ran ahead to erect tents. Crawling into the first of these I examined my patient. He was now a normal colour, his lungs were dry and he had no papilloedema*. I wondered if I had imagined the altitude sickness so obvious 1500' above.

Next day's breakfast, porridge with honey and malt whisky, was superb. Everyone felt better and we continued but all were at risk of mountain sickness. We regained the ridge with a view over the whole Nanda Devi sanctuary. Hanuman, named after the monkey god, at 20,000' led to a long ridge extending to hide the northern slopes of Nanda Devi. Further North high peaks shielded the Chinese border. Eastwards Trisul towered 8000' above what was to be our top camp at 15,500'. I asked the guide why it was called a sanctuary? He was praying but a moment later he made namaste and answered: 'Because God made it a sanctuary, sahib'. This simple sentence combined with mountain ecstasy made me weep.

We descended to camp beside a stream, washing for the first time in days. Now, though we were going higher, we had acclimatized and I was less anxious about altitude sickness. The Rishi Ganga, a magical, talismanic name, is one of the highest tributaries of the sacred Ganges... now we were to walk through its valley, the legendary sanctuary of Nanda Devi. We started through forest to emerge into the sun high above the river. Massed lilac and white gentians made a rock garden above which Lammergeier and Alpine Choughs soared on thermals. Colourful White-capped Redstarts flitted along the river far below. Once there was the sudden polychrome flash of a rare Impeyan Pheasant, Nepal's national bird. We climbed through a birch forest glimpsing Nanda Devi and the distant, twenty-two thousand foot tiger tooth of Changabang. Here the scenery was different. A huge glacier cascaded over a cliff crumbling emerald ice cubes as big as houses.

---

*Retinal swelling, an early physical sign of brain swelling due to altered water metabolism associated with cerebral altitude sickness.

190

Next day a friendly starving collie, left behind by another climbing party, attached herself to the group for a steep climb. Missing my own dogs I befriended her and gave her the food I felt too ill to eat.

During that last climb to top camp at 15,500' fatigue confounded co-ordination. Once, reflecting that help for severe injury was three days away, I fell twenty feet with boulders crashing round me. I landed with pain but nothing that cursing did not cure. Rubbing at bruises I watched a stoat chasing hyrax among the rocks and high above there was a herd of bharal, the blue Himalayan sheep. I was intensely glad to be alive and felt I could lie there forever but struggled to rise and catch up the others. At top camp I had never been so close to total exhaustion. Watching my companions on the last steps before rest I saw them staggering; faces set, eyes glazed with the effort of reaching base.

Even after nitrazepam and whisky I had a terrible night; with all spare clothing on in a down sleeping bag it was still extremely cold. I developed Cheyne-Stokes respiration*. The minute long periods of apnoea were calm; nothing mattered–not even the next breath. Then there was a wave of nausea and panic before a crescendo of gasps. Perhaps this was how it felt to die. I dreamt of the dog I had not seen for days. In my dream I felt her leaning on me from outside the tent drawing warmth from my body.

Waking to the beauty of the sanctuary and a cry of "Chai, Sahib" we found a porter, his feet bare in the new crisp snow, bearing a huge kettle full of tea. How feeble and inferior these porters made us feel. We had lost so much fluid through respiration the tent's interior was festooned with icicles and I drank my tea gratefully, watching dawn bathe the summits pink. Suddenly the hot sun was upon us, temperatures rose 60-70° in minutes and everyone was happy again.

When I stepped outside the tent there, clearly stamped in the new snow were the large pugmarks of a snow leopard. These creatures are extremely beautiful but shy and elusive. It must have been he who leant on me in the night, seeking my heat through the canvas. The knowledge of having slept with one of the world's most rarely seen mammals, combined with the incredible beauty of the high

---

*A pattern of breathing text-books describe as a prelude to death.

Himalaya heightened the knowledge that I had tested myself as never before. Suddenly I felt my father would have been more proud of me for this than for anything else I had done, or might ever do. Remembering him made me weep again.

Chapter 9 A Globe-trotting Academic

When Owen Wade became Dean of the Medical School our GP unit was still part of the department of Medicine but had advanced to superior accommodation on the main corridor of the school and Michael and I had our fingers in many pies. This had come about by our first making ourselves universally useful so that others came to see the newly named General Practice Teaching & Research Unit (GPTRU) as extra manpower for their own departments. With extra commitments the unit expanded with GP lecturers David Morgan, Andrew Carson, Richard Hobbs, and Kate Thomas joining us from local practices. Sheila Greenfield a sociologist and Barbara Stilwell, nurse-practitioner brought new skills to the team and for a short time Dr Phil Hammond kept the students on their toes before he went off to the BBC as a comedian.

Owen Wade was a great support and a marvellous dean. He had a happy knack of remembering names of the hundreds of students and staff. Once Owen and I were using adjacent urinals in the gents while a cleaner was on his knees scrubbing the floor. Buttoning up, (a manoeuvre he sometimes performed rather inadequately) Owen tapped the cleaner on the back and said: "Well done George, this is the cleanest bloody bog in Birmingham." That must have made George's day!

I managed to persuade Owen to put one of his road shows on television because I felt his unique way of teaching should be recorded. We set up the usual panel of students in the television studio but without the whole year being present. A physician and I were the 'experts'. Owen performed magnificently, but I think was dissatisfied by what he saw. At the end of the play-back he put an arm round my shoulder and commented: "You know Robin, I've got a face just like a chicken's arse!" I felt it improper to contradict my senior but when I related this at home three teenage daughters went off into peals of laughter and forever after referred to Owen as 'Old C.A.!'

Though the support from colleagues was enormous the real strength of the GPTRU was Mrs. Lyn Shields our secretary and general organiser whom both Michael and I referred to as "*The* Department Of General Practice" for neither of us could have functioned without her. Lyn came to us as successor to Sue Magwin who had married and gone off to raise a family. By now it was necessary for us to have our own secretary and this began our slow separation from the Department of Medicine and the beginning of a shift to being a department in our own right. Lyn came to us from running a nightclub after which the comedy duo of Drury and Hull came as second nature. Lyn was a brilliant organiser and soon became the envy of other departments. She planned the logistics of all our courses, managing students in practices all over the Midland Region and was always making helpful suggestions. The students regarded her as an agony aunt and often dropped in to see her to talk about their troubles. To Michael and me she was an endless source of strength dispensed with a million coffees she brewed for us.

Michael had always championed non-medical staff and one of his most successful books was *The Medical Secretary's Handbook*. With Lyn he set up a course for practice ancillary staff. At first the course was known as 'Miss Piggy' for she like, the practice staff, was always in the middle; the receptionist was sandwiched uncomfortably between the patients and the doctor. This course was explosive in its success and with help from the new Association of Medical Secretaries & Practice Administrators grew to become first Region-wide as the Practice Receptionists Programme; eventually it became so big 'it could not,' in Michael's words 'be run by amateurs.'

Some time before Michael had met a young publisher who was keen to set up his own publishing house dealing with medical titles. We had many meetings with Andrew Bax and it was he who took over the organisation of the Practice Receptionists Programme and made such a success with it that it helped to establish his firm, Radcliffe Medical Press, which subsequently published several books from the GPTRU and many more from general practice as a national discipline.

Meanwhile Michael's comet was rising, with a tail of brilliance. In 1978 he received an OBE. By 1981 the GPTRU had become a department in its own right and Michael was given a personal chair. In 1984 he became President of the Royal College of General Practitioners and he was knighted in 1989.

When Michael became a Knight Bachelor I was on holiday in Skye and on an early morning walk I pondered the awful problem of what I was to give my friend to mark his knighthood. By then I was a fairly well established medical writer and the idea of a biography came to me. When I got home I asked Michael about it. "Nobody will read that," was his comment but I could see he liked the idea. I approached Andrew Bax whose response was immediate "I would be honoured to publish that;" and so, in 1994, it was issued*.

During the eighties I was growing increasingly restless; The world seemed so much bigger than Wellesbourne. I was happy enough in the practice but development at Birmingham was slow and seeing that I could never be anything but second fiddle to Michael I began to look at other possible openings. For some time I had served on the board of the MSD foundation, an organisation set up to improve the teaching of General Practice at all levels. This was chaired by Professor Pat Byrne with several other GP luminaries on its board and had led to a number of interesting teaching adventures including a television production based on City and Country Practice revealed. We also produced an excellent documentary on days with French, Dutch and German doctors based on Update's "*A day with the doctor*", which explored the effects of differing health care systems on the routine work of doctors in different countries.

I made a number of tentative enquiries about chairs in other departments, even editorship of Journals and, after Pat Byrne's death, made a serious bid for directorship of the MSD Foundation. I was runner up to the much more able Professor Marshall Marinker from Leicester. Once I was interviewed for a chair in New Zealand. I had an uncomfortable meeting with two Scottish Professors whom I knew well and fell out with them. After complimenting me on my long list of publications I was criticised because only a small proportion were in refereed journals. This was always a sore point and I argued that if we were to advance

---

*Just A GP, a biography of Professor Sir Michael Drury.

195

standards of General Practice we should not labour to make small improvement in the high fliers but should try to advance the worst rump of our colleagues where comparatively little input could achieve great effect. I argued that the lesser but widely read journals, such as Abraham Marcus's Update, though lacking the academic respectability of the refereed journals, actually had a greater effect than the often rather unreadable College Journal. I still think that is so and on publication of my hundredth Country Practice Revealed I received a crate of champagne from Update along with the following letter: -

Dear Robin,

I have never had the pleasure of congratulating an author on his one hundredth contribution. In your case the opportunity to do so is particularly welcome because as well as being one of our most durable authors you are also one of our most distinguished in style, content and in effect.

I hope you will accept this token of our thanks and appreciation. It is sent on our own behalf and on behalf of all the readers who have, I know, enjoyed your pieces and who have acquired from reading them some deeper sense of their vocation. We look forward to your continuing with Update for many years; With very best wishes from us all.

Bram Marcus

Writing certainly kept me busy: 'Practice Revealed' meant a steady thousand words a month with between a dozen and twenty other articles and papers a year. From 1975 to 1984 I was a member of the board of examiners at the RCGP. This meant a lot of work with two examinations a year which involved marking exam papers and taking part in viva voce examinations. Actually all examiners enjoyed the 'chore' of the vivas when we would each spend two or three days at College headquarters in Princes Gate, London or in Edinburgh. Most of us regarded these days as the best possible refresher course and it was a joy to meet up with friends and colleagues from all over Britain especially under the enlightened and good-humoured chairmanship of the Chief Examiner Professor Johnny Walker from Newcastle.

Often there would be foreign observers, especially from the Antipodes at the exam. One also met them as visitors to the university or as travelling lecturers. I had long had an ambition to visit Australia but was doubtful that I would be able to afford such travel. However, in case such an opportunity were to arise, I used to accost every visitor from downunder and say "I'm Robin Hull, I live in Stratford on Avon, come for the weekend." It never failed and Gillian always rose to the occasion with good meals. Antipodean academics responded well to good grub and free grog.

In 1983, ten years after we had six months away from the practice at the University of North Carolina, I put in an application for a second sabbatical. The rules really only allow one such long leave for a doctor but because I had been officially employed by North Carolina the first trip did not seem to count. I worked on this chink in regulations and soon had six months leave on full pay from both Birmingham Medical School and my official employers in the NHS. This effectively meant the practice was reimbursed for my locum. and I set off on a self organised tour of Australia, New Zealand and the United States to study methods of teaching and assessment of primary care. I was expected to produce a comprehensive report for both the College and for Birmingham University.

Now all those weekends of guests bore fruit: I had invitations to every medical school throughout Australasia where Paul Morby's productions made a welcome addition to teaching programmes. Negotiations with a number of medical journals fixed contracts for articles written during my travels, many organisations came up with paid lectures and of course hospitality was showered upon us from those generous hosts down under who had dined at my table.

Before I went I knew I would hate Australia and love New Zealand. This preconception was based on a number of uncouth Australian registrars I had met in my hospital days. In any case was not the whole of 'Oz' a vast cultural desert?

Emma was deeply involved that year in A Level so Gillian delayed coming with me until the exams were over. I arrived horrendously jet-lagged in Perth, Western Australia to be dragged straight to a dinner party of senior University folk. The talk was all philosophy and the state of British poetry, and would I like to go to the opera next week? Clearly flying had disturbed my mind, the sands of the cultural desert seemed obscured. Later I found myself in an art gallery and was astonished at my first introduction to painters such as Hans Heysen, Tom Roberts, Frederick McCubbin and Albert Namatjira. Surely these were not co-national with all those beer-swilling, womanising registrars who called me 'a bloody pom'!

I decided it would be unfair to tell the kind host who took us to Don Giovanni that I had recently heard it at Glyndebourne. In fact I enjoyed the performance in Perth's delightful 'Her Majesty's Theatre' even more than at Glyndebourne. Western Australia with a population of a mere 1.7 million could certainly sing more than Waltzing Matilda!

I was completely captivated. The University of Western Australia was as idyllic, but for different reasons, as Chapel Hill. It was set on the great curved bay of the Swan River estuary and its campus was resplendent with unfamiliar trees filled with exotic birds with strangely strident voices. Max Kamien, professor and head of the department of General Practice had worked at Warwick Hospital and not only knew of me but was a regular reader of my column in Update; he had even detected my anonymity and, like so many others, he had week-ended at my home in Hampton Lucy. He had found free university accommodation for my three weeks stay in Perth. Gillian joined me a fortnight later to find an Australian convert completely smitten with this new country, its culture and, above all, its natural history. Like me she was carried off to dinner as soon as she arrived. This time it was with the Kamiens and she had to pinch herself when she found herself talking of mutual friends near Hampton Lucy.

Max Kamien had established a thriving department and I was soon involved in meetings with his staff such as Senior Lecturers Peter Underwood and Douglas McAdam; the latter I had known when he worked at Liverpool Medical School. Max had worked in New South Wales where he had done much for the underprivileged, and, in Australia, that means the Aboriginals. They suffered the fate of ethnic underclasses everywhere in the world. Marginalised by the successful white majority they were condemned to poverty, alcoholism and the carbohydrate diseases consequent on poverty: diabetes, obesity and hypertension. Shunned and ignored by the majority the health of the Aborigines was a blot on Australia's health care*.

Gillian also adored Australia and we spent an idyllic week together exploring the environs of Perth in a battered rented car. We were lionised by friends and loved the wildness of the outback. In the centre of Perth, only a few minutes walk from the University lay King's Park a virtually untouched area of wild bush. It was a paradise for birds and plants. We kept thinking how Banks must have felt when, as the world's leading botanist, he first set foot on this magnificent continent and did not recognise a single plant.

Attached to Max's Department was part of the Australian Family Medicine Postgraduate Department which was a National scheme similar to Vocational Training for General Practice in Britain run from headquarters in Melbourne. Its director in Western Australia was Dr Richard Nowotny. Richard invited Gillian and me to travel with him to visit training practices in the Southwest corner of the State particularly to a local beauty spot called Margaret River. We jumped at the opportunity of seeing so much rural Australia as well as learning about vocational training. Poor Richard, he was not used to ornithological enthusiasm as I kept demanding a stop to check new birds. At one point he became quite abusive and I had to suppress my excitement†. The trip was fantastic and one practice we visited was that of Dr. Kevin Cullen at Busselton. Dr. Cullen

---

*Slowly as a result of people like Max Kamien in Australia and Ann Macaulay in Canada this is improving worldwide.

†*vide infra*

199

and his wife Di were leading viticulturalists and had a superb vineyard at Willyabrup in the Margaret River region. We visited the winery and dined with the Cullens. Di was to become one of the great among West Australian wine producers. The friendship made then has been remembered in Chardonnay ever since.

Another adventure I had was a day flying with the Royal Australian Flying Doctor Service. This allowed me to see much of the south coast of Western Australia near Albany and to learn about this incredible service which provided emergency care for the great wilderness of Western Australia. The pilot told me a story about one of his cases. Early one morning a voice crackled in from the outback announcing that 'Sheila was fair crook'. Taking a history by radio the doctor thought it was nothing serious but to make sure he promised to look by later in the day. In the meantime, he told the farmer, to look in his medicine box and give 'Sheila' one tablet of 'number twelve'. Hours later he touched down at a remote dirt airstrip and met the owner of the voice. He was full of praise for those No.12 tablets which had settled the patient completely. Then he grinned rather sheepishly and said 'Trouble was we didn't have any No. 12; so I just gave her two No.6!' Such is faith!

We had been advised to travel by train in Australia; flying is a much quicker way of getting around the continent's unbelievably vast area but fails to convey the wonder at its sheer size and emptiness. We boarded The Indian Pacific in Perth at quarter past nine in the evening to be shown our day cabin complete with shower and loo. A steward showed us round and suggested we made our way to the bar for a drink before dinner. On our return, he assured us, our bedroom would be ready for us. Dinner was seafood such as only Australia can offer. A good chardonnay helped conversation with a retired couple sharing our table. It seemed most of our fellow passengers were retired and it appeared that crossing the continent by train was an experience many looked forward to on retirement. After dinner somebody started playing the piano in the bar and we waltzed with Matilda across the Nullabor Desert.

We woke at six after a comfortable night to find the train stationary at Kalgoorlie for reprovisioning. Everyone disembarked for a coach tour of the gold rush town. In its heyday Kalgoorlie had been a bustling town whose main street was wide enough to turn a camel train. We saw the mine workings and were taken on a tour of the brothels; there was not much else to see except the red dust of central West Australia.

The desert impressed one with the hardiness of the explorers of this huge continent. More than anything one began to have respect for the Aboriginal whose land this was and who had adapted to its incredible harshness. Impressed by Max Kamien's seminal book* about them I became fascinated by these human beings whose way of life, of thought, behaviour and even physiology was so different from my own. All over the continent I managed to get time with these real Australians, to try to understand their dreamtime and complex art forms. The history of their persecution by the white man, especially in Tasmania, makes shameful reading.

From Kalgoorlie we travelled on through 360 degrees of damn all in the red heart of the Nullabor Desert to reach Adelaide to visit and teach at Flinders University Medical School with Dr Dean Southgate who had also worked with me at Wellesbourne. Then on to Melbourne to visit Professor Ross Webster at Melbourne University and Professors Neil Carson and John Murtagh at Monash. We had a weekend at Lorne on the Great Australian Bight watching a superb display of surfing before an intensive natural history course, wandering in eucalyptus forests hunting for exquisite blue wrens and lyrebirds.

A brief stay in Tasmania allowed a little teaching at the smallest medical school I have ever been to at Hobart and a brief glimpse of the early penal settlement. Tasmania has to be my favourite state in this magnificent continent. It is as wild as the rest of Australia but, like Scotland, it is wet and lush with splendid mountains and semi-tropical jungle alive with magnificent birds and marsupials. It also teems with highly venomous snakes and, some say, the Thylacine, or Tasmanian Tiger, still prowls the dense jungle of

---

The Dark People of Bourke 1978] which Max had inscribed for me just after I arrived in WA 'In appreciation for the warmth of your entry and the whimsy of your thoughts.'

its west coast. I learnt new respect for my phlegmatic wife who calmly showed me a leech fattening itself between her fingers. Most people become hysterical at even the thought of leeches but she regarded it with fascination!

Back at Melbourne we hurried on to Sydney and relatives. Gillian flew home from here while I had shorter visits to the capital's two medical Schools. Then it was north again for a longer spell at Brisbane where I stayed with Professor Geoff Ryan and his delightful English wife, Doris. While teaching at Brisbane I travelled by 'The Sunlander' as far as Cairns from where I hired a car with a Dr Gregory, a fellow academic from Newcastle whom I met on the train. Echoing the meeting between Stanley and Livingstone he greeted me with "Oh Hallo Robin; they told me you were in Australia I thought I'd run into you!" We drove to the base of Cape York to an aboriginal centre at Laura. I particularly wanted to visit this sacred place of the dreamtime to study the magnificent 30,000 year old petrography paintings: so much for the cultural desert; art had been alive and well here for millennia! I am not sure how much Gregory enjoyed exploring the bush to find the paintings, he was so terrified of snakes that he wrapped layers of newspaper round his shins.

After three months in Australia I was besotted by this new continent and had learnt enough of its history and natural history to realise the size of my ignorance; I was hungry for more. By contrast New Zealand, which in anticipation had seemed so much more attractive was disappointing. I was welcomed at all the medical schools, particularly by Professor Rae West at Auckland, and enjoyed teaching but there is a dullness about New Zealand that reminds one of wartime Britain which contrasts sharply with the zinging enthusiasm of Australia. Perhaps my biggest disappointment was in the ecological despoilation of the country. Successive invasions of Polynesians and white men had exterminated the Moas and introduced sheep and rats that destroyed much of the native bush and wildlife. Writing to Gillian in October I described walking in bluebell woods, under the new green of beech trees listening to blackbirds and chaffinches and asked 'Have I crossed the World for this?' However the scenery was stunning and the fishing out of this world. With a borrowed rod I caught bigger trout in the rivers than I had ever caught before... but it was still not as exciting as Oz!

From New Zealand I returned to Warwickshire for a few days' recovery and then flew back to North Carolina to see how the programme I had helped to start ten years before had progressed. I started in Georgia visiting several medical schools, from whom I had had visiting students who welcomed me back and organised paid lectures for me. At Emory Medical School, considered very much 'Ivy League', they really did not accept family medicine as respectable. I was invited by the student body at the instigation of Craig White, the son of an avocado rancher in California, who had visited me in Hampton Lucy in May 1981. The students were delightful and thirsty for news of what is so disparagingly dubbed 'socialised medicine' in the States. I was introduced by an internationally known epidemiologist with the shortest introduction I have ever had; He said 'Gee I only know of one other guy from Stratford on Avon', then he sat down!

Gillian and the girls, to whom we had promised Christmas in Chapel Hill, flew to Atlanta and we drove through Appalachia, visiting Will Hamilton and other friends near Asheville before joining Peter and Carolyn Curtis for Christmas Dinner. Peter had left Chapel Hill at the same time as I had, ten years before, on the completion of our respective tours of duty but, unable to settle in England, he had returned to UNC to carve out a very successful career as Director of Family Practice.

After Christmas Gillian took the family home while I toured the Carolinas giving presentations at Duke, Bowman Gray, Asheville and Charlotte. As ever, American Universities were always interested in a different approach to medicine and my enthusiastic support of both the National Health Service and British General Practice was so different from their own experience they always listened attentively.

Two days before I was due to return home a letter came from Gillian that was to change our lives. In her note she said 'this letter has just come I thought you should see it straight away rather than wait till your return.' The letter, from a man I had never heard of and from a University I had never heard of began 'Dear Dr. Hull, Will you come and be our professor.....'

That day I was due to dine with Rob Sullivan, the man who had so influenced my life ten years before when he had written across my naïve application for the post at Chapel Hill 'get this chap'. I showed him the letter which had come from the department of General Practice at the Free University of Amsterdam.

Rob considered the letter, asked what I knew about the Free University and at my shrug of ignorance he said "This smells of politics, of course it could be fun but my advice is protect your back!"

That was to prove very sound advice.

Chapter 10 Holland

Gillian and I had a lot to talk about when I returned from the States. The trip had been extremely successful and I brought home a host of new ideas for Birmingham and the College. On top of it all was this inexplicable approach from Amsterdam. It seemed utterly crazy, for how could anyone as inept at languages as me, hold a post in a Dutch University? However the letter could not just be ignored. We decided that, if nothing else, we would explore further. So, as I plunged back into work in Wellesbourne and Birmingham, I wrote to Professor Cor Spreeuwenberg about his invitation expressing guarded interest.

A few weeks later I met Spreeuwenberg and neuropathologist Professor Frans Stam, Dean of the Free University Medical School* at Birmingham Airport. They told me afterwards that my first words to them were "You're mad!" The whole project seemed hare-brained. The Dean spoke English very well and, though Cor's English was poor it seemed his intentions were clear. I showed them the department at Birmingham before driving them to Wellesbourne to see my clinical base, the practice. Then they came home with me where they were to spend the night. The Dean was easy-going and, like so many Dutch people relaxed when off duty. He was clearly set on enjoying himself on this free mini-holiday in Britain. He drank half a bottle of whisky before dinner and explained how the extraordinary invitation that the 'VU' had issued had come about. The Dutch Government, deciding that primary care, or the 'Erste Lijn', must be strengthened, had voted millions of guilders into a programme by which two medical schools, the 'VU' and the school at the University of Maastricht should advance the organisation of primary care in the Netherlands. My job, they told me, was to help spend those millions of guilders. Put that way the job did seem to have its attractions.

Over dinner they explained how they had come to approach me. The Emeritus Professor of Huisartsgeneeskunde, or General Practice, at the VU was Jan van Es, a wise old political fox who had made a name for himself in international medicine. He had

*Vrije Universiteit or 'VU'

205

approached two former Presidents of the RCGP, John Horder and Ekke Kuenssberg and asked for suggestions. Both came up with my name and on that basis they invited me.

Gillian excelled herself and dinner was superb; the dean ate and drank heartily; he had three desserts and when tempted to a fourth declared "Why not? I am a diabetic!"

On a miserably cold day the following March, when the wind blasted straight across the north European plain from the Urals Gillian and I arrived in Amsterdam. We faced the question of whether we could relocate. By now Emma, the last of the daughters, was accepted at Cardiff Medical School but more difficult were the three Labrador bitches; Guilder, Florin and Pfennig. Gillian shrugged the canine problem off saying "They will be no problem we'll find a way"

In freezing cold we looked at the medical school and worried at house prices in the city with increasing gloom. The reception committee seemed to sense our despondency and became artificially enthusiastic. Eventually I asked for half an hour by ourselves so that we could talk alone. Cor Spreeuwenberg looked at his watch. "You can have twenty minutes," he said.

We walked in the wind, freezing to the marrow, and reached a decision. At the end of the twenty minutes I announced that we had decided to decline the offer. Cor spoke again: "The reason you could only have twenty minutes is that now we have to go to the celebratory dinner to mark your appointment." Flabbergasted we were escorted to one of the best dinners we have ever had.

The dinner of five courses, each with different wines and with palate clearing sorbets between, was fantastic... But, since we were refusing the appointment, extremely embarrassing. I was sharply reminded of Rob Sullivan's prediction of political overtones for my hosts were distracted by an empty place at the table. A senior university official, after accepting the invitation to this fabulous dinner, had failed to turn up. Rapid, concerned Dutch discussion speculated on the significance of this absence. I had not the slightest idea what was going on and paid reverent attention to my plate of mixed smoked fish at which Holland excels. The copious wine helped to suppress my embarrassment which soon turned to maudlin amusement; after all it was not our fault that someone was spending a small fortune on fêting the Hulls. After dinner Cor Spreeuwenberg suggested we repair to his house where we were staying. There he poured me a very large brandy. Swilling the amber liquor in the glass I stared at it reflectively. "Of course," I said, "I am only part time at Birmingham; suppose I remained there part-time and spent the rest of my time here?"

Cor was immediately positive "That's how we'll do it!" he exclaimed and for the second time in my life an important and far reaching decision was taken *in vino veritas**.

Michael Drury was in New Zealand. With difficulty I ran him to earth and explained the situation over the phone. He was not happy and made his objection plain. This was unusual for he, like Lawrence Mackie, was usually so supportive of my plans. However over the next few months we worked out a *modus operandi*. My post at Birmingham as Senior Lecturer was unchanged; I resigned from the Wellesbourne practice and accepted half a professorial salary from the VU, plus accommodation and a return airfare from Birmingham to Amsterdam every month. In Holland I was subject to academic terms so that I had a long summer vacation. Most of this I worked at Birmingham but a considerable part I spent as a long term *locum tenens* in Hamish Nicol's practice in Stratford so that I was keeping my hand in with clinical work.

On New Year's Day 1985 Gillian and I went to Holland on the first of some 25,000 miles of commuting; just about the circumference of the planet. That first visit was in arctic weather when all the canals were frozen solid and people were skating everywhere. We had come by car to bring books and papers and the second hand bicycle I had bought in keeping with the Amsterdam transport. We arrived at the Akademisch Ziekenhaus, the teaching hospital. Everyone was still away on holiday and nobody was expecting

*As when I met Gillian.

us. Eventually officialdom was summoned and it was discovered that we were to be housed in an extremely basic flat attached to the hospital. We went to bed to keep warm while outside the temperature plummeted. Across the road lay the Amsterdamse Bos* with many large lakes linked by a network of canals. My memory of that flat is the sound of halyards banging in the wind against the masts of yachts frozen into a marina close by. The flat consisted of a tiny bedroom, bathroom, kitchenette and small sitting room. We did our best to make ourselves comfortable and explored. Nothing happened. At the weekend, fed up with inaction, we drove north to explore the villages around the former Zuyder Zee now renamed the Ijsselmeer. It was so intensely cold our noses ran and formed icicles in our nostrils. Nobody had warned us about the Calvinistic Sabbath in Holland and the place was deserted but slowly things came to life and from everywhere people appeared with skates. At the attractive little town of Hoorn the Ijsselmeer was frozen to a depth of several feet. As the day progressed we were resuscitated by ertwesoep† and watched merchants putting up stalls with braziers way out on the ice selling soup and coffee to the skaters. Later in the Rijksmuseum we were to see a late sixteenth century painting by Avercamp; the scene was almost identical, even to the peculiarly long skates favoured by the Dutch.

Slowly life returned to normal but intense frost is a time of recreation in the Netherlands. Children seem born on skates and the great winter festival is the Elfsstedetocht, when madmen skate some 120 miles over frozen canals for as long as six hours. This race began as a sort of pub crawl in the sixteenth century and has grown into a national sport. Of course it was only in exceptional seasons such as January 1985 that the race could be run. People spent the whole year training for it, some sleeping in commercial freezers to adapt to extreme cold. Even so several skaters were admitted to hospital with cold damage; some had to have their eyes unfrozen.

---

*Amsterdam's very extensive park with much open water - a wonderful bird-watching venue.

†A typically Dutch, spoon-bending, pea soup with sausage sliced into it and delicious in cold weather

The cold was the chief memory of that first visit to my new University. The other memory was a lesson in history. My school history books had hardly touched on Holland as a great nation yet it had been so during its golden age of the sixteenth and seventeenth centuries when Dutch merchants controlled much of the commerce between Europe and the spice lands of Southeast Asia. Commerce has always been the life blood of Holland and the national character is forged from strict Calvinism and a shrewd bargaining ability. Their ability to corner the spice markets through the Dutch East India Company and their anti-catholic religion brought them into conflict with Spain whose Dutch wars were destructive and punitive. It was hard for me to realise that late sixteenth century history was to cast its shadow onto my life in late twentieth century Amsterdam.

William the Silent [1533-1584] is the great national hero of Holland. A member of the Dutch nobility, a Stadhouder, he inspired resistance against the Spaniards. In 1575 'after relieving the Spanish occupation of Leiden' William rewarded the citizens of that great city. He offered them freedom from taxation or, if they wished, he would found a university in the city. Leiden chose the latter and from that foundation grew the custom that Dutch Universities would have complete autonomy free of governmental interference. Many times during the next three years I was to have occasion to regret Silent William's legacy. However he got his come-uppance at the hands of a Spanish agent who assassinated him in Delft in 1584. The bullet hole is still carefully preserved in the wall of the stairway where he was shot

John Parr, or UJP as he was known to our children, on learning of my appointment at the VU, gave me an interesting insight into the Calvinist mentality. In 1940, he told me, when Hitler's heel was on the neck of Holland* the professorial faculty of the VU was split by dilemma. The question was: did the serpent actually speak to Eve when offering apples in Eden?

---

*Even forty years after the war its effects were still apparent and wartime memories lived on among colleagues who remembered starvation and their recourse to eating tulip bulbs. The Anna Frank House is a cherished but awe-inspiring relic of those years.

The University was called 'Free' to indicate its freedom from Catholicism. However it was as deeply Calvinistic and devout in its regulation as many a Hebridean 'Wee Free' kirk. Meetings of senior faculty were always intensely formal and started with prayer. I had to keep my laughter-loving, impious mouth firmly buttoned. But I did like the monthly professorial breakfast when all the senior faculty were bidden to a cup of coffee and a bun to discuss current medical affairs. At my first 'breakfast' I was formally introduced to the heads of all the other departments and it was then that I began to have the uncomfortable feeling that there was a big problem and that somehow that problem concerned me. That problem turned on large sums of money and if there is one thing Dutchmen do not like to talk about it is the mis-appropriation of cash.

It was all due to William the Silent. His establishment of the relationship between State and University was that the latter should have autonomy. In effect this meant that when the State awarded a University a great research grant for a particular purpose the University could receive the funds and then spend them on something else.

I could hardly believe this and almost the whole of my first year was spent fighting. I have files of carefully written notes of frequent long meetings with the Dean (by now Frans Stam had been succeeded by Professor Louw Feenstra, an Ear Nose and Throat Surgeon.) I have sheaves of copy letters to officialdom, to members of Faculty and I had almost daily meetings with Professors Spreeuwenberg and van Es. We argued for a year but were unable to break down the vested interest of the faculty who more or less told us that mere 'huisartsen' would waste the government money.

So there I was; a professor in a foreign land with a good salary, by now rather better accommodation and travel expenses but no job! In fact I was very busy because my real love of medical school life, the students, were all around me. The school was larger than Birmingham with 200 students in a year compared with 160. The course lasted six years of which the first three quarters was spent on preclinical subjects. In the early days, whenever I could, I would sit in on formal lectures given by other professors. I was horrified at what I heard. Teaching at the VU was more didactic than anything I had ever come across before. Students wrote down exactly what their professors told them (even using the same colours the lecturer employed, though this meant finding the appropriate crayon to make their notes an exact copy of what teacher said!) Some professors were sexist to the point of obscenity, much to the distress of many women students.

I began by trying to meet the heads of all the other departments offering my services. This was met by attitudes that varied from blank astonishment to puzzled but open-armed welcome. Strangely, the professor of oncology, Bob Pinedo, perhaps the furthest removed from General Practice, was the most supportive. I soon found myself making a presentation on the importance of general practice to this ultra-technical branch of medicine. With the professor of paediatrics, Guus de Jonge, I launched a family attachment course similar to that in Birmingham. I managed to inveigle my way into outpatients in the department of Medicine where I met Ab Donker, one of the professors of medicine. Ab worked with a quiet, scholarly, widely read and cosmopolitan physician called Frans Westerman who became my closest friend in the medical school. Frans saw my wish to teach and through him I started small group teaching among the students attached to medical outpatients. I really loved this; at first the students were terrified for they were startled that anyone should expect them to *think*, much less express their ideas. Slowly they came to realise that this strange bearded Briton believed that medicine was fun and not something that had to be wrapped up in Calvinistic morality and leaden seriousness. Not only that but he listened to what they said, gave praise where it was due and laughed with them, not at them.

On 18th October 1985 I gave my professorial inaugural lecture before the Rector Magnificus*, university professors, clinicians and students in the great Aula of the university's main building. This was an awesome occasion of great pomp and circumstance with all senior members in academic dress. Wearing the gown of a Fellow of the RCGP, borrowed from Michael Drury and Owen

*The Rector Magnificus at the VU is much the same as the University Vice Chancellor in Britain. When I complimented him on his splendid title he commented 'It is rather celestial, isn't it?'

Wade's mortar board I gave my carefully prepared address on Medical Ecology. In this I set out my philosophy of general practice stressing the importance of good, personalised primary care. Reading the printed version today I see my views have changed little for I spoke of Ryle, of Gilbert White and of Boerhaave, of ethologists Konrad Lorenz, Nico Tinbergen and Robert Hinde* and touched on the wide ranging philosophy of Lewis Thomas, the

Dressed for the innaugural lecture, Amsterdam, October 1985.

*Years later I was to have the pleasure of dining with Robert Hinde as guests of a neighbour in Strathtay.

renowned oncologist, bacteriologist and writer, President of the World famous Memorial Sloane-Kettering Cancer Center in New York [vide infra].

'Medical ecology' I explained' is about balance between man, his disease and his doctor and about communication. It is an immense subject and one which requires an educational background which is very broad: one which teaches not just about disease but teaches equally about anthropology, culture, behaviour. psychology, and cybernetics. It needs a thorough grounding in ethical principle and above all it needs wisdom. You may well argue that wisdom cannot be taught but I would suggest to you that in our slavish obsession with the explosion of medical fact we are 'unteaching' wisdom.' Later I expanded this expressing the fear 'that in stuffing them [the students] with knowledge we may displace wisdom: the ability to use knowledge and to translate it into the idiom of humanity and caring.' I quoted my own research showing that when a television examination designed to assess an individual's ability to communicate and appreciate the significance of patients' behaviour was shown to audiences of schoolgirls, medical students and trainee general practitioners marks diminished as medical training advanced.

I concluded 'Medicine is a bridge between nations and a lingua franca, we should use international exchange from students to greybeards like myself, so that we may debate and discuss our likenesses and differences. That way we will learn from each other, increase our medical ecology, lessen the risk of Armageddon and find the way to Alma Ata*.

In Holland I made great use of the televised teaching material made with Paul Morby in Birmingham and even made two video-tapes in the VU's own television department. One of these, 'Rats', was about a young man with AIDS which forcibly brought the topic into the arena of student debate. The Dutch audio-visual department was much more sophisticated in its equipment than that at Birmingham but seemed to lack Paul's imaginative innovation.

---

*A 1978 declaration made at Alma Ata had a vision of complete social, medical and physical well-being for everyone by the year 2000.

Soon there was regular tap on my office door when students would come for a chat. They discovered that one of my jobs in Birmingham was helping with student electives and asked if I could help by fixing up foreign travel for them. Through an organisation called Nemsic (Netherlands Medical Student International Cooperation) I helped to fix foreign contacts. Needless to say many of them came to stay in Jasmine Cottage while observing British general practice. Some went as far as Australia and America. So I began to have a little coterie of students who followed me around, and I even got to know some of their families.

Another task fell to me with the delightful Professor of Gynaecological Pathology, Hermann van Kessel. Hermann was the chairman of the committee running the Actualiteitscollege*, which involved student interaction and debated subjects of general interest. This closely resembled a series I was involved with in Birmingham called 'Co-ordinated studies' which attempted to set current medical affairs in the context of student experience. This was fun, far ranging and often took us deep into ethical questions about fertility, abortion and euthanasia. van Kessel and I held many meetings, usually over a beer when he would always begin by saying "Comes the question... what about our next Actualiteitscollege...?"

With the new job it had become necessary to cut back on some of my activities. The first to go was examining at the RCGP which I had done for ten years. I was sorry to leave the board of examiners because I always enjoyed my fellow examiners' company. True, marking papers was a chore but the twice yearly viva voce examinations were always stimulating especially so under the chairmanship of Professor Johnny Walker from Newcastle Medical School. Johnny's wit, immense capacity for work and perpetual good spirits always made the meetings fun. There was a continual striving after excellence and, particularly, consistency between examiners and to this end we held an annual workshop at a hotel in Ullswater in the Lake District. On my last of those workshops a casual meeting was to have lasting repercussions.

*Loosely translated as 'Actuality lectures'in which topical ethical questions were debated.

One of the examiners was Dr David Haslam of Ramsey near Huntingdon. I had known David since he had been a trainee with my neighbour and friend Dr Hamish Nicol in Stratford. Even then David was a bright star clearly destined for big things. Our ways parted but it was perhaps difficult for either of us to be completely separated for David was a much more prolific writer than I ever was. One could not open a journal or a medical newspaper without seeing the writing of David Haslam*. His particular forte was writing easily read articles about common complaints which became extremely popular with patients. At Ullswater it was natural for two old hacks to get together over a lunchtime beer. We talked about writing, one of the world's loneliest occupations, we spoke of finding topics and how we developed themes, and how we tried to act as change agents. The hour and the beer slipped away effortlessly and it was time to get back to work. As we parted we said simultaneously "that was good, there should be a forum where writers can meet and talk like that. "

We met again at teatime, reiterated our agreed need and said we would do something about it. The first requirement was support and funds. I wrote scores of letters which produced enthusiastic replies but no hard offers of help, least of all cash. Then, when I was on the point of giving up came a letter from Ian Munro, editor of the Lancet. He had found my letter at the bottom of his in-tray and wrote 'good idea–come and see me.'. That was the key that started opening doors: with the support of the Lancet funds started coming in so that within eight months of our meeting at Ullswater David and I could mount an open meeting in Birmingham with eighty or more attendees and speakers from the world of medical writing. So the General Practitioners Writers Association (GPWA) was born. It grew rapidly and soon we had an active membership and an energetic committee. We published a register of members with details of their writing from which many members were commissioned to write. Gillian Byrne, my former practice manager, took over as general secretary, David Haslam was editor first of a newsletter and later a journal called The GP Writer and, later still, *The Writer*.

---

*I still have a letter from David congratulating me on an article I wrote about an exquisite piece of early Worcester porcelain in which I likened it to life because each embodied the qualities of durability and extreme fragility.

We held regular committee meetings at Jasmine Cottage which were full of ideas, drive and energy. When the meeting was over we repaired to the pub across the road* while Gillian cleared the table and set up a bread and cheese lunch. I have never experienced a committee which was such fun and so effective. GPWA grew and pharmaceutical houses vied to offer prizes, awards and funding for administrative costs and meetings. Along with a committee including David Haslam, David Brooks and Gillian Byrne I worked hard, first as chairman and later as president of an association that looked as though it was going somewhere fast. We were joined by a retired professor of English, Wilfred Hopkins, who was a tower of strength taking on publication of the register and the journal and indeed several books written by members. Wilfred confessed he had an ambition to write a novel and eventually he became a best-selling novelist. There was no doubt the GPWA was an exciting vibrant organisation drawing widespread interest from a growing medico-literary world. Among many endeavours the GPWA published three books of medical humour: *Alimentary my dear doctor* 1988 (edited by Clifford Hawkins), *Myocardial Medley* 1990 (edited by Ian Gray) and *Nervous Laughter* 1991 (edited by Merton Sandler) all were published by Andrew Bax's Radcliffe Medical Press. Wilfred Hopkins set up Limited Edition Press with the aim of producing low cost short runs of books which members wished to publish but for which they could not find commercial publishers. Among such volumes were my *A Schoolboys War* - memories of Christ's Hospital 1994, *Evening Surgery: an anthology of Verse* by GPWA Members, Marie Campkin's hilarious *The G.P's Songbook and How To …. Guide* advice on writing about everything from Antiques to Women's Health published in 1997.

With such activity at home I was writing hard in Holland publishing some 130 articles and papers published in eighteen journals in five countries during my stay. I also wrote a book *Infective Disease* published by Chapman and Hall. Professor van Es was editor of a weekly Dutch medical magazine called '*Medisch Contact*'. Talking to him one day I said that my schizophrenic job between

*The Boar's Head, which the children called 'The whore's bed' it was the model for 'The Olive Branch' the pub so often mentioned in Country Practice Revealed.

two countries was so unusual he might like an article about it. "OK, he replied give me six!"

Surprised I started scribbling and soon had some draft material for him. He received it in total silence and after some days I tentatively asked what he thought of it. "It's OK," he said, "but *Medisch Contact* is a weekly, where are the other 46 essays."

Though used to producing monthly copy I was astonished at being asked for so much. We worked out a scheme whereby I wrote my pieces in long hand on ferries, planes and trains; Gillian bashed them out on her old typewriter and they went to translator Eva ten Velde who translated them so perfectly that friends said they could hear me speaking off the page. These tales appeared under the unoriginal title *Een Verhaal van Twee Steden* (A Tale of Two Cities). Writing for journals in England rarely produced response unless one made a flagrant error or upset someone. In Holland it was quite different; almost every week the postman brought comments, brickbats and praise from all over the country. One essay on the impact of different plumbing arrangements between the two cities and how such a basic difference in bowel function altered national characteristics brought an avalanche of amused, if scatological, comment.

It seemed that I never stopped talking: I chaired or spoke at fifteen conferences in Britain*, six in Holland two in Germany and one each in Portugal and Italy. I made innumerable contributions to postgraduate and undergraduate courses and, with Frans Westerman, set up a continuing education programme for established Dutch GPs.

Though the major research plans never took off because funds were appropriated by the VU several small programmes advanced to publication. Among these was a study comparing prescribing habits of family doctors in Britain and the Netherlands with Frans Westerman and pharmacist Roy Jonkers. Another study looked at the standards of referral letters from Dutch GPs to their specialist colleagues. One of my students commented on the poor quality of referral letters saying "some doctors did not care very much for

*Including an excellent conference for Trainee GPs from all over Britain organised by Dr Kate Thomas of the GPTRU.

their patients and perhaps not very much about themselves either". Frans Westerman and I published a highly controversial paper in the British Medical Journal. The paper was not well received in the Netherlands where one critic wrote of it "It was a pity this research had been written and a mistake that it was published" (and he was a friend of mine too!). However the facts were there and a subsequent study compared referrals in Birmingham and Amsterdam. The doctor who so harshly criticised the first study took part and he not only retracted his criticism but said our earlier comments on the poverty of many Dutch referral letters were far too lenient!*

My stay in Amsterdam coincided with the start of the World AIDS pandemic. I repeatedly tried to start research into HIV related disease but found in both Britain and Holland an attitude of denial of its existence. Then AIDS was of such extreme rarity for most GPs that it was disregarded in those early days when, had it happened, intervention with health education could have saved countless lives. There was in both countries a combination of ostrichism and ostracism towards the syndrome and its sufferers. This was particularly true in the Calvinism of the VU.

One place where AIDS and research did combine was at the Kruispost. One day a middle-aged doctor knocked on my door and asked for advice. He explained that he represented a Christian Mission in the city's red light district. The mission had set up a clinic to provide care for the underprivileged, the down and out, the illegal immigrant and the drug addict. My visitor explained that the clinic was manned by what amounted to medical missionaries but that officialdom refused to accept that their work had any value. He asked for help. I told him to set up a recording system so that the mission could document, measure, and publish researched statistics. That way I assured him people would start to notice. The visitor looked blank "We don't know how to!"

The upshot was that I said I would go and show them. That was to lead to the most extraordinary part of my whole bizarre Dutch experience. I was nervous when I visited the red light district. I

---

*Comparison of Referrals to Medical Out- patients in Amsterdam and Birmingham - British Medical Journal 1986.

parked my car outside a sex shop whose window display left little to the imagination. I met the Pastor, a charming grey-haired man called Rolf Boiten, and his wife Georgina* who showed me round the beautiful old canal house at No. 100 Oudezijds Vorburgwaal or 'OZ100'. He was delightful and explained that he had set up his mission where it would do most good. Inside there was peace and an almost monastic air of contemplation and faith. Outside was all that made Amsterdam infamous; masses of stateless illegal immigrants with no means of support, street crime, prostitution, drugs, syphilis and AIDS.

The pastor took me to the Kruispost but the clinic was shut as early afternoon is never a brisk time in the Red Light district. It was set in the basement and had the air of a very simple city lock-up surgery; the sort I was doing my best to get changed for the better. He suggested that I return late in the evening when the clinic would be busy. As I took my leave I patted my pockets for the car keys. They were missing; we turned up the chair I had been sitting in. They were still missing. "I bet you've locked them in your car!" said the Pastor, but don't worry one of my residents is the number one cracksmith of Amsterdam. He'll sort you out."

I wandered back to my little Peugeot 205. Sure enough the car was locked and the keys were visible in the ignition. I knew forced entry to this make of car was practically impossible. I went back to the mission and was introduced to a young man in his twenties. He grinned when he heard the problem and made me promise not to tell his probation officer what he was about to do. He walked round the car slowly examining it, then, with the side of his hand he struck a blow on part of the body work. All three doors immediately flew open.

After that I was committed and, whistling hard, I visited the Kruispost clinic many times late at night dodging the invitations from open doorways. In some ways this reminded me of the SHAC clinic in North Carolina in that the Kruispost was providing care for the lowest level of the social strata. Later in Birmingham when I told of my work in the red light district I used to add "after all one has to make the family fortune somehow."

---

*Pronounced in Dutch 'Cheorchina' where the 'ch' is like that in 'loch'. Dutch is hardly a euphonic language!

At the Kruispost I soon realised that here was Mother Theresa-like work going on among the bordellos of Amsterdam. I met Bianca aged 28, she was German, highly intelligent, polyglot and articulate. She was also a heroin prostitute. Her boyfriend, by whom she had a child, was HIV positive but her HIV status was unknown. She was a nice girl much loved in the mission where she came for refuge from the streets outside. Another patient was a male illegal immigrant resident in Amsterdam for four years and working in a club for homosexuals and receiving methadone from an official source. He reported with a macular rash and generalised gland enlargement. The diagnosis of secondary syphilis was confirmed after referral to the genito-urinary clinic. The mission was full of such people; lunch there was interesting since one's fellow guests were committed either to saintliness or sinning. Several were HIV positive, one was a retired terrorist awaiting his final encounter with AIDS-induced pneumocystis pneumonia and another was my accomplished friend the cracksmith.

Between us, two dedicated Kruispost staff, Dr Leen van Tright and Dr Helen Kreuger, together with Frans Westerman published *Morbidity at an Amsterdam Inner City Clinic in Relation to Drug Use*. The paper concluded: 'The need for Kruispost is sometimes questioned by those involved in the official health care system. In such a deprived community, which has been described by one of the Kruispost staff as 'fourth world', the clinic provided by the mission serves a real and important need for primary care. The importance of this clinic lies in its low threshold of free consultation offered to a severely deprived community at high risk in whom suspicion of officialdom may act as a deterrent to seeking medical advice.'

Sometimes walking home from the Kruispost I hurried through the very early morning streets. Petty crime was rife with drug users seeking money for their habit. Six times in two years the locks on my car were forced in search of anything that could be used to pay for drugs Some street people had unpleasant habits. A used syringe needle laid on skin was a very effective wallet opener... it was probably safe but who would take the risk of being infected with HIV? Such threat to property was rarely associated with personal violence but the screwdriver was becoming a popular weapon. Such small instruments as one chooses to wire electric plugs make interesting daggers. When held in the clenched fist, with the business end protruding from the ulnar border of the hand and delivered with a firm blow to the chest a screwdriver leaves only a tiny entry wound; the victim is aware of little more than a playful thump on the chest until his tension pneumothorax builds up later.

So three academic years passed in a mixture of frustration and exhilaration. I loved the students and though there for only a short time made permanent friendships with many who, years later, were still sending me postcards of their travels and letters about their progress in life and the profession. But the reason for my being in Amsterdam never materialised. A pompous board of enquiry was set up and found in favour of the university faculty; Goliath had won and poor David, the *Huisartsen Instituut Vrije Universiteit* (HIVU) waved goodbye to all those millions of guilders. In disgust both Cor Spreeuwenberg and I resigned on the same day.

But I had remembered the advice of Rob Sullivan given the day I received the ill-fated letter of invitation from Amsterdam: "watch your back" he had warned. So I did not resign from Amsterdam until I had regained a place in Michael Drury's department at Birmingham.

It was remarked when we resigned from the VU that nobody remembered students throwing a party for a leaving professor. It was a mark of great personal pride that they did this for Gillian and me. One student made a speech in which he described coming to my cluttered room where every flat surface was covered in piles of books, journals, files and papers for I was forever doing several things at once. It was impossible to sit anywhere. "Professor Hull your room is a mess"! he expostulated to cheers and laughter. The hosts for the party were the Kramers, the delightful parents of Marten Kramer, who along with Marieke van Schoot, Boony Thio, Elspeth Vischer, Desiree van der Feltz van der Sloot (who lived in the house of Paulus Potter the painter in Enkhuizen) and Bart

Rottier were prominent among my student following. The evening was heart-warming and delightful.

Gillian and I also gave a party at which she with the HIVU choir (called the 'Bel Canteeno' because they practised in the canteen!) sang madrigals and I gave my valedictory talk called, after Juliet's farewell to Romeo, "*Such Sweet Sorrow.*" In this I reviewed the success and failure of my professorship. I have to say that as a means of academic advancement Holland was a disaster but as life experience of incredible variety and stimulation it was superb. For Gillian, who had two weeks holiday a month, it meant total immersion in music, art and the culture of an exquisite, if sometimes rather sordid city. She became very active in the International Women's Contact of Amsterdam where she made many friends and for whom she organised two meetings in Stratford-on-Avon. Together at weekends we explored Holland from the Wadden Islands in the north to Maastricht in the south with frequent excursions to Germany, Belgium and even as far away as Switzerland and Florence. We developed a love of raw herring, smoked eel and Genever, made many friends and, more than anything else we had a great deal of fun.

Chapter 11

Return to Birmingham

I had heeded Robert Sullivan's advice and by keeping my contact with Birmingham Medical School I was in a position to hear of developments in the school's General Practice Department. Michael Drury had advanced the department enormously and as his half time senior Lecturer I had helped in this advance and was by now responsible for the design and organisation of several teaching programmes.

Michael, ever keen to attract funds to his department, had negotiated with The Cancer Relief MacMillan Fund for the financing of a five year Senior Lecturership in Palliative Care. At the age of 55 this was exactly the period I was looking for if I was to retire as I planned at 60. The trouble was I had no experience of Hospice work, though I had always regarded care of the terminally ill as an essential part of good General Practice. I discussed the post with Michael who made it clear that he wanted me back in his department full time.

The interview was long and searching for the interviewing board was divided in its opinion. There was only one other real contender in the short list. I was up against a Welshman, Dr Dewi Rees. I had known and respected Dewi for several years ever since our paths had crossed at a research meeting some years before, though in the intervening years I had seen little of him. However I had never forgotten his presentation of the work which he had done on bereavement on which he had based his successful MD thesis. For some years after he left full time general practice Dewi had been Medical Director of St Mary's Hospice in Raddlebarn Road, only half a mile from the medical school at Birmingham. The post for which we had both applied was full time and the successful candidate was to work at two hospices: St Marys and at St Giles at Whittington near Lichfield.

The choice facing the appointment board lay between two doctors of very different experience: Dr Rees was better qualified with his MD and years of experience as hospice director, but he lacked academic experience especially in the field of teaching. The board kept us waiting for a long time as argument raged between those representing the hospice movement and my colleagues from the medical school. I was to learn later that it was a very close run thing but the board eventually decided to appoint me. This was very encouraging after my rather ignominious retreat from Amsterdam which had severely dented my confidence but now, back in my familiar hole, even if short of palliative care experience I hoped I could soon learn.

Starting work at St Marys Hospice with the man I had beaten for the post was strained. I had enormous respect for Dewi Rees and learned much from him but our relationship was never relaxed. At St Giles Hospice things could not have been more different. Mr. John Taylor, the Director was a man after my own heart. He had been a surgeon in Canada before returning to Britain to the medical director's post at St Giles. John was a brilliant teacher whose wide experience in oncology and his natural philosophy made him ideally suited to care of the terminally ill.

There can be no doubt that this work does not appeal to all doctors. There was an unwritten philosophy which pervaded the therapeutically powerful, late twentieth century medicine that the doctor's task was to cure and, to all too many of my colleagues, it seemed that 'once there was nothing that could be done' for cure the patient represented failure to the doctor and was abandoned. Though many hotly denied this in many cases it was plain to see. In consequence those who threw themselves into care of the dying were often unusual people. Often of strong, even evangelical faith, they brought an air of piety to their work which often seemed at odds with the dispassionate but effective care which I felt was needed. I felt this most acutely when I visited that Mecca of palliative care, St Christopher's Hospice in London. It is impossible to separate spirituality from the deeply personalised care of those who know their days are numbered, indeed it needs to be brought out and discussed as I did with my students. However there was an air of pious 'good-doing' quite absent from the normally dispassionate attitude of curative medicine. I soon saw that this was something that I had to address among my students.

Before I could teach I had a lot to learn for the care of patients, some of whom suffered unbearable pain, vomiting, depression or a host of other symptoms. This required knowledge, skills and attitudes for which I was ill prepared. In John Taylor I had an outstanding teacher and I was at his side in one-to-one teaching for hours every day as we travelled round Staffordshire seeing patients in their homes or doing ward rounds at St. Giles. John was a first rate clinician who, had he not chosen a surgical career, would have made an outstanding general practitioner. He combined a compassionate personality with great personal warmth and infectious humour.

The problem with St. Giles was distance; it was an hour's drive there from home or Birmingham and the logistics of ferrying students there from the medical school was impossible. With much regret I had to withdraw from St. Giles, where I was happy working, to the slightly strained atmosphere of St. Marys. But this had to be; the hours spent driving between distant places of work meant less time devoted to my principal tasks of teaching and research. So, as soon as I had absorbed as much of John Taylor's wisdom as possible, I opted out of St. Giles though not before I had made a television programme about it. I used this extensively in teaching and St. Giles used it for fund-raising.

During the time I had been in Amsterdam the Department of General Practice had grown further with the addition of a number of part-time teachers. Of course the stalwart Lyn Shields, by now the envy of every other department in the hospital, conducted this disparate and opinionated orchestra, organised it and made it function extraordinarily smoothly under the overall direction of Michael Drury. By now we were involved in teaching all five years each consisting of 160 students. Much of this was done in small groups and covering, as general practice should, every aspect of medicine. I was involved across the board of this teaching but, as the only full time academic in the department, was responsible for co-ordinating much of the programme. My chief input came at that crucial point in a student's career when he or (increasingly) she changed from the largely theoretical laboratory based anatomy, biochemistry and physiology of the preclinical years to the more practical, hands-on clinical, patient-oriented medicine. This is an exciting juncture when students at last feel they are doing what they came to medical school to learn and they are as enthusiastic as a litter of labrador puppies ever wanting another stick thrown for them. This Clinical Introductory Course (CIC) lasted for three weeks and was largely set up for the didactic, lecture-theatre teaching which I had so criticised in Amsterdam. But how else can you teach 160 students at a time for many hours each day with a severely limited number of teachers? And there was so much to prepare them for. For the most part they were still children (though they would have hated to be called so) with little experience of the emotional trauma of serious illness, death and dying. Many of them had no idea how to cope with the physical proximity of patients of opposite sex and the challenge of embarrassing personal examination of other people's bodies. Though they had strong views on rights and wrongs they had little understanding of principles of moral philosophy and regarded such a topic with disinterest. Then they had so much to learn not only about life but also about bread-and-butter techniques of medicine such as interview skills and physical examination.

Given these problems we devised a course of mini-lectures, drawing on the best teachers from many different departments in the school. Rapid, short punchy talks about 'what I do' from physicians, surgeons, obstetricians and pathologists were interspersed with interview skills from Tim Betts the psychiatrist, talks from midwives on birth and nurses on dealing with female genital examination. Co-ordinating all this was a major task: each speaker had to have written briefing to understand where he or she fitted into the whole and each day culminated with one of the video programmes I had made with Paul Morby or sometimes with the television team in Amsterdam. I would show a little television and then literally by running round the theatre would pick on a student at random and ask for his comments on what he had seen. The air became electric, later students told me they loved it but were often very scared when my finger pointed at them. As Lawrence Mackie once told me 'probably only your students know what sort of a teacher you are and they won't say for all your assessment forms.' There were plenty of those and in usual laid-back student language the assessment forms showed that the students clearly found them interesting, thought-provoking and challenging of attitude. It was only many years later that more positive feed-back came to me accidentally. My daughter Janet, on changing her GP after moving house, happened to ask her new woman doctor where she had trained and on discovering a Birmingham graduate mentioned me; the reply was immediate: "Your dad was inspirational!"

Another problem was how to assess this course. Birmingham had a system of continuous assessment, unlike my own experience of an examination system where for years there was no exam only to be followed by the trauma of finals which, with written papers, orals and practicals in all major subjects lasted for six interminable weeks.* So, at Birmingham, this meant that we had to devise a way of assessing how much our students had learned from the frenetic three week CIC. We tried to teach them some of the knowledge they would need in their clinical work; more important were skills of gathering clinical data through history-taking, physical examination and interpretation of that information. Still more important were uncovering attitudes and prejudices and getting each student to come to terms with them. Much of the course turned on the behaviour of doctors and patients and we found ourselves puzzling about how one can possibly assess what was beginning to be known as behavioural medicine, especially when that assessment must also teach. At one of our departmental discussions I asked "Suppose a patient gives the doctor a meaningful look, it could be highly significant, but you can't ask a student to write an essay on 'a meaningful look.'

Amid laughter I realised that I was on to something. I designed an examination by television in which a young woman with a breast cancer was followed from her first presentation to the doctor with a breast lump through to her death and the subsequent bereavement of

---

*In student parlance this was known as 'sudden death examination!'

her husband. The tape consisted of fifteen short sections averaging about a minute in which the patient was seen with doctors, surgeons and nurses as her disease progressed over a period of some two years. This demanded accurate and tight scripting and put an enormous responsibility on the role players especially the actress playing the patient. This brought out all my former experience of tripping the boards of amateur dramatics. Paul Morby and his team rose to the occasion and our 'Televised Modified Essay Question' was used for several years in assessing the CIC.

I borrowed the four laboratories of the anatomy department which were set up to seat forty students apiece, and each with excellent television monitors. Students were provided with a book of 15 pages each with questions on them. I controlled the video warning students when each section was to start, After viewing the short clip they had a timed five minutes in which to write an answer to the questions. The exam lasted about an hour and a half during which the students wrote like mad in concentrated silence. With completion of the exam there was an explosion of conversation for the story was compelling and the issues raised stark and controversial. After collection of the completed exam books they were dismembered and each page was distributed to a single examiner so each of the fifteen sets of questions was assessed by one examiner. There are always hawks and doves among examiners and this avoided inter-examiner variation since when the marks were summated each student had papers assessed by both hawks and doves. The first time we ran the exam we were anxious to find out how it had worked. Student opinion suggested that for the most part they had found it interesting and challenging. The results were fascinating; statistically the marks fitted the usual Standard Deviation or 'top hat curve' but closer study revealed two distinct curves for women and for men. Women students tend to be harder working and win most of the prizes and at first we thought the gender difference was simply due to this but increasingly we thought we had chanced on a means of discriminating between a difference in ability as opposed to one of application. We tried hard over the next few years to prove this but were unable to do so. Nevertheless we were left with the strong impression that women were better than men at communication and empathy. Naturally the women, be they students, staff or wives, said 'Of Course'... but it would be nice to have proved it.

Two particular results fascinated me. Within a few minutes of the results being posted a furious young man burst into my room "I have come to tell you your exam is punk," he said at the top of his voice. I waved him to a chair. "Interesting," I said, "tell me why."

The lad then recounted that he was a high-flying student who in every exam he had taken had received the highest grades... Until he came to mine where he had failed miserably. This, he claimed, proved my test to be 'punk.'

I was beginning to get irritated at his arrogance and said that perhaps he was not comparing like with like. Was it possible I suggested that different examinations assessed different things?

But he would have none of it and became all the more vociferous till he got up my nose.

"Listen," I said, "you obviously are a very bright student; one day you may win the Nobel prize for medicine but you won't win it in psychiatry or in general practice. I suggest you take up anaesthetics or pathology because so long as your patients are either asleep or dead you will communicate with them very well."

The student got up, walked out and slammed the door leaving me cross with myself for I do not like getting angry with those I have to teach. But in one respect he was right, he was a very bright student. Three days later there was a timid knock at my door and the same student returned looking rather sheepish. "I've come back," he told me "to say two things: I'm sorry I slammed the door and to thank you for teaching me more about myself than anyone else since I came to medical school."

The other interview with a student could not have been more different. One student had done so well in the exam that her mark was two standard deviations above the mean and the best for the year. I sent for her and congratulated her and asked how she had managed it. "Well," she said, "I'm a woman, I'm a good deal older than the rest of the year, I'm a mother and before I started medicine I was a nurse. Your exam assesses wisdom, maturity and life experience and I have advantage over the rest of the year. I probably need your teaching less than the others, but keep it up for most of my year need it desperately badly."

However my most important and most concentrated teaching was in the final year. In this last year every student had a fortnight's attachment in general practice which included one and a half days in Palliative Care. The 160 students were split into ten groups of 16. On the Tuesday and Thursday afternoons they met me in groups of four at St Mary's hospice and later there was a full day for all 16. In the afternoon sessions I gave them a short introduction to what they might expect in the hospice and explained that we would first be visiting the day care centre where I would introduce each of them to one of the patients. "Just talk to them as people; I don't want you to take a history... chat about anything you like and I think you will find them very interesting people." I then sat watching the interaction while ostensibly appearing to be reading. Of course the patients were forewarned and had become very good with the students and at teaching them, for that's what they did. It made them feel they were important and contributing to educating young doctors. After a quarter of an hour I took the students away and asked each to tell the group how things had gone. They were all astonished at finding how easy it was to talk to these cancer patients. One who was particularly good was an ex-barmaid called Lily. Lily had come to us to die with her whole body riddled with secondary growths from breast cancer; that had been years before. She was indomitable as a result of an extremely hard life. She and I got on very well. One day she asked "'Ow long's this going to go on Dr. 'Ull?" I put my arm round her and said "Lily I really think you'll have to be shot!" and she cackled with laughter.

Lily talked frankly about her cancer from the first appearance of the lump when her husband had died, and through the impersonal business of mastectomy, radio- and chemotherapy. Nothing altered the rate of advance of her disease. Eventually she was sent to St Mary's with an expectation of life measured in days.

Students recounting what she had told them were astonished to find that a patient could not only say the forbidden word 'cancer' but could discuss it rationally and unemotionally. For students the word was always in capitals, thought about continually, but not spoken for fear of upsetting patients. Suddenly the taboo was lifted and they could talk with Lily and her friends quite openly. For many this was a great eye-opener. The discussion led on to why Lily was still alive years after expert opinion had said she would not last a week. Seeming to change the subject I asked if any of them had had glandular fever. Many had and remembered it as the 'kissing disease' of their teens which had struck them before exams. Why, I asked, before exams? They usually offered something connected with being run down before important tests. Changing tack again I asked why more people failed to get cancer. "By the time you get to my age," I told them "you will all have malignant cells lurking about somewhere but not everyone develops cancer. Why?" Someone would offer a suggestion about the response of the immune system and that would lead us into talking about the function of a particular white blood corpuscle that sought out and destroyed cells which were foreign and not part of us. That brought us to AIDS in which the virus destroys those self same white cells that prevent small clusters of malignant cells developing into cancer. Now how did those white cells stop working apart from their destruction by the AIDS virus? The students did not know but I explained that as a result of stress, chemical transmitters were released by the brain which resulted in diminution of white cell function. Thus before exams one was vulnerable to glandular fever. Students, bled before major exams in medicine, could be shown to have a depleted white cell count. So could people who had experienced loss, bereavement, divorce or some other crisis. Lily's cancer had followed her husband's death. "So," I argued, "if being unhappy can impair your immune system to such an extent as to permit the development of cancer perhaps it is possible, by increasing happiness, to improve the immune response and, if not actually curing the malignancy, at least allowing the patient to live with it. Lily had led a hard life in Birmingham. She told me one day she had never experienced so much kindness as she had at St. Mary's. I think Lily was telling us all to be kinder to each other."

I told the students that patients were referred to the hospice because someone had decided that there was nothing more that could be done and said how I hated this phrase and that in the hospice it was our job to find something more and do it. Sometimes that was difficult and I gave the example of a lady with motor neurone disease. This patient was a typically outspoken Brummie lady who was totally immobile but could just speak in a whisper. One day standing by her bed I confessed that if I ever was in such a state my chief problem would be boredom.

"Too right," she whispered, "what are you going to do about it?"

I had not expected that and I remembered a time when virus labyrinthitis had laid me low. If I lay perfectly still with my eyes closed I felt fine but as soon as I opened my eyes I vomited with extreme giddiness. I was going mad with boredom and started composing poetry in my head.

"Write poetry," I said to the patient.

She regarded me silently for a moment and said "Piss off!"

Next day when I asked for poetry she was even more emphatic: "Bugger off!"

On the third day she whispered "Dr Hull came round again / and said that I should use my pen."

I immediately printed this simple couplet up on my word processor and showed it to her. There is something about seeing one's first writing in typescript; she was delighted. After that everyone passing her by had to write down her next lines She wrote verses for the doctors and nurses and for the other patients. She died a week later with a grin on her face!

After that we went round the wards. I would shake every patient's hand reiterating to my round the importance of touch. I would have a few words with each patient, many of whom were very sick. After we left each ward there was an opportunity to explain the cases we had seen to the students. With some, whom I had warned before, I would ask the students to bring chairs so we could sit beside the bed and not stand, vulture-like, at its foot. That way we were not superior to the recumbent patient. Then for a few minutes I would invite the patients to talk about their experience of cancer, of their encounters with the white-coated specialists and what it was like in the hospice.

One young man, little older than my students, asked me to bring them to his bedside. He was dying from a melanoma which had appeared under a big toenail. He described to them how it felt to be dying and then said I have a message for you all "The fear of cancer is worse than cancer." That simple sentence was afterwards incorporated into every lecture I gave such that students would chant it back to me*.

That comprised the half day session which I always found so tiring I would pull into a lay-by on the hour's drive home to have a little sleep.

By the late eighties in Birmingham we were beginning to see more AIDS. It was interesting to see how, although it was the gay community that were hit hardest, there were other groups at risk. In Edinburgh most AIDS cases were in drug users, in London they were largely among homosexuals, in Amsterdam both but in Birmingham, which was a major haemophilia centre, many cases had been caused by transmission of the virus by infected blood products administered before the risk was understood. We were now getting AIDS cases referred to the hospice.

Looking back it is hard to realise how ignorant most of the medical profession was about this new and terrible disease. I was lucky to have had early experience in Amsterdam. Shortly after I took up my post at the hospices my eye was caught by a notice from Help the Hospices offering a travelling fellowship to New York for the express purpose

---

*This closely resembles Sir Philip Sidney's [1554-86] 'Fear is more pain than is the pain it fears.'

of studying AIDS and palliative care. I applied and since I was the only one to show interest in AIDS as well as in cancer care I was awarded the fellowship. I negotiated visits to several medical Schools in New York State as well as my attachment to Memorial Sloane Kettering Cancer Hospital in New York City. I asked if it would be possible to have an extension so that I could visit Montreal to see what Ann Macaulay was doing with her work on the Indian reservation at Kahnawake. She offered me a lecture and an introduction to Dr Balfour Mount, internationally known for his teaching of Palliative Care. I hated New York apart from the splendid ornithology of Central Park which just happens to be on the migration line for the spring southward journey of warblers. Gillian, on the other hand, loved its museums and art galleries. To me Sloane-Kettering typified American medicine where ultra-scientific technology was focussed onto disease and where the rest of the patient was of no interest. I found this sort of medicine distasteful: I would not want it for myself and found myself thinking it was all for the advancement of the superdocs who practised it rather than for their patients. I could hear my old mentor Lawrence Mackie snorting in disgust.

But I learned a lot in New York though most of it was pretty depressing. I saw queues of fearful young men waiting to be seen, all clutching at hope that something could be done about AIDS. I knew, as I suspect they did, that all were to die a disgusting, humiliating and terrifying death within months. I saw Kaposi's Sarcoma, pneumocystis carinii pneumonia, and appalling dysenteries. I saw pain, fear and inevitable bereavement and there was very little that could be done. It made me feel as I imagine an earlier generation of doctors must have felt when confronted by cholera or plague epidemics. I was also shown some of the New York drugs scene and learnt about the then innovative crack cocaine and the incredible sexual orgies its habit released. Crack, though not as risky as heroin since it was inhaled rather than 'mainlined' was every bit as likely to spread AIDS through the intense promiscuity it unleashed.

Despite this depression I was impressed at the way in which the population was responding. Gillian had noticed the poverty of window dressing in Fifth Avenue. The artists famous for these displays came from the gay community; most of them were sick and many dead. But the word had got out; the large and highly promiscuous New York gay population were heeding warnings and using safer sex. Partly because so many were already dead and partly because of the condom the peak of the epidemic began to wane.

From my depressing experience in New York it was a joy to travel north to Montreal. Here I did a little teaching in Ann Macaulay's department and saw what she was doing in her Indian reservation* and my spirits began to lift. One disappointment was that Balfour Mount was leaving Montreal the following day. I attended one of his teaching rounds and took part in discussion. Afterwards he asked who I was and took the trouble to ring me and apologise that he was out of town. "I am off on a lecture tour for several days and I'm sorry because I heard you wanted to meet me. Actually I am driving to Ottawa I suppose you wouldn't like to come with me?"

My reply was immediate "Give me a little while to get organised and if I can possibly do it I'm on!"

That is how I came to spend three days in the company of the man I came to admire most in palliative care. Bal Mount and I never stopped talking; he was a fascinating man; himself a survivor of cancer and of a major air crash but also of incredibly wide literary knowledge and with such a witty way of talking that much of our long journey was filled with laughter. He was also quite informed about the birds we saw on the way. I probably learned more about palliative care on that journey and from attending his lectures than at any other part of the fellowship.

Back at Birmingham I realised that I must make AIDS a major thrust of my teaching. I wrote a television script about a young heterosexual Birmingham couple in whom the man became infected by dirty needles when using intravenous heroin. This tape called 'Nigel and Sam' was shot quite brilliantly using students from Birmingham University Drama Department as main characters

*For which she was later awarded The Order of Canada.

and David Morgan, from the GPTRU and Rosemary Lockie, wife of Dr Cameron Lockie of Alverston. Rosemary worked as an AIDS counsellor in Warwickshire It was to be one of the last videotapes I made with Paul Morby and was probably the best. Nigel and Sam won awards from the BMA and internationally. Like the modified essay question it moved fast through very short sequences from Nigel experimenting with heroin to his death from pneumocystis pneumonia. This was to become the major part of the teaching at the whole day at the hospice for the sixteen students in the final year. I was astonished to find that the group were very ignorant despite the fact that, as they recognised themselves, AIDS was predominantly a threat to their own age group.

I kept careful records of the comments made by students for I wanted to submit a report on the five year Macmillan Senior Lecturership at its conclusion. Two of these student comments revealed how little they were taught on what by then was beginning to look an apocalyptic killer: "The AIDS Afternoon was particularly interesting–probably so as it was new material." "The AIDS session was very good–as well as from a Dr's point of view it is actually relevant to our age group and we can relate to the scenario. It is good to try and promote discussion... From shy people too."

Wide ranging discussions explored aspects of human behaviour which surprised many students by challenging attitudes. Students were apprehensive about the responsibilities that were soon to be thrust upon them as young doctors one commenting "A useful way of addressing a difficult subject. We are none of us given any other opportunity to explore our own feelings about death and the dying patient and I know that for me the first time I tell a patient, or relative, of their incurable illness will be a difficult moment. We are told that there is no lesson like experience but I feel that preliminary discussions of this sort can only be beneficial and hopefully improve what is likely to be an initially inadequate performance. Thank you for a useful approach to a difficult subject."

This and many similar comments from students led to a major research study in which I examined students' experience of, and teaching about, death and dying. In concluding a paper on Death and the Medical Student* I wrote... "students become doctors with little formal teaching about death and dying. Such experience as they do acquire is more likely to have come before entry to the medical school or in their social lives. This is bound to have a bearing on their communication skills as young doctors when they are thrown in at the deep end of house jobs."

Cancer Relief Macmillan had funded my senior lectureship for five years. As my tenure of the position began to close I tried hard to get alternative funding so that the post would survive for a successor. I circulated reports of my activities and student feedback. Of course Michael Drury was supportive and a letter from the Dean, Professor Sandy McNeish of 20 Feb 1990 to Dr Michael Harrison Regional Medical Officer endorsed 'completely the view expressed by Michael Drury, namely that this has been an outstandingly successful venture' and hoped that the Regional Medical Officer would 'see merit in exploring possible mechanisms to continue the post beyond 1992.' But all universities were hard pressed financially and eventually the Professor of Medicine broke the news to me:

"Palliative care is a luxury we cannot afford."

I wonder if things have changed.

Despite being fully occupied at medical school and Hospice I was busy writing, travelling the world lecturing on my work at Birmingham. In 1989 Andrew Bax published 'Teamwork in Palliative Care' co-authored by myself, Mary Ellis and Vicki Sargent, two senior teaching nurses at St Mary's. I also put together a series of lectures given at the medical school on drugs used in Palliative Care in "A Pocketbook of Palliative Care" subsequently published by McGraw-Hill in Australia. I was still completing research work from Holland and had to return there to read papers and give lectures. As chairman of General Practitioners Writers Association I made a short trip to Brisbane to be keynote speaker of a conference of the Australian Medical Writers Association. At

---

*Death, dying and the medical student. Medical Education 1991,25, 491-496.

home I was an honorary consultant in Palliative Care and a Member of the West Midlands Region AIDS Task Force from 1986 until my retirement. With social psychologist Angela Ryan, who had wide experience of counselling in serious disease and bereavement. I set up 'Oncare', a programme attempting to ease the lot of a series of patients undergoing disfiguring facio-maxillary cancer surgery.

In 1991 my old friend and much respected colleague Professor Sir Michael Drury retired and for a few months I was acting head of the department until the appointment of the new Professor of General Practice, Richard Hobbs. This taught me how much sweeter life was as a senior lecturer than as head of department where interminable and highly political committee meetings obtruded on time so that it was difficult to get anything done.

Jasmine Cottage still seemed a meeting place for doctors from around the world to such an extent that in the pub across the road it was called International House. That pub, The Boar's Head, must have quenched the thirst of doctors of many nations. To my three daughters and their friends it was always spoonerised. People would be surprised at teenage shouts in the village street of "see you in the Whore's Bed!" All three daughters grew up with Shakespeare particularly Janet whose best friend at school was a member of the Dench family who lived nearby. Judi Dench and her husband Michael Williams occasionally drank at the Boar's Head. One evening Jan and friends including Julian Harris, the young musician who dog-sat for us when we were in Amsterdam, decided they would put on a performance of *A Midsummer Night's Dream* in the local Charlecote Park (such is the arrogance of the young to stage amateur Shakespeare in Stratford!). They consulted their diaries: there was a window of opportunity in the late summer which gave them six weeks from start to finish. They dragged everyone in: Gillian was wardrobe mistress and I took on the small part of Peter Quince the carpenter and director of the rude mechanical's play within the play. This brought back my old love of amateur dramatics which, though I had not had time for over the last many years, had undoubtedly profoundly influenced my teaching techniques. The production was a fantastic success so much so that the following year I played the philosophical shepherd Corin in *As You Like It*. Doing this part made me realise how skilfully Shakespeare writes even his tiny parts leaving much that can be interpreted by the actor. Again the Rural Theatre Company's As You Like it played to full audiences in the open air of a glorious Summer. The following year we planned *Romeo and Juliet* in which I was cast as Capulet but upheaval in the lives of the young caused them to scatter and the production did not survive the first few rehearsals. The Rural Theatre Company had other productions too, putting on a Christmas show in the church with poetry and music and that was fun too. The Hampton Lucy and Charlecote vicar, Canon Cyster, was great and welcomed innovative use of his church. We once held a sponsored hymn sing when we sang all the hymns in Ancient and Modern without pause and continuing in relays through the night for a total of nearly 17 hours. I promised the 6am shift and for the only time in my life attended church in dressing gown and pyjamas. The Boar's Head did well that weekend for singing hymns is thirst-producing but we raised a lot of money for the church roof.

Another interest was growing rapidly. All my life I had always been interested in ornithology and my peripatetic lifestyle, which involved so much intercontinental travel, gave me the opportunity to study birds wherever I went. With family education largely behind us there was more money for exotic travel. In 1988 we visited Australia stopping over in Singapore and later visited Oregon as guests in Professor Bob Taylor's department in Portland gaining ornithological experience all the time. In 1989 we booked our first bird watching holiday in Kenya with the RSPB 'Sunbird' company and fell in love with Africa and its wildlife. 1990 took us first to Tenerife on holiday in pursuit of the Blue Chaffinch, *Fringilla teidei* and later to my last professionally subsidised international conference in Vancouver. This Conference of the World Organisation of National Colleges and Academies (WONCA) was to prove especially productive for birds and also for later travel. By 1990 I had mustered a respectable list of nearly 1000 bird species, a bare 10% of the possible total; I resolved to do better.

We still kept an interested eye on the Wellesbourne practice which, with large areas of new housing of the 1980s was expanding rapidly. The Palace which Lawrence and I had thought would see us through to the next century had to be modified and enlarged. Lawrence himself on retirement from the practice had gone on to a distinguished career in the diplomatic medical service working as PMO to the British Embassies first in Moscow and then in Warsaw. Lawrence was a superb correspondent and sent regular letters detailing his life 'behind the curtain' where he was doctor to the ambassadorial team at a crucial period of East-West relations. It was sometimes tough going but he clearly loved the intrigue which seemed to complicate the already confidential aspects of his work. His descriptions of Muscovite life from the sophistication of the Bolshoi to the practicality of having to pee on the frozen locks of his car made fascinating reading. It was a great disappointment to Gillian and I that we had to cancel a proposed visit to see him in Moscow due to the illness of Gillian's mother.

When Lawrence returned to his old home at Rana House in Wellesbourne I decided to nominate him for Fellowship of the RCGP. This is an honour to which one is elected and to be elected one has to be known. Lawrence, though devoted to his doctoring, was a retiring man who did not write, teach (except by precept) or research and so lacked those attributes which drew attention to him. It was easy enough to find two local Fellows prepared to support my nomination but we all wondered if he would be elected. It so happened that Michael Drury was chairman of the committee on Fellowship and he told me what happened when Lawrence's name came up.

"Who?" asked the members of the committee "What has he done?"

Michael then weighed in "It is all very well honouring people like his partner Robin Hull but I think we should give thought to men like Lawrence Mackie who keep the shop running and allow the Hulls of this world to advance general practice for without the Mackies there would be no Hulls. "

I was delighted to see Lawrence wearing his fellow's gown. Alas he did not wear it for long before his sudden death in 1988.

Two Fellows, Lawrence Mackie and Robin Hull, Spring 1988.

Chapter 12 Retirement

Part IV A third Career

The 1992 WONCA Vancouver meeting was full of old friends from all over the world. I had work to do presenting papers, taking part in discussions and exhibiting a poster about GPWA. The poster next to mine was about the medical school in Oman and was presented by Swedish Bengt Linder. He was an old friend from EGPRW days and now Professor of General Practice at Sultan Qaboos Medical School in Oman. Within five minutes we had fixed up a visit to Muscat.

Then Professor Neil Carson from Monash Medical School invited me there as a visiting professor. It looked as though retirement was going to be busy! But my real memory of Vancouver was birding in Stanley Park and a visit to bird reserves at Reifel and Iona sewage works*. I hardly attended any lectures except when giving them myself, skiving off on my own or with Richard Nowotny who was among the Australian contingent.

I had decided that after forty years of medicine I was going to launch a new career. After general practice and then academia this third career must be completely different and a challenge to give purpose to whatever time was left. I decided it would be based on natural history, travel and writing. Gillian and I formed a formal business partnership becoming Wordwise Writing and Lecturing Service. With my contacts in medicine and Gillian's in tourism we felt we could raise a small income to supplement our pensions from the state, the NHS and Universities and support the launch of 'the third career'. By now Gillian was working as a Heart of England tourist guide, was writing and was increasingly in demand as a speaker. But there was a problem; the spondylolisthesis which had started causing severe back pain in Amsterdam was now getting much worse. Fearing a rather gloomy future I encouraged her writing as much as possible and she became an active member of GPWA, contributed many articles to its journal and expanded her interest in medical history. With her earnings from writing, speaking and tourism, she made an important contribution to Wordwise.

---

*Some of the best birding is to be found at large sewage works.

By now I was amassing a huge data base on British birds which I was hoping would become a book*. However, though it was attracting little interest from publishers I was still earning quite well from speaking to medical audiences and from journals at home and abroad.

My experience in Africa had made me thirsty for travel. Hitherto funds had been short and I was glad of professional travel grants but now, with maturation of life insurance and inheritance we had some spare cash. Education was almost finished, one daughter married and one engaged, so we could travel. I set myself a target of identifying a third of the World's birds before taking wings myself and to this end we had many holidays with 'Sunbird' and 'Ornitholidays' sometimes by ourselves but often with a bird-watching friend, architect Rodney Melville. To many people ornithology is a bizarre hobby, typified by 'twitchers' who are solely interested in ticking checklists and communicating with each other electronically before rushing hundreds of miles to see and tick a new species. This is quite different from the slow, patient study of bird behaviour and variety in their natural setting. I became as besotted with ornithology as I had been of medicine. This meant my life was coming full circle; I was returning to the natural history of my childhood but applying to its study some of the rigour of science. That meant that instead of birds being incidental to medicine they became my *raison d'être*. Though I was always thrilled to see a new species I could still wonder at the behaviour of common garden birds and their relationship with man.†

In the autumn of 1989 I met a young enthusiastic Japanese Doctor called Tsuneo Kato. As was my wont I invited him home for a weekend. At that time I had no knowledge of Japan other than prejudice as a hangover from the war. I had grown up with horror

*Later much was used, with generous acknowledgement, in Birds Britannica by Mark Cocker and Richard Mabey (Chatto & Windus 2005) and in my own Scottish Birds Tradition & Culture (Mercat 2001).

†As I was typing this a robin flew into the house where it attacked a Worcester porcelain figure of a North American cardinal. Tinbergen, the ethologist, would have been delighted at such aggression at a fellow red bird. Unfortunanely the Worcester figurine was damaged.

stories and I had also seen pictures of the devastation of Hiroshima and Nagasaki. My feeling towards the Japanese was a mixture of fear and guilt. My friendship with Tsuneo and the many colleagues he was to introduce me to changed my attitudes completely.

As a house guest Tsuneo was unusual; he had clearly never been in a western home and was gauche and ill at ease. Despite this, his was such a delightful, if intensely formal, personality that we immediately took to him in what was to become a lasting, though distant friendship. I arranged for Tsuneo to live in at St Mary's Hospice so that he could observe the work of the staff and their interaction with patients round the clock. At first the staff were nonplussed by this strangely formal person but soon his personal warmth and hunger for knowledge won them over.

A year later Tsuneo again stayed with us writing in the visitor's book 'Please come to Japan in the near future.' The following March brought a visitation from Professor Naoki Ikegami, a hospital physician from Tokyo. More cosmopolitan than Tsuneo he was an easier house guest who thanked us for 'a lovely time'. At that time neither Gillian nor I realised that for Japanese it was exceptional to get into western homes and that inviting them to stay with us had given them a novel insight into western life.

Then, in the summer of 1991, came an invitation for Gillian and me to travel to Japan as visiting lecturers and guests of the British Council and Dr Hinohara of the Life Planning Center of Tokyo. The invitation included funds for a nurse to speak on her role in connection with terminal illness. I asked Hannah Coetzee, one of the Wellesbourne district nurses, whose South African husband Peter was also invited. When we arrived in Japan we were met by the Life Planning Center's liaison officer, Methodist minister Mr Takeshi Saito, who had graduated in theology in Atlanta. In the foyer of the hotel Mr Saito flicked open an attaché case to reveal more banknotes than I have ever seen in my life. This represented airfare, honoraria and expenses for us all during our stay in Japan. As we signed receipts Mr Saito explained 'from now on you pay everything'. Faced with such largesse we agreed at once when he beamed from ear to ear and ordered champagne to welcome us. Apart from the odd fares, snacks and shopping I don't think we were allowed to pay for anything while we were in the country.

I had been briefed by the Life Planning Center to speak on the mouth-watering topic of 'The Organisation of the National Health Service'. I spent much time researching a most boring lecture. Predictably within minutes my audience was asleep. I stopped, bowed to Dr Hinohara in the chair and said "this isn't working please may I do it my way?"

At a nod from the chairman I tore up my notes and told them about my work at Birmingham. Then I showed them videotapes springing questions on them just as I did in Birmingham. But this audience were not students, rather they were some of Tokyo's leading medical men and women. In Japan you don't ask anyone anything which might make him lose face. However an overriding rule in social behaviour was courtesy; after initial reserve the audience felt a need to be polite. Some of them answered, there was laughter and in a few more minutes the whole audience was sitting up and taking notice. There was no doubt that the videotapes made our presentations real because the Japanese doctors recognised in the television the everyday problems they faced themselves; they could identify with these 'foreign devils' and see different ways of dealing with shared problems. From boredom and apathy the meeting sprang alive and I was glad I did not have to give that dreary bureaucratic NHS lecture. Hannah, a vivacious redhead was the success I knew she would be describing her work in the community. Gillian spoke so well on the Heart of England, her research on the history of the Wellesbourne practice and the role of voluntary work in general practice that she was commended by Dr Hinohara and invited to speak to the Life Planning Center's volunteers when we returned to Tokyo.

Later we went to Okayama, Tsuneo Kato's home town, where another formal programme had been arranged. This focussed on cancer and the palliative care of terminal disease including AIDS. Again Paul Morby's excellent videotapes helped to bridge cultural and linguistic difficulties and our hosts were delighted, fêting us at lavish receptions. There was plenty of time to explore Japan, travelling by bullet train to visit Kyoto and the ancient castle at Himeji. There was even time to list seventeen new Japanese birds thanks to help from the Japanese Wild Bird Society to whom I had written in advance. To my astonishment a fax awaited me on arrival, informing me that an official guide had been provided for me to show me local species.

Our greatest pleasures were invitations to two Japanese homes. Tsuneo took us first to his clinic where we saw him at work. Again I had the extraordinary experience of watching a skilled doctor, speaking a tongue I could not understand talking to a patient. He was telling her that her illness had reached a point from which there was no return. He had warned me beforehand that he was going to tell her she was dying but not how he would do it. I saw him greet her and ask to examine her distended abdomen. He laid a clinical, examining hand on her belly palpating gently with his finger tips, slowly the gesture changed from questioning to supporting; the hand gently caressed the woman's abdomen more like a lover's than a physician's touch. Eye to eye he spoke firmly but gently. When he took his hand away the woman said the only Japanese I knew; "thank you." This experience, witnessed without intelligible speech, convinced me more than ever that non-verbal communication, among the very skilled, was universal.

We walked round the wards full of elderly people who had prepared themselves for the doctor by kneeling on their beds. At his approach each patient bowed, her forehead on the sheets in front of her, then straightened to greet him with a smile. At first this seemed obsequious, but it soon appeared that this was not subservience, but rather reverent thanks to a physician whose care was so transparent that it was he who was serving them. This was a revelation of the interdependence of the doctor-patient relationship which, for all my teaching, I had never fully appreciated. It was very moving.

Afterwards Tsuneo took us to his tiny home to meet his family. We took off our shoes at the door before entering onto tatami matting of the floor. By the door there was a painting of water lilies. Seeing me admiring it Tsuneo said almost apologetically "by my wife". Hisako was widely travelled, westernised and an accomplished painter; she was also a brilliant cook. We sat at a table only fifteen inches above the floor with our legs extended under it, for me uncomfortable, extremely painful for Gillian. Our host and hostess knelt by the table to eat. Dinner was superb; Chinese chicken consisting of breast meat opened flat and cooked like steak with ginger and herbs. This was followed by a paella filled with shellfish with noodles and salad. Their three adolescent children ate with us. We wondered how they all fitted into this tiny house, but that is typically Japanese where houses are not measured by rooms but by the number of tatami mats needed for the floor space.

After this insight into domestic life we returned to Tokyo to visit Naoki Ikegami's hospital and to dine at his home. Naoki lived in a much larger house which he shared with his parents. After another delicious meal Naoki asked me, as a special favour, if I would spare a minute or two to meet his mother. We went to his father's side of the house where his mother was totally paralysed by Parkinson's disease. Naoki had to prise open her eyes so that she could see me. With no idea what was expected of me but knowing she had spent many years in England and had complete command of the language I held her hands and spoke of my respect for her son. I told her about my patient at St Mary's, paralysed with motor neurone disease, whom I had got to write poetry. I thought I saw recognition in her eyes. Naoki seemed touched that I had spent so long with her.

Another episode helped to reverse my boyhood attitudes towards these people whom I had feared as barbaric enemies. When Takeshi Saito our guide and brilliant interpreter had to leave us he became quite emotional. Clearly the whole of the organisation of our visit had been a tremendous responsibility to him. In totally un-Japanese fashion he enveloped Gillian in a bear hug. When released she presented him with a little gift we had brought from home. His eyes filled and he choked out "I have to go or I might make crying!"

So much for the inscrutable, unemotional Nipponese of my preconception.

I had such memories of my 1977 trek in the Garwhal Himalaya that when I spotted a 'Sunbird' birding holiday centred on Naini Tal in February 1992 I decided I wanted to show Gillian something of that vast country. With Rodney Melville, a former patient, we travelled by Tata bus across the never-ending Gangetic plain. We saw tigers at Corbett National Park, wondered and photographed at the architectural splendour of Fatepur Sikri and the Taj Mahal and were dazzled by the profusion of birds at Bharatpur. In Naini Tal, birding in the cemetery of this old 'Raj' hill station we were appalled at the number of British graves, especially of children, from cholera. But the birds were magnificent and I was able to show Gillian the distant peaks of Nanda Devi and her sister mountains 75 miles to the north. On a walk with Rodney Melville we came across a simple shelter constructed by placing loose sheets of corrugated iron together. Gillian wanted to look at it but I restrained her saying that is someone's home. As we approached we heard John Arlott's voice giving the cricket commentary from England. Somehow this summarised India in its poverty, its Anglophone simplicity and its love of cricket.

Towards the end of this trip Gillian was severely incapacitated by back pain. Shortly after we got home she developed a high swinging fever and I got her into hospital fearing malaria. After being practically exsanguinated by an enthusiastic house physician trying to prove an interesting diagnosis it turned out to be pyelitis and she made a complete recovery. However this was a prelude to severe and potentially crippling back problems.

In November 1992 we flew to Melbourne where I was to be part of a secret. My visiting professorship was for a month after which I was supposed to fly home. In fact we had extended our visit for a holiday so that we could make a surprise return for Neil Carson's retirement and give a short tribute to him during his valedictory party. I enjoyed being back in Melbourne where, by now, we had many friends. I spoke at three hospices in Victoria and at the departments of GP at Monash and Melbourne Universities.

Meanwhile Gillian spoke on three occasions on Medical History and spent time researching on Dr William Redfern 'the father of Australian Medicine' subsequently publishing papers about him.

Even in Australia I had British deadlines to meet for I was publishing regular articles and monthly crosswords in a number of medical journals. One day John Murtagh, the department's second professor came to see me, noticed the crossword grid I was working on and was intrigued. At the time John was editor of the monthly Australian Family Physician. As a result my crosswords appeared regularly in his journal providing a small but regular trickle into my Australian Bank. During that month at Melbourne we explored Victoria at weekends visiting Gillian's cousins in Ballarat: Joan Steele and her son Richard. 'Rick' was a surveyor who had built a superb stone house where he and Kathryn and their family welcomed their English 'rellies' and so began a lasting friendship. I have always found it easy to make friends with people who own a vineyard! In addition Rick and I explored the bush together seeking birds.

After staying in Lorne, where in 1983 we borrowed the summer home of Ross and Jill Webster and where it was a delight to return we took the opportunity to drive the stunningly beautiful Great Ocean Road to Port Fairy to visit Dr. Andrew and Judy Gault. Judy looked exactly like her mother Bonnie Carson and she and Andrew had visited Hampton Lucy in 1986 before they were married. They made us most welcome and after supper they took us to Griffiths Island where Andrew guaranteed 'mutton birds' or Short-tailed Shearwaters which were so common early settlers ate them instead of mutton. We waited long after dark but they did not arrive. Andrew was mortified and, whenever we meet afterwards, he refers to the birds that did not come!

We dined with Chris and Ruth Hill. Chris, my predecessor in Wellesbourne, had emigrated to Perth where divorce left him penniless. He and Ruth got in the car and crossed the Nullabor Desert to Victoria where he settled in practice. Ruth was lovely and we had a delightful evening comparing our lives. I think that though I would have loved a lifetime in Australia I have had a much more varied life than Chris.

Among many birding trips our best was with Richard Nowotny, whom I had so infuriated in 1983 in West Australia. He had driven Gillian and me to Margaret River and I kept asking him to stop for birds; eventually he got quite cross. I am not sure how much influence I have had on the people to whom I tried to teach medicine in Australia but am sure my influence on Richard's life was considerable: from knowing nothing about birds he had, in nine years, become one of Australia's foremost amateur ornithologists. Together, on a day so blustery we could not hold our telescopes still, we visited Werribee, the Melbourne sewage works and Mecca for birders which is among my top world favourites. We saw many species despite the weather.

From Melbourne we booked a week's holiday in Tasmania which I loved on my brief teaching visit in 1983. Now all the time was ours to explore this, the wildest, exquisite and most pristine state of an enthralling continent. Much of Tasmania is mountainous; some of it, on the west coast, largely unexplored. Tasmania has a large number of endemic species of birds and it was these that we were after.

It rained incessantly and we drove our hired car for miles round this beautiful island, so reminiscent of Scotland. At one point the rain grew too much and we retreated to a small restaurant for coffee. We were the only people there and the proprietress, Charlotte King, chatted to us. She had been born in St Albans and was fascinated that we had been married in the Abbey there. Charlotte gave us several ornithological contacts and then said "What you really want is Langoona."

"Where's Langoona?" I asked.

Charlotte's finger descended on a completely featureless area on the map, which the restaurant used as a table mat.

"There," she said, "where there's nothing else." A few moments on the telephone and we were booked.

Next day we set off following Charlotte's directions. The highway dwindled to a side road which, becoming narrower and more potholed, was soon reduced to a grassy track. Feeling we must be wrong we remembered Charlotte's words "Just keep on going even when you think you're lost, it's miles from anywhere in the Leven Valley, considerably further than the back of beyond!"

Eventually we found a number of wooden chalets. I noticed that the 'paddicks' were littered with animal droppings. We were greeted by Len and Pat Doherty who showed us our chalet which was capacious, comfortable and well equipped. I said I was interested in wildlife and had also brought my fly rod. Len assured me that "I'd be right for wildlife but, though the trout fishing was usually good, the river was too high after the rain. Mind," he added, "if you catch fish leave the guts on the doorstep."

I agreed, for where else does a gentleman leave fish offal? Len left us briefly before returning with a load of logs for our fire. "You'll need these... Get's cold at night even in November, sometimes snow on the tops."

We had brought a little food and plenty of wine and settled to supper. It was while washing up I noticed something odd. Things were moving in the dusk outside; they were thirteen pademelons* feeding quietly right in front of the house. Len came with a special mash he makes and these small wallabies tucked in, oblivious of us on the porch outside the floor to ceiling window which made up the front wall of our sitting room. Len dumped some of his mash beside my elbows on the hitching rail. Then Gillian pointed at my feet. I looked down to see an endangered species, a Spotted Tailed Quoll, sniffing at my boots. While I was admiring this rare marsupial a Common Brush-tailed Possum climbed down from the roof and fed on the mash on the hitching rail. He was so close that I stroked this wild creature as he ate.

---

*The smallest of the Kangaroo family, little bigger than brown hares.

Next morning I was up early and caught two half-pound brown trout–just as well as we wanted to stay a second night and were short of food. In the afternoon, in better weather which increased my anxiety about snakes, Gillian and I went out again finding the exquisite flame and scarlet robins and had a fine view of a white goshawk; three new species. Len came to the chalet and offered to show us platypus as the river had gone down a bit. For a long time, though he kept pointing to them, we could not see them.

"Look for what looks like a bubble going upstream," he said. Then we identified them and as we watched we saw these little animals lift their beaver-like tails as they dived. Once we knew what to look for we saw plenty.

That night I did as bidden and left the fish guts on the doorstep. After a delicious supper of fresh brown trout I watched the cast of our evening show: the pademelons, the quoll and the possum, but I was tired after a long day and dozed by the fire. Suddenly there was commotion on the other side of the picture window: the quoll bolted and the possum let out a squawk and fled. There, on the other side of the window was a wild Tasmanian devil, about the size of a badger, eating the fish offal. At their best these are ugly creatures; this one was old and battered with a scarred face and a missing right ear: no wonder he was called a devil.

Neil Carson's party was formal and I had not thought to bring a dinner jacket. Professor Doris Best, with whom we were staying solved my problem. She hugged me and told me she was going to a formal reception where she would hug every man till she felt one of my size. The resulting Pierre Cardin suit fitted very well!

In February 1993 we went to Oman where I had not been for 35 years. The change was phenomenal. Though oil had been discovered in the 1960s the old Sultan did not hold with Western technology: despite considerable revenues, the country remained as poor as it had been before. Meanwhile the Sultan's son, Qaboos, was first an officer cadet at Sandhurst and later studied local government in Warwickshire where, in all probability he sent me my rates demand! In 1970 he deposed his father in a bloodless coup and reorganised his country.

I was invited to teach at the medical school at Sultan Qaboos University, designed by an English architect and set in the desert outside Muscat. The university campus was vast with wide expanses of sandy gravel between its buildings. There were frequent trees, mostly acacias, each with its own irrigation supply and filled with birds, such as bulbuls, palm doves and purple sunbirds.

The staff of the General Practice department took us to brunch at a hotel near Muscat. What a transformation; nothing I had read had prepared me for the extent of change. The city was modern with Arabic architecture and no high rise buildings. An excellent new road, the Corniche, between Muttrah and Muscat climbed high to a pass with a stunning view of Muscat Harbour with the forts of Merani and Jelali apparently unchanged from my visit in HMS Loch Fada in 1957. The Al Bustan Palace is reputed to be among the five best hotels in the World. The interior is like a cathedral with a magnificent domed roof nine stories above decorated with blue and green ceramic tiles. This is a popular place for Friday brunch which was a superb buffet, especially crayfish, crab and smoked Kingfish.

When I met Allan Burrell, the director of the Centre for Educational Technology at the University I realised the importance of my old 8mm ciné films which I had had converted to videotape. The Professor of history was particularly enthusiastic and, later the Secretary General of the University himself, an important person in Oman related to the Sultan, thanked me for the videotape and presented me with a handsome commemorative medallion and asked me to try to retrace the steps taken in 1957 to update the film with a modern video-camera.

I was instructed to meet Gus, an American-trained Omani cameraman, who took me first to Muttrah to find the hospital where, in April 1958, I had helped operate on the gunnery officer's perforated stomach ulcer. The primitive disused operating theatre was still there divided by a partition wall into offices. We tried to find our way by old roads over the steep pass to Muscat and found the al Akshar Mosque which I photographed in 1957. Then it had stood alone with no buildings near it; now it is surrounded by new blocks of shops and flats. By climbing on a roof (the charming owner of the house seemed pleased to help us and even found a ladder for us) we found a vantage point from which to take shots of the mosque and the nearby school.

The University was delightful with extensive gardens ablaze with petunias, antirrhinums and a host of exotic tropical shrubs. The professorial staff were largely European and teaching was all in English. Male and female students were segregated: on double-decker cloisters, men walk below and women above; in lectures men sit on the speaker's right, women on the left. Islam is more than a religion here it is a complete way of life, where curriculum timing is modified to fit religious practice. The students are, like all Omanis, delightful, attentive and extremely well mannered quite unlike the students in Europe, America or Australasia! Like medical students everywhere they are overburdened with factual learning but at Sultan Qaboos Medical School subjects such as ethics, communication and human behaviour are paramount.

Sultan Qaboos has been described as a benign dictator; certainly he is universally loved. In twenty-three years he had modernised his country. An anecdote hints at the personality of this remarkable man. He is said to like driving his own car 'incognito'. He appeared at an army check point where a corporal, unimpressed by the Sultan's claimed identity, refused him entry. Two days later the corporal was sent under armed guard to the palace where he was marched into the Sultan's presence. Qaboos dismissed the guard, congratulated the corporal on his devotion to duty and promised immediate promotion. As the surprised and relieved soldier left the palace he was shown his personal gift from the Sultan; a new Mercedes.

We both were kept busy teaching in Oman: I lectured on Palliative care and Ethics and Gillian gave a formal lecture on Medical

History and held informal discussions with women students. We both learned a great deal about Islam and came to appreciate how Ibadhi, the variety practised here, was peaceable and tolerant. We met Omanis from professors to peasants and all were welcoming and, where we could speak English with them, informative and entertaining. I was struck by their tolerance such that in a supermarket there was a special door through which infidels like me could go to purchase bacon!

In the early spring evenings we walked out into the desert and were surrounded by stone mountains changing colour in the sunset; it was incredibly beautiful and full of birds. We were fortunate that the staff included internationally famous ornithologists Hilary Fry and Jens and Hanne Eriksen all of whom took us off on birding trips. Unlike my former visit I could not wait to return.

But Gillian's health was deteriorating and her back was increasingly painful. For some time after Oman we travelled little apart from an experimental trip to Holland in the spring of 1993 visiting old friends Anneke Arbouw and Otto Sigling in Amstelveen and travelling with them to former haunts among the birds of Texel.

Gillian was spending increasing time resting and I began to fear the condition might progress to paraplegia confining her to a wheelchair and in desperation I said to her "You'd better learn to use the bits of you that work; start writing." That was harsh but she took it to heart and began writing seriously on a light Amstrad Notepad she could use while resting in bed. The resulting articles soon began to appear in medical and lay publications*. In October 1993 she underwent surgery including a spinal fusion at the Nuffield Orthopaedic Hospital in Oxford. I spent the day while she was under surgery in Oxford with Fiona watching red kites from her garden in Watlington. The kites, with their marvellous flight, took my mind off anxieties for the outcome. For months Gillian was laid up and meanwhile I donned the apron of a house-husband and learnt to cook. The back operation was a great success, my fears of paraplegia removed and we began to feel that travel was again possible. Gingerly we planned a trip to Israel but

---

*Ironically, as I stopped writing about medical subjects, Gillian had several medico-historical papers published in refereed journals.

following a massacre there a telephone call to an old friend Professor Max Polliack in Tel Aviv deterred us and we went to Cyprus where I had not been since naval days. Gillian loved it, particularly the history and the wild flowers and I found new Mediterranean birds.

Australia still called so we returned in November 1994 with a stopover in Thailand. This time in honour of Gillian's new back we flew club class and arrived in far better shape. We found Bangkok very polluted and flew to Chiang Mai where we had had an introduction to the British consul. He took us to meet Tony & Yurie Ball who are very keen birders. Yurie, who is Japanese is ebullient and great fun. We should have had several days with this delightful couple but I was smitten with a fever that cost me precious time. However we managed to find new birds.

During the Australian summer of 1994/95 Gillian and I toured Australia from Cairns to Adelaide visiting many friends and working on natural history. I had visited the Barrier Reef from Cairns on a previous trip and was anxious to show it to Gillian. In Townesville we learned about the ecology of the reef, which is about six thousand years old and abounds with animal life but no plants. The basic organism is a *Zooxanthellum* which acts like chlorophyll in the coral polyps and lives symbiotically with them gaining shelter and providing nutrients for the coral. The coral secretes an exoskeleton which dies to leave huge limestone cliffs rising from the ocean floor.

Early one morning we boarded a catamaran for the two hour trip out to Kelso Reef. Near the pontoon where we moored an attractive guide led my group away to snorkel round the corals, while Gillian studied them from a glass-bottomed boat. There were many different corals: blue staghorn, table corals and huge pyrites corals. The fish were incredible and it seems beyond belief that there should be such combinations of colour and shape. The Parrot fish, which specialise in eating coral, rasp off great chunks of coral with savage-looking but quite harmless teeth and excrete pure limestone sand behind. It is this function which builds up the huge sand deposits that lie in the deeper water between coral outcrops.

Of all the Parrot fish the most exciting were the big Humpback Parrots or Bison Fish with an estimated weight of 80Kg.

The fish that suck out the polyps from the coral have long siphon-like mouths and come in the most varied shapes with many butterfly fish, often in brilliant yellow with complex patterns. Just as one thinks a particular fish so extraordinary that it must be unique then a whole shoal swim by all identical. Among the coral there are delicate little clown fish, blue and brown or red and white. They have adapted to live in the coral and are immune to the deadly nematocysts and so protected from predators while they serve symbiotic function with the coral colony. Another fish I was able to identify among the myriad was the Humbug so named because its black and white pattern recalls an old fashioned humbug or, as my Mother called them, 'wee strippit ba's'.

Meanwhile Gillian enjoyed the glass-bottomed boat but after an excellent lunch she tried snorkelling and immediately realised how very much better it was. I cut lunch short and swam to a moored buoy where the brown boobies, black and common noddies and sooty terns were roosting and got quite close to them. Gillian and I swam through the coral forest together, sometimes I had to take her by the hand to show her some special fish especially the Humpbacked Parrot fish. When the siren called us back we were tired out and drunk on colour. We were both badly burned on the backs of the legs despite sunscreen and even after swimming in a tee-shirt there was a gap between trunks and shirt that was painfully red.

At Townesville Hospital we had a fascinating conversation with a hospital chaplain, who had spent years living with aboriginals, spoke their language and clearly loved them. I asked him if he had seen ever seen 'the pointing of the bone', a form of Aboriginal voodoo that I had read about. I expected scepticism but he had experience of this tribal punishment and was entirely convinced about it. He spoke of Aboriginals being "sung" to death and that there were many ways of causing fatal cursing apart from pointing bones. When I asked how the victims died he said "it seems that their immunity collapses, they get cancer, strange infections and just waste away". He had never seen AIDS and was astonished when I told him he had described something very similar.

We travelled on by train to Brisbane to be whisked off to Geoff and Doris Ryan's new house in Ormiston. Geoff was thinner and more frail since a cardiac ordeal a year before but Doris was her usual ebullient self. In Queensland the highlight was a trip to O'Reillys in Lamington National Park which was swarming with birds especially Regent and Satin Bowerbirds driven there by the drought in the outback. Arriving in late afternoon we had tea at the hotel watching the bowerbirds and I had the first glimpse of a male Riflebird. At dinner we sat beside the feeding table window watching a Sugar Glider, a pretty Australian marsupial, having his supper.

Next day, on the morning bird walk, we saw the bowers of the satin and great bowerbirds. The bower is built entirely by the male as a seduction chamber into which he lures the female. It is made to precise measurements to secure the female for mating. These bowers are decorated in blue with tail feathers of crimson rosellas and blue straws, plastic and other things whose colour the male satin bowerbird thought might induce his lady to enter.

Christmas was spent with Gillian's niece Kathy and her husband Rowan Atkin and on the first day of 1995 we drove to Botany Bay National Park where there was a very good museum exhibition of the "Eight days which changed the World" when Cook, Banks and Solander were here. We walked through the woods to the shore seeing a four foot black snake by the side of the road which made off hastily. I mentioned this to the next person I saw who happened to be a Czech immigrant, who was with his family, to warn him. He told me not to be frightened of black snakes and that he ate them. He had come out to Australia just after the war and lived in the bush with only a cat for company and was very lonely. He told me how he caught snakes with a cleft stick, whirled them round his head and cracked them like a whip thereby breaking their backs and killing them.

On a visit to the NSW Art Gallery we visited the Aboriginal section and enjoyed the pictures until, distracted by the sound of a didgeridoo, we found a young Aboriginal playing and dancing to a large and obviously appreciative audience. He was wearing ceremonial paint worn for dancing and fighting and which was intensely spiritual. The red paint represents Mother Earth (all Aboriginals have two mothers: their flesh mother and the Earth; the origin of all things). They also have two fathers of whom one is human and the other the Father of all things who, God-like, knows everything and sees all. This second father is represented in paint by the circles round the eyes capable of seeing all. The red paint representing the Earth Mother is in lines all of which originate in the navel which is the spiritual centre of each person's identity.

In the beginning, the actor told us, there were no men but strange God-like creatures who created the Earth and laid down social law and rules of behaviour. In time they changed back into rocks, trees and animals and gave rise to man. Thus all creation existed and exists in one continuum in which present is also past; each individual is of the past, in the present and part of the future. They have no possessions and everything belongs to everyone and to the dreamtime. History, the law, religion and way of life is one in the past, the present and the future. Aboriginal dancing shows this relationship in nature; their hunting, their spirituality and their law. It is very rhythmic and stylised often imitating creatures such as kangaroos or emus.

Rick Steele and his family drove us from Ballarat to the Grampian Mountains where Rick has just bought a house. We walked through magnificent gullies full of tree ferns, seeing a very handsome male gang-gang cockatoo and had good views of crescent honeyeaters. Back at Ballarat we had a superb dinner cooked by Rick and were led down into that holy of holies, the cellar, where he opened a special bottle a 1982 Coonawarra Cabernet Sauvignon saying "I can't give you anything better than this and I doubt you'll find better anywhere in Australia". It was his last bottle saved for a special occasion and was indeed wonderful with a beautiful bouquet. Rick said good wine should be shared with friends. It is quite extraordinary how our friendship has burgeoned; I really hardly got to know him last time we were here, now I find him the warmest most approachable Australian I have met.

Next day we were up at dawn to meet Richard Nowotny and Diana Bryant for a day's bird watching first at the You Yang's, where Gillian and I had stopped briefly in 1992. The place was full of birds including diamond firetails. This new species is an exquisite little finch chequered on its flanks with a scarlet rump.

Back in Melbourne we had dinner with John and Jill Murtagh and heard that my crosswords were going well in The Australian Family Physician. We again visited to Chris and Ruth Hill in Mount Eliza. They will be coming to UK next summer so I did my utmost to persuade them to come to Hampton Lucy but I don't think Chris has very happy memories of Wellesbourne*.

After two months in Australia Gillian felt that she would rather have gone home than meet an entirely new culture, but she soon adapted in a brief stopover in Bali. For me, after concentrating on Australian birds I found myself disoriented with a whole new avifauna. On a brief visit to the volcano (1717 metres) we saw many plants we had never seen: cocoa pods, salak which is grown on a palm tree and coffee beans. Everywhere there were women carrying baskets on their heads: as in India women seem to be the chief beast of burden.

In Ubud, hearing of a bird watching tour, we booked and next morning we reported to Beggars Bush Hotel where we met our guides, Sue and her assistant Lilli. The heat was appalling and Gillian had walked further than at any time since her back trouble started and both of us were beginning to flag. But Sue, delighted to have keen birders with her, wanted to show us everything and we were lucky enough to see several ruddy breasted crakes and a different rail which Sue and I identified as a band-bellied crake which she had not seen before. She brought us back to Beggars Bush by a lane with an enormous culvert running under it where white-bellied or cave swiftlets flew in and out to nest. Then she became extremely excited at seeing an Emerald Dove which was extremely difficult to see but

---

*They did come and we spent a delightful day remembering our old practice of forty years before.

261

a very good bird. We ended the morning with 37 species including 16 new ones. Sue was delighted since it was one more species than her boss, Victor Mason's best for a bird walk.

In late September 1995 Gillian and I flew to Calgary to explore a very rainy British Columbia. One of the first locals we met was the grey jay, who became our constant companion whenever we stopped for a picnic. These birds seemed particularly fond of cheese which they would steal from our sandwiches as we held them. One laid a proprietorial claw on Gillian's hand as if to prevent her lifting cheese to her mouth. For sheer cheek the Grey Jay has to be the most irrepressible bird I know. There were many other new birds and we added black bear and porcupine to our mammal list. The latter lumbered short-sightedly quite close to us, realised his mistake and hurried off into the forest

We stayed with Owen Mackie, Lawrence's brother, and his wife Gillian who were most welcoming. We were fascinated at meeting my partner's brother for the first time and poor Lawrence's ears must have burned (if such posthumous embarrassment is possible!).

Barry Lovell was at St. Marys with me, we had spent a few days in Paris together and had last met in 1958 in Aden when we climbed Shamsan together. He was now practising on Galiano Island. He and Mary Hope, his wife, entertained us in their beautiful island where Barry showed me his practice and we compared our lives. I wondered if I could have lived there among bald-headed eagles and ospreys, but reflected that I would just bird-watch and write, so it would be little different from anywhere else. Clearly Barry and Mary Hope adored it.

Gillian and I walked in the woods seeing few birds but watching seals and admiring the *Arbutus menziesii* or Madrona trees. Gillian was becoming very interested in plant collectors particularly Douglas and Menzies about whom she was to write.

In Seattle we visited Bob Stever whom I knew through GPWA. We had long literary discussions with him and explored the arboretum with its fine views of Mount Rainier 17000 feet above us beyond the ridge of the Cascades. In Portland we stayed with Bob and Anita Taylor, old friends from North Carolina. Bob was now professor and chairman of the family practice department at Portland where I spent a day before hiring a hire car to drive through fantastic Oregon scenery along the Columbia River following some of the route of pioneer explorers Lewis and Clark*. There were superb views of Mounts Hood, Jefferson, Adams and St Helens (less 1500' following its eruption in 1980). We walked in the John Day Fossil beds, an incredible lunar landscape with excellent information boards and copies of fossils placed where the originals had been discovered. The Painted Hills revealed another extraordinary landscape formed by huge piles of multicoloured volcanic dust from different eruptions. One hill, several hundred feet high, was shaped as though it had been turned out of a jelly mould and, with its alternate red and green layers looked like an enormous blancmange; we spent hours here finding the fossil beds and the Painted Hills as interesting as anything we have seen in North America.

Then we went on to visit Dick and Florence Foster at Sun River where we had been in 1987. These two old stalwarts had sent Gillian's family food parcels during the war. Florence was far from well but she and Gillian had a good chat which seemed to cheer her up. I found a lot of birds along Sun River and spent some time watching, and listening to, coyotes.

We drove to Sisters along an excellent road with fine views of the Sisters Mountains and Mount Washington to cross the Mackenzie Pass. This was a slow road but a marvellous drive through a raw landscape of aa† lava. This is granular with each grain a foot or more cube. Though not beautiful it is awe-inspiring when one thinks of the heat and pressures involved in its creation. The lava field is 65 square miles and was produced as little as 2700 years ago. There were magnificent views of the mountains including one with the splendid name of 'Three Fingered Jack.' Seeing these great geological upheavals made us appreciate our Scottish landforms all the more.

---

*They both have eponymous birds: Lewis' woodpecker and Clark's nutcracker and their names also live on in plants such as lewisia and clarkia.

†Pronounced 'ah-ah' and a useful word for scrabble!

We flew on to North Carolina to a great welcome from Jim and Betsy Bryan for a brief stop before going to Fairview in the Appalachian Mountains, where we had had such happy visits before. We met up with Dr. Will Hamilton who had married Susie Clark the daughter of Senator Jamie and Elspie Clark from Hickory Nut Gap Farm. Will recalled that years before he had come to me for advice after which he had given up his practice in Ealing and returned to Susie's home in NC. It is frightening what influence one has on other people's lives; but I could reflect with gratitude on many who had influenced mine. Will was a devout Christian and he clearly adored Appalachia. He showed me a Great Horned Owl behind his house and together we fished the Tuckasegee River, a clear amber coloured stream, under a canopy of trees. I caught a Brook Trout *Salvellinus fontinalis*, the first char I had ever seen, let alone caught. I took it on a Montana Nymph tied by Robin Pinsent and sent to me on a Christmas card just before he died. He would have been delighted.

That evening we again supped with Will where fellow guests were Jim McMillan and Carol Kauffman* and dinner was a most enjoyable feast. Carol had hardly changed and is one of the most delightful of all the many Americans who have passed through Jasmine Cottage and the Wellesbourne practice.

Back at Chapel Hill we were again in the most comfortable house we have stayed in throughout this trip where Jim and Betsy Bryan are so welcoming. Gillian spoke at Grand Rounds at Duke on Medical History. She was not introduced, people came and went, ate all the time and seemed bored. I was rather fed up for her for I knew what preparation had gone into her talk. I had better reception when I taught at UNC on a Birmingham videotape 'Telling the Truth'. These students were as I remembered them from before, hungry for knowledge and eager to engage in discussion. One of them was attached to Joe Fesperman who was a student of mine at UNC in 1973 and from whom he brought greetings.

---

*Carol had visited us at Jasmine Cottage in 1982 writing in the visitor's book 'Thanks for the matchless fortnight! Would love to stay longer particularly as there is a bottle of "Newkie" (Newcastle Brown Ale) remaining. Love Carol.'

To my astonishment I found ancient ornithological books by Frances Willughby, John Ray and Thomas Bewick in the marvellous North Carolina Collection with splendid pictures of birds by Mark Catesby. I do wish I had known of this before when I had more time. However I managed to get permission to photocopy several documents and read others into my tape recorder for copying into my bird archive at home. These were subsequently to be much quoted in my own writing.

After several lectures at Duke and UNC we visited Lewis and Nancy Thorpe at Rocky Mount where I made another presentation. Afterwards I could have used a dram but Nancy did not allow alcohol in the house. I am glad Gillian is not like that! I was horrified at reading papers Lewis gave me by extreme fundamentalist Christians supporting white supremacy. There are forces at large in America that I begin to fear. To my astonishment I several times heard talk of civil war. In discussing this with Rob Sullivan he dismissed it "for it to happen one side would be black and they were too widely scattered both socio-economically and geographically for that to be possible."

We spent a few days at Williamsburg where, while Gillian researched in the library on William Small, on whom she was to publish a number of papers, I went birding.

On our return home to Hampton Lucy I felt more than ever that I preferred the American countryside and natural history to the majority of its people who, before long, were to give George W. Bush two terms as their president during which time World History took a turn for the worse. We had learned so much about our beautiful fragile planet that we both felt a great urge to write about it and to try to encourage its preservation.

Part V return to natural history

Chapter 13 1996 Scotland

For a year before Gillian's sixtieth birthday there had been much subterfuge. Fiona was the prime mover. She had taken me aside shortly after Gillian was 59 and, swearing me to secrecy, told me that she, Jan and Emma were planning a surprise holiday in Arran for the whole extended family for the 'sixtieth' and that they had already booked a cottage large enough to take us all and our dogs.

It was to be an eventful year.

Perhaps my second greatest adventure, after the Himalaya, started as a joke. One Sunday morning we were on our terrace at Jasmine Cottage reading the papers. Gillian passed me the travel section which had an advertisement for a trip to Antarctica. I looked at the cost and exclaimed "Far too expensive anyway you'd be seasick."

"Oh! I don't want to go I'd be ill all the time."

At that point the doorbell rang and Jan burst in and 'yes, she would like a drink and yes, she would stay for lunch.' She was in her usual muddle because of work problems. I listened for a moment and then went thoughtfully to replenish the drinks. When I returned I fixed Jan with a frown and said "Can I ask you a personal question?"

I was given the sort of look one might expect from a thirty-two year old spinster and a heavily qualified "ye-es."

"Jan, are you thinking of getting married in the near future?"

She shook her head.

"Well I've just married your two sisters at vast expense. Why not come to Antarctica with me but mind, if you get married afterwards you pay the bill."

"Done!" she said and that was why we went.

As a geographer Jan had always wanted to see the southern continent but never thought she would. The trip proved so enthralling that we wrote a book about it together–alas it remains unpublished. But it was splendidly full of whales, icebergs, birds and the history of exploration. Perhaps more than anything it brought father and daughter closer than they had ever been before at a time when she seemed undecided about her future.

That summer after Antarctica I was working hard on a book about birds which was beginning to take shape and I was approaching publishers. None seemed interested. By chance I heard of 'Ocean Books' a firm in Northamptonshire not far from home. I wrote to them and had a quick reply from its director, Philip Gosling. He explained that he was not a publisher but a provider of books for cruise liners. He added as a post script 'I also provide lecturers, why not come and see me?' We drove over the following week, when we discussed books for a few moments before he turned to cruise lectures. 'Would we take on the job?' he asked only five minutes after he had met us. He told us he could offer a cruise on one of the Queens in a few weeks. That was impossible for us but we left his office committed to a lecture tour in Royal Viking Sun less than three months ahead.

In September 1996 Gillian and I joined the ship in Copenhagen extremely nervous and wondering at what we had let ourselves in for. We duly reported to the Cruise Director who, when not wearing his host persona was a nice chap... At other times he seemed to belong to Butlins. We were glad of the privacy of our delightfully spacious cabin where we could read and work. The seven course dinner was excellent after which we went to the evening cabaret where the cruise director did his Butlins stuff and introduced Gillian and me as the 'Cunard World University Program'!

Breakfast next day was most enjoyable as there were few people there because of sea-sickness. I ate quantities of smoked salmon and scrambled eggs whilst reflecting that all this luxury was free...

well, almost. The day after sailing and after a fulsome introduction from the cruise director Gillian and I gave the first lecture of our carefully planned series 'From the Baltic to Barcelona'. This was an introduction to the cities we were to visit. There were about 40 people present who seemed quite lost in the enormous Norway Lounge but because the lecture was televised throughout the ship several times during the day many people heard it. We had good feedback and people were beginning to recognise us about the ship.

At Zeebrugge we met Gilbert and Lydie Temmermann, old EGPRW friends from Ghent*, and spent a good day with them at a bird reserve at Zvin. Next day Gillian gave her talk 'They started from here' about World explorers, including Henry the Navigator, who had set out from Lisbon. I thought she was excellent and though there were only thirty in the audience she had some nice comments afterwards. At brief stops we explored as much of La Rochelle and Santander as we could during the short time ashore. In the next leg of the cruise I gave my second talk on the food and drink of the countries we visited. This was much lighter and the feedback was more positive.

Then we woke to find ourselves in the Tagus. We explored the fine old city of Lisbon in a day and only just made it back to the ship where they raised gangway as soon as we got back. As we sailed in the evening the Tagus with its bridge was very fine and we enjoyed views of Henry the Navigator's statue and the Belem Tower.

Gillian gave her talk on architecture to about twenty people: it was excellent but over the heads of her audience. We watched a televised replay of it in the afternoon when she was good, authoritative and fluent; what a pity so few were interested. We decided, if we were to do this again, to pitch our lectures at a less informed audience. However, when I gave my final lecture on medicine in different countries to about forty people a quietly spoken man pushing his wife in a wheelchair agreed with my views on current medical education; he was an American neurologist.

---

*The Temmermanns had been exchanging ideas on disease classification with me for over twenty years on many visits between Warwickhire and Ghent.

We wondered whether we had acquitted ourselves adequately during the trip; we had some fans but most of the passengers seemed to be brain dead and some seemed too young at 70 to be abroad alone. The cruise director was pleased and stressed how much he liked having a couple as speakers. We were ambivalent about the trip; there was no doubt it was an interesting experience but convinced me that though I did not mind stupid or rich people I found them tiresome when both rich and stupid. If nothing else I had added four new seabirds to my list. We decided to wait and see what Philip Gosling had to say before accepting several thousand pounds worth of free travel again.

We disembarked at Barcelona and visited Jill and Michael Byrne in the French Pyrenees. Jill had been so important in my life as a young doctor in Wellesbourne that it was great to see her again. She and Michael seemed completely settled in their new home within sight of the peak of Canigou. After a delightfully nostalgic visit we set off to explore the Pyrenees where we loved the scenery and wildlife as well as seeing six new species of birds including the Dartford Warbler that I had never been able to track down in the south of England.

In the Spring of 1996 we went to Jordan with Rodney Melville on a Sunbird tour travelling from Amman via Petra to Aqaba. This trip was more historical than ornithological and was largely revision of birds in other parts of the Middle East though I did find 15 new species. Petra was terribly crowded but we managed to dodge disgorgements from tourist busses and walked through the Siq without too many people. The Siq is a seismic split in the mountain each wall of which is several hundred feet high. The passage has been eroded by severe but intermittent flash floods*. An important aspect of the Siq is that it forms a perfect defence where a handful of men could hold an army. When Petra was at the height of importance this was the only approach to the city.

---

*One such flood had earlier drowned a party of French tourists.

So we reached 'The rose-red city, half as old as time*' which, at its height of importance, had been a thriving city of 25-30,000 Nabateans. The Siq widened at the El-Khazneh or Treasury, carved out of the living red sandstone before narrowing again as we reached the next major building, a Roman Theatre. The irrigation was carefully engineered at the junction of two wadis where the Nymphaeum stored water. I commented later that I enjoyed writing about Petra more than visiting it for it was incredibly hot.

By now the great day of the sixtieth birthday was getting near. I had managed to fend off many questions about the proposed summer holiday, speaking vaguely about a cottage in Arran. Fiona helped by sending a letter duly signed by our landlord-to-be and written as from him and addressed to me. It was full of the sort of information one might expect in response to a booking. When this letter arrived I was able to sound more convincing.

We set off to exploring Dumfries and Galloway which we hardly knew. For a long time I had wanted to realise a dream of living in Scotland but this had been postponed because of Gillian's back. Now that surgery had improved things so much it was beginning to look possible again. I yearned for the west coast but Gillian said she could not stand my language when the midges were bad: I think she knew all the time where it would be if we ever got around to moving.

The day of the great big surprise started with a grotty drive through Ardrossan, such a pity that the sail to Arran starts so unpleasantly. Nearing Brodick I soon spotted the reception committee. As if putting her onto a bird I told Gillian to focus her binoculars onto a man in yellow working on the pier. "Now pan a little higher and left." The effect was immediate: she burst into tears! So against all odds the secret had held. A few minutes later, tears gone, she was greeting them. It was well worth so much economy with the truth!

We were both happy to be back in Arran, the island I knew so much better than the others and where it was good to be with

---

*Archbishop Ussher of Armagh in 1650 calculated, from biblical references, the date of creation as 4004 BC. This was accepted as 'gospel' truth so much that another cleric, the Rev. John William Burgon [1813-1888] penned the famous line about Petra: 'A rose-red city half as old as time'.

grandchildren after so many holidays with Fiona, Jan and Emma. On a beautiful evening Gillian and I walked to the great standing stones on Machrie Moor amid hen harriers and short-eared owls with superb views of mountains purpling in the crepuscular light. Another day the middle generation climbed Goatfell while grandparents and grandchildren visited my old campsite in North Sannox. The stones of our old fireplace were just as Pater and I had left them two thirds of my life before. To me they seemed as monumental as the sarsens of Machrie.

On another peerless day I decided to brave the hills. Leaving young Edward with Gillian we set off into Glen Rosa for what was to be Hannah's first mountain... and I wondered if it would be my last. She was six and I was 65. I chose Beinn a Chliabhainn, or 'Ben Chilblain' as I called it as a boy, as a very respectable mountain though only just over 2000 feet. The summit is exposed but with good holds so Hannah was thrilled but quite safe. On the way down, while the girls skinny-dipped in a deep pool in the Garbh Allt, I found a slow worm to show Hannah. She was reluctant to handle it at first but soon had its burnished gold twining between her fingers as she marvelled at its beauty. Fiona subsequently described that incident in her World-selling *Nature's Playground**.

"You're getting on a bit and if you are to move to Scotland you'd better get on with it," the daughters said. So we drove to Aberfeldy and, after two days, found West Carnliath. We instantly recognised this as our fourth house in nearly forty years and started the complicated business of Scottish house purchase the same day. By November it was ours.

The business of selling Jasmine Cottage was not so easy and for nearly a year funds were too tight for travelling other than trips to Perthshire to work in the house and garden. I usually went alone with the last of the Labradors, Pfennig, who was old and arthritic. She slept all of the seven hour drive and was so stiff I had to lift her out of the car. She sniffed the air, wagged her tail and ambled down to the Tay and had a swim. She came out grinning as only Labradors can as if asking "Why the Hell didn't you bring me here before?"

*Nature's Playground Fiona Danks & Jo Schofield. Frances Lincoln. London 2005.

Fortunately the time waiting for sale was filled with activity and when not showing would-be purchasers the house there were many friends to say goodbye to. Reactions were extraordinary varying from "What will you do in that cultural desert?" or "What about all your friends?" to "We do admire your courage, we could never do such a thing at our time of life!" We on the other hand had no doubts and felt sure that moving to so beautiful a place would provide new stimulus slowing the inevitable slide into geriatric gloom. The hospitality of Perthshire ensured we had no difficulty in making many new friends.

And so it proved. Sonia and Watty Yellowlees in Aberfeldy threw a welcome party for us introducing us to their friends among whom were several writers including Campbell and Maisie Stephen and James Irvine-Robertson. Before long we were competing with Campbell at bird-watching.

A stranger, an elderly lady called Olive Holden, knocked on our door. She explained she was a neighbour and said she would like to throw a party for us to meet her friends. At a dinner-party with Carol and James Irvine-Robertson we met a strange long-haired man dressed in a tartan suit with oriental slippers. My first reaction was that I thought Oscar Wilde was dead. This strange apparition turned out to be the Laird, Henry Steuart-Fothringham. Looking back after years of friendship with this charming, erudite man I still find that first meeting bizarre for since then I have never seen him except as a well, if comfortably, dressed Scottish gentleman. Henry enquired what I did and, when I confessed to writing, he offered the use of his library. To my shame it was some time before I took him up on that and then only after fishing with his son who told me that 'if Dad said that, then he really meant it'. When I went to the house and met Henry again in a library filled with old books I asked a question and, after a moment's thought, he named the page of the book that held the answer to my query. That is how he knows his extensive library. For years afterwards I borrowed from both Henry's library and his extensive knowledge to enrich my own writing.

Shortly after we arrived in Strathtay we went on another of Philip Gosling's cruises. This was cheese to the first cruise's chalk. We loved every moment of the voyage from Leith via Norway to Iceland and returning to Glasgow. This down-market ship, the Southern Cross, was full of kindred spirits and a great change from the gin-palace of Royal Viking Sun. One man, a plumber from the East Neuk of Fife was a great birder who taught me a lot–when I could penetrate his Fifer's accent.

I lectured on the geology and vulcanism of Iceland and on natural history especially whales and seabirds. Gillian spoke on Viking history and Arctic exploraion. Bergen, the Lofoten Islands and Iceland gave us sightings of new auks and sea duck. We also saw minke and sperm whales and had frequent views of white-tailed sea eagles off the northern shores of Iceland. These magnificent birds, often described as 'flying planks' because of their huge wing span and relatively short tails and heads, had been reintroduced to Scotland where I had seen my first pair near Portree in Skye a few years before.

For some time I had had a month's birding planned in Argentina. Gillian, still unsure how she would cope with roughing it, decided not to come. This was a magnificent trip, a few months after our move to Strathtay, covering much of the enormous country from Iguazu to Tierra del Fuego. In Patagonia I nearly stepped on a magnificently camouflaged venomous snake lurking in tall grass. Friends marvelled that I had seen it but there are compensations for colour blindness. At the Valdez Peninsular, we saw seabirds and Southern Right Whales before flying to Rio Gallegos and driving to Calafate near Lago Argentino in the Los Glacieres National Park. Here, among the magnificence of the mountains we watched condor soaring on thermals and saw icebergs calving off a glacier flowing into the lake from the Andes. Calafate was spectacular for the masses of scarlet *Embothrium coccineum* which, rather hopefully, I had recently planted in my garden at Strathtay*. Finally I spent a week birding on the altiplano of NW Argentina close to the Bolivian border. Here the avifauna was quite different bringing us up to a grand total of 384 new species for the trip and I had seen over 2000 species worldwide before flying home.

*Embothrium, or Chilean firebush, flowers well on Scotland's west coast. Mine, though it grows well has not flowered in ten years.

That Hogmanay we had a houseful with Fiona and Peter Danks, their Hannah and Edward as well as Emma and Saul and the still unmarried Jan. Just after New Year we were all walking at the Linn of Tummel and I was searching the river for dead kelts because I wanted to tell my grandchildren the life history of salmon. Not looking where I was going, I tripped on a root and fell vertically ten feet to land on my heels on rock. I knew at once that my back was broken. My right foot was hurting badly; a good sign, I wiggled my toes and was relieved to feel them move. Whatever I had done I was not paraplegic. The family had seen me fall, rescued me and half carried me to the car. At home I managed to crawl to bed where I was given half a pheasant carcase which I could gnaw without moving too much in bed. Next day I was sent for x-rays when the radiographer brushed my pyjamas saying ' 'ye're fu' o' wee beady things'. The shot from the pheasant was responsible and I must be the only patient to have an x-ray report reading 'compressed fracture of L1 and gun-shot wound'.*

Birding on the Tay, from sleeve of audio tape 'Birds and Words',
Photograph by Ian Sadler, Strathview Photographic, Pitlochry.

*The visitors book contains comments: 'I saw a red squirrell' (Edward 7)
'We went on a three mile walk & we stayed up until midnight' (Hannah 8)
with commiseration from them all for my injury.

In pain and immobile I was transferred to Aberfeldy Cottage Hospital where I had worked nearly 37 years before. As soon as possible I managed to get home where I was bored to tears by inactivity. Watty Yellowlees came to the rescue by organising visits by James Irvine-Robertson and Brendan Murphy. Brendan was the tireless editor of *'Comment'* the local news-magazine. He soon had me composing crosswords and writing a monthly column on natural history. Gillian also started writing a similar column on 'Short Breaks' which detailed excursions to places of interest all over Britain and sometimes further afield.* James I-R was broadcasting every Saturday with Henry Steuart-Fothringham on Heartland Radio's programme *'The Long Good Morning'* brilliantly compèred by Sandy Goodyear and as soon as I was fit I started a weekly broadcast called 'Birds and Words' which explored the etymology of bird names and culture; it continued for over two years. These activities not only cured the boredom of enforced inactivity but began to get Gillian and me widely known in the community. A collection of these talks was published as an audio-tape. I had a few fans particularly granddaughter Hannah who said she couldn't go to sleep without it! Another fan took me up on mispronunciation of Scottish place-names after a talk on fieldfares;-

A fieldfare once said to his wife,
'Although you're the love of my life,
If you said Kill-conker'
I really would conk yer,
It's Kilconqhuar as a' ken in Fife!'

Sonia Yellowlees was the secretary of the Breadalbane Heritage Society, a splendid organisation which met monthly during the winter to hear speakers talk about local archaeology, history and natural history. On Halloween I spoke on Witchcraft in Scotland, we were regular attenders at the Society's meetings and because Sonia knew of Gillian's interest in history she asked Gillian to take over the secretaryship. Gillian was by this time enrolled in Pitlochry & District Choral Society and later served on its committee as publicity officer..

---

*Over 130 issues later both these columns are still continuing at the time of writing.

We had thought, as regular visitors to Scotland that we knew the country well. Now, living here, we realised our ignorance and spent as much time reading and travelling our new country as we had done in Holland. We loved the incredible beauty and diversity of the landforms of Highland Perthshire. We immersed ourselves in its history and natural history and were soon writing for Scottish periodicals at home and as far away as America and Australia. There was a theatre in Pitlochry and the whole strath seemed musical and full of writers, potters, poets, painters and smiths of iron, silver and gold: so much for the cultural desert predicted in Warwickshire!

Jimmy Knox, an old friend and former professor of General Practice at Dundee introduced me to a local fishing syndicate on an exquisite hill loch and my cup ran over. One fly in the ointment was the winter, which, so far north is both long and dreich. We escaped it by our third cruise, a rather dreary trip to Lisbon in QE II. This cruise culminated in the funeral of Pfennig, the last of our beloved line of Labradors in the garden of West Carnliath. She died in kennels while we were away.

We decided against any further Gosling trips even if they were free but also decided that we were too old to take on the responsibility of another dog especially as we wanted to travel widely. In later winters we went to Cyprus, Madeira, Costa Rica, Morocco, Venezuela and South Africa bringing my World bird list to nearly 3000.

By 1997 my third career as a writer was developing but it was difficult to know if I was succeeding. How does one measure success? I was approaching a thousand publications in magazines at home and abroad but nobody would look at my books. In addition to 'Going South', written with Jan after Antarctica, I wrote a book on Birds of the Old Statistical Account with Campbell Stephen and, in conjunction with Richard Cutler, a poet from the GPWA, another on birds and poetry. None of these had raised a flicker interest from publishers. By chance I was put in touch with David Fletcher, a literary agent in Penicuik and soon discovered that both he and his wife shared my interest in birds. He rang me and asked if I knew *The Scots Herbal* by Tess Darwin. I didn't, but David told me to buy it "for," he said, "if you can write a book like that about birds, I think I can find a publisher." That was how *Scottish Birds: Culture and Tradition* came to be published by Mercat of Edinburgh in 2001.

For some time I had been publishing articles in the Scots Magazine. One was about the locum I had done for Watty Yellowlees in 1960. John Methven, editor of the magazine commented 'that it was a pity I had not been there longer or I could have done a Herriot.' That started me writing a series of adventures of a doctor in the mythical Scottish island of Laigersay, somewhere between Arran and Cape Wrath. John published them suggesting the idea of trying a novel. On the advice of Christopher Rowley, then the only bookseller in Aberfeldy, I wrote to six small publishers. Most did not reply but one, Steve Savage, replied immediately. Steve had seen the articles in the Scots Magazine and was interested. So *The Healing Island* was published in early 2004.

Meanwhile extraordinary events were unfolding under the wing of Schiehallion. In November 2001 an 1100 acre parcel of land in Highland Perthshire came on the market. This was Glengoulandie Farm which, apart from a small neglected stand of Scots Pines, had been grazed and browsed by deer, sheep and goats into a bare hill. The hill was Dùn Coillich [572 metres] and to the west, the eastern shoulder of Schiehallion [1083 metres] belonged to the John Muir Trust. Asked if they might be interested in the land the John Muir Trust declined but suggested that the property was suitable for a community purchase.

The story of that purchase appears in another book, however in May 2002 the land became the property of the newly created Highland Perthshire Communities Land Trust. The Trustees included several professional foresters but most of them were ecologically–minded folk from backgrounds as varied as medicine, farming, tourism and local government. I was one of them. We set out, as one Trustee put it "to return the Dun to the state it might have been in had man not messed it about for several thousand years."

I set out to discover as much as possible about the history of Dùn Coillich for, unless we knew how man had "messed" the hill about it would be difficult to know how it might have looked without his intervention. The resulting book, *Ravens over the Hill*, was the culmination of many months research. However it is difficult to uncover the past of a small mountain on which only a handful of people have lived. The history of the land is as old as the planet whose birth pangs caused the shaping of the continents. Aeons of contortion, erosion and deposition of the surface rocks have shaped the geomorphology of the land. More recently it was carved and shaped by the glaciers of the Ice Ages in an all-sterilizing deep freeze. After the ice, life returned and man's history in Scotland began. From then on the history of Dùn Coillich mirrors that of the people who lived on and worked the land, of the armies who marched on their way to war, of road-builders and cattle drovers, and countless tourists including royalty. It records the adversity that its people suffered illustrating how the modern Scot has evolved. Throughout its turbulent past Scottish history has moulded the land and the characters who live in it.

Though Dùn Coillich does not merit the title 'Munro' or even 'Corbett' it is at least a 'Marilyn'. This term is applied to any Scottish mountain that has a 500 foot drop on all sides of its summit, thus ensuring spectacular views. Indeed the outlook from the summit of Dùn Coillich is quite magnificent. Schiehallion fills the western view; to the south the deep cleft of the Tay Valley Fault leads down to Coshieville. To the north Loch Kinardochy fills the foreground, with Loch Tummel behind it against a backdrop of the Atholl Hills.

In this book the history of Dùn Coillich is recounted as seen by the people who have lived there... or as it might appear to an unkindness* of ravens over the hill. *Ravens over the Hill* was published by Perth and Kinross Libraries in the autumn of 2004.

Now with three Scottish books David Fletcher was even more helpful. "What about a Mammal book as a sister volume to the birds?" he asked. Three years later *Scottish Mammals* was published

---

*An 'unkindness' is the collective noun for ravens.

279

by Birlinn*. Even though he does not like novels he encouraged me to write a sequel to *The Healing Island*. As a result *Silver Sea* was published by Steve Savage in May 2007. At the time of writing the manuscript of *Black Sand, Gold Sand* has been completed and the fourth in the quartet of the Laigersay Saga; *Madgie* is nearly finished but, so far, neither has been published.

But my writing was eclipsed by my eldest daughter. Fiona and her friend, photographer, Jo Schofield, hit on the idea of writing a book about using the natural world in education. This book, *Nature's Playgound*, published by Frances Lincoln, was an immediate success and was soon translated into many different European languages and reprinted in America. The book was aimed at parents and their children under 12 and the publishers have now commissioned two further books for the early teenage years. At my suggestion this has included fishing and in the summer of 2007 Fiona and her family visited Strathtay where various fishing expeditions were arranged and are to be included in the forthcoming book.

During this time I continued to record bird sightings for the Perth and Kinross annual bird report and for the 2007-11 bird atlas of Britain. Many of these observations are made on summer Saturdays when I fish the Atholl Estate's beautiful Loch Dowally in the company of Jimmy Knox, Ivor Gordon, Chris Bluer, Chris Mallon and Bill Hoare. Bill also serves with me on the board of Trustees of Highland Perthshire Communities Land Trust, which administers the community property of Dùn Coillich. With the help of a committee consisting of professor of geology Russell Coope, ornithologist Wendy Mattingley and silversmith Malcolm Appleby, Bill and I have raised funds for an Observation and Education Facility on Dùn Coillich. Just before Christmas 2007 the shell of this building was erected and future residents of Highland Perthshire and their children will be able to watch and learn about the natural history of the Dun.

---

*Like many of my books I celebrated this publication by commissioning a piece of silver from neighbouring silversmith Malcolm Appleby. Malcolm also contributed several of his quirky silhouettes to the book.

In retrospect that is no mean marker of a long and varied life. But slave master David Fletcher has said "What about an autobiography? That seemed the height of egocentricity but I reflect that perhaps the grandchildren might be interested... Well that's my excuse!

So, for my genetic extension in time; Fiona's Hannah (20/2/90) and Edward Danks (29/12/91), Emma's Hamish (1/8/98), Isobel, the splitting image of her great-grandmother Lottie Chalmers (16/6/00) and Oliver Miller (24/2/04), who copes with translocation of the great vessels as though it was not there. Jan and Darren were the last to marry in June 2002. Wasting no time Jan bore George Peter Hull Waters (20/8/03) and Elizabeth Gillian Waters known as Libby on 20/10/05, the day before my 74th birthday. I can only hope that their lives will be as filled with interest as mine has been–though I foresee greater problems in such 'interesting times' as the rest of the 21st century.

Good luck and God bless.

Robin Hull
Strathtay

Grandchildren, Oliver, Edward, Hamish, Hannah,
George, Libby and Isobel on Colonsay, 2007.

A

Adams
Fanny, 96

Amphitrite
Queen, 92, 93

Appleby
Malcolm, 280

Arbouw
Dr, Anneke, 256

Archbold
Mr. TE [Archy], 57, 61

Ariss
Mrs. Mary, 151

Arlott
John, 249

Atkin
Kathy, 259
Rowan, 259

Atkins
Dr. Toby, 168

B

Bailey
Dèdè, 30, 33, 61
Pauline, 30, 31

Ball
Tony, 257
Yurie, 257

Banks
Sir Joseph, 172, 199, 259

Barnard
Surgeon Rear-Admiral Peter, 61, 62, 77, 81, 108
Winsland, 77

Barrie
JM, 37

Barton-Wright
Dr., 61, 62, 63, 68
Mrs., 61, 62, 68

Bax
Andrew, 194, 195, 216, 237

Belcher
Frank, 139
Luke, 140
Ms., 139, 141
Violet [Wig], 139, 140, 141

Best
Professor Doris, 253

Betts
Tim, 142, 183, 184, 226

Bewick
Thomas, 265

Bianca, *220*

Birdseye
Mr., 67

Birlinn
[publishers], 280

Bliss
Ms C., 37

Bluer
Chris, 280

Boerhaave, *13, 212*

Boiten
Georgina, 219
Rolf, 219

Bolivar
Simon, 74

Bosch
Dr. Donald, 107

Boucherat
Jean, 69

Brinton
Dr. Denis, 58

Brooks
Dr. David, 175, 216

Bruins
Dr. Chris, 176

Bruusgaard
Dr. Dag, 176

Bryan
Betsy, 264
Jim, 166, 264

Bryant
Diana, 261

M

Mabey
Richard, 244

MacGregor
Dr. Malcolm, 147

Mackie
*Dr. Lawrence, 119, 120, 128, 129,
130, 132, 136, 139, 144, 154,
169, 175, 177, 186, 207, 227,
234, 240, 262*
Elizabeth, 129
Owen, 262

MacWhinney
Dr. Ian, 154

Magwin
Sue, 179, 194

Malins
'Gaff', 49, 51, 57
Mrs., 51

Mallon
Chris, 280

Malvolio, *58*

Marcus
Abraham, 175, 196

Maria, *145*

Marinker
Prof. Marshall, 195

Marshall
Tim, 183
Walter, 152

Mason
Victor, 262

Matthews
Tony, 135

Mattingley
Wendy, 280

McAdam
Dr. Douglas, 199

McConell
Mr., 55

McCubbin
Frederick, 198

McMillan
Dr. Jim, 264

McNeish
Prof. Sandy, 237

McPhee
Hughie, 122, 123

McTavish
Mrs., 125

Meadows
Dr. Henry, 133, 154, 177

Melville
Rodney, 244, 249, 270

Menzies
Archibald, 262

Mercat
[publishers], 244, 278

Methven
John, 278

Miller, 50, 55
*Dr. Emma, 133, 149, 152, 157, 178,
188, 198, 206, 267, 272, 275,
281*
Dr. Saul, 275
Hamish, 281
Isobel, 281
Oliver, 281

Montrose
Duchess of, 36, 37

Moran
Lord [Corkscrew Charlie], 152, 153

Morby
*Paul, 1, 142, 183, 184, 185, 197,
213, 226, 228, 236, 246*

Morgan
Dr. David, 193, 236

Mount
*Dr. Balfour, 170, 234, 235, 261,
263, 265*

Munro
Dr. Ian, 215

Murphy
Brendan, 276